P9-DTT-867

# On-Scene
# Commander

**POTOMAC TITLES OF RELATED INTEREST**

*Hide and Seek: Intelligence, Law Enforcement, and the Stalled War on Terrorist Finance* by John Cassara

*Thinking Like a Terrorist: Insights of a Former FBI Undercover Agent* by Mike German

# ON-SCENE COMMANDER

## FROM STREET AGENT TO DEPUTY DIRECTOR OF THE FBI

Weldon L. Kennedy

Potomac Books, Inc.
Washington, D.C.

**Library of Congress Cataloging-in-Publication Data**
Kennedy, Weldon L., 1938–
On-scene commander : from street agent to deputy director of the FBI / Weldon L. Kennedy. — 1st ed.
p. cm.
Includes index.
ISBN 978-1-59797-136-2 (alk. paper)
1. Kennedy, Weldon L., 1938– 2. United States. Federal Bureau of Investigation—Officials and employees—Biography. 3. Oklahoma City Federal Building Bombing, Oklahoma City, Okla., 1995. I. Title.
HV7911.K38A3 2007
363.25092—dc22
[B]

2007006174

Printed in the United States of America on acid-free paper that meets the American National Standards Institute Z39-48 Standard.

Potomac Books, Inc.
22841 Quicksilver Drive
Dulles, Virginia 20166

First Edition

10 9 8 7 6 5 4 3 2 1

**To my family,
who means everything to me:**

My wife, Kathy;

Our sons Milton and Darrell and
their spouses Beth and Angie;

Our daughter, Karen, who recently married
Scott Anderson;

Our grandchildren Cody, Ciara, Savannah,
Collin, and Zadie;

My departed father and mother,
Weldon and Arlene;

My brother Dale, my late brother
Gary, and my sister, Sherry Foshee.

# CONTENTS

# PREFACE

I really was not interested in writing this book. For years friends and family had encouraged me to do so since I was personally involved in the Oklahoma City bombing investigation and the riot at the Atlanta Federal Penitentiary. From time to time I would tell stories—really just snippets of information—concerning these incidents to friends or family and they were always asking for more. While I was still in the FBI I lectured extensively to law enforcement groups, civic groups, and students at the FBI Academy concerning lessons learned and leadership issues involved in these landmark cases.

While in the FBI and for many years afterward I was interviewed frequently by the media, and even friends in the news business encouraged me to write a book. I still resisted because I have seen more than one autobiography that made it sound as if the author was the sole reason for the success of everything in which he or she was engaged. In my case, the principal reason for my success was the people of the FBI. In every situation they performed magnificently even in the face of extreme personal danger. The last thing I want to do is to claim credit when it rightfully belongs to the men and women of the FBI.

What finally convinced me to write this book was that Ira A. Lipman, my boss after my retirement from the FBI, talked to me about leaving a legacy for my grandchildren. I have always been interested in the lives of my grandparents and great-grandparents but know very little about them. I have talked to many people younger than age twenty who know almost nothing about the success of the FBI in the Oklahoma City bombing and who have never even heard of the Atlanta Federal Penitentiary riot. Unfortunately, what they have heard of are cases in which the FBI was not as successful such as Waco and Ruby Ridge, cases that became the focus of a lot of criticism.

When my oldest grandson, Cody, was a small child he saw me frequently on news stories about the Oklahoma City bombing and could not understand why his "papa" was on TV. His father, Milton, attempted to explain why I was on the news but Cody was too young to understand. Eventually he gained a partial understanding when Milton told him that I was a "bigwig" in the FBI. The next time he saw me on a news conference he proudly told a visiting friend that I was his grandfather and that I was a "pigwig" in the FBI.

So I undertook this project for two main reasons—first, to give testimony to the wonderful work done by the men and women of the FBI, and, second, to tell my life story in order that my grandchildren and any future great-grandchildren would know how I earned the lofty title of "pigwig" in the FBI.

# Acknowledgments

My first thank you is to Ira A. Lipman who convinced me that this book should be written and who provided moral and financial support for the project.

I also owe a huge debt of gratitude to Caroline Waxler without whom I could not have completed this book. She patiently listened to and questioned me for hours on end while taping our conversations. She then transcribed those conversations and organized our efforts for my rewrite, review, and editing. She is a brilliant young writer who, I believe, will have a very successful career.

There are many, many others who provided support and encouragement and I hesitate to list them for fear that I might omit someone. However, I must make special mention of Phoebe Neal of Guardsmark LLC whose administrative support in preparation of the manuscript was invaluable.

# 1 Growing Up

## "If You Want It Well Done . . ."

"There's been a major explosion in Oklahoma City at the Federal building," my secretary Jackie Cooper calmly told me. "It's too early to tell what's going on but there's been some loss of life. Louie wants you to proceed to Oklahoma City." Immediately.

It was around 9:30 AM by this time. The explosion, as we later learned, occurred at 9:02. I had barely sat down at the border conference in El Paso, which I was attending to talk about drug enforcement, when I saw Jackie's page.

Before I could even register what had happened I was home in Phoenix to pick up some more clothes and to say good-bye to my wife, Kathy. Then I turned right around and went back to the airport. I called headquarters only to hear Louis Freeh, director of the Federal Bureau of Investigation (FBI), relay the unfathomable result of a meeting between he and Janet Reno:

"I want you to be on-scene commander for the bombing case."

I'd come a long way. I was born September 12, 1938, in a town that no longer exists: Menlow, Texas. And, in fact, I wasn't even really born there. Menlow had only a house that served as a country store/gasoline station/post office out in the hill country of central Texas. Since my father was sharecropping a small farm very near to this little store our mailing address became Menlow. I was born in that house; a doctor came out and delivered me in the bedroom. A few years later the store caught fire and burned to the ground, and that, in essence, was the end of Men-low. There's still an exit off of the freeway that says "Menlow," but there's no town.

The "big town" relatively nearby is Abbott—one that shows up on a few more maps—where my father's family lived. My relatives settled there in the late 1800s after leaving Kentucky. I'm not sure why they chose Abbott, an area later famous (well, somewhat) as the home of Willie Nelson. He's a little older than I am, and as a small kid I used to see an old school bus around, painted white with red lettering on it for "Willie Nelson and His Boys."

My father, also named Weldon, and my grandfather, Upton, did all sorts of odd jobs. They worked carpentry and farmed—you name it and they did it. Upton was what you would call a general contractor today. He built houses, literally, from the ground up: he dug the foundation, laid the brick, did the plumbing, did the wiring, and finished the carpentry. He built a lot of the houses in the little town of Abbott.

At the time of my birth, my father was farming and working as a part-time carpenter. I don't know exactly at what age—I was still very young—we moved off the farm and to a little town nearby called West, but it wasn't long before we nomads were to pick up again. This time it was to Vancouver, Washington, where my father had accepted a job building ships right at the beginning of World War II. He first moved there by himself to work as a welder in the shipyard, but the place badly needed help so he decided that my mother, Arlene, should join him working there. By then my sister, Sharon (known to everyone as "Sherry"), had been born, so there were two children to consider now. I can remember—and it's the first real memory I have —traveling by train for days with my mother and sister from Texas to Washington. Once we got there we settled into a house near the shipyard and my mother went to work. She was a riveter—just as in the Rosie poster—doing riveting and sheet metal work.

We stayed in Washington until my father was drafted into the marines a year or so later. It was a pretty simple deal, really: The draft board had all potential candidates lined up. The marines came in, took a good look at the men, and said, "We want you and you and you and you." Dad was six feet two inches tall, so—no surprise there—he was picked. A few days later he got the draft notice. My mother, sister, and I immediately headed back to Abbott, where I entered the second grade, and my father went to Parris Island, South Carolina, to begin training in the U.S. Marine Corps.

Abbott was really a part of my family. All my father's family had lived in and around this little town. My teacher there was my great aunt Vida, one of my grandmother's three old-maid sisters who lived together in Abbott. She also taught my father in the second grade; but sadly, none of my siblings—my younger sister, Sherry, and two much younger brothers, Dale and Gary—would have the experience of sitting in her classroom.

• • •

When the war was over and Dad got out of the marines in late 1945, we moved to Dallas, where he worked as a mechanic, repairing tractors for Oliver Farm Machinery. Right after the war there was a critical shortage of housing throughout the United States, so we had no choice but to settle on what had been a military base. No house for us. Instead, we lived in one of the Quonset huts that decorated the entire base. Remember the Quonset hut? Picture taking a big round metal cylinder, cutting it in half, and then laying it down on the ground. Within that, frame in walls and doors and you've got two two-bedroom apartments in each unit. Our Quonset hut was freezing in the winter and boiling in the summer. We didn't have air-conditioning in those days. I can remember my father going down to the icehouse and buying a big three-hundred-pound block of ice and bringing it back to the hut on weekend afternoons. He would set it in a big washtub and aim an electric fan to blow over the big, huge block of ice. We got in front of it to try to cool off.

Mercifully, we were only in Dallas and that hut for a few years—although as a kid I did think it was sort of fun—before we were off to wander around Texas. Our first stop, in 1949, was San Antonio, where Dad worked for another farm machinery company called Minneapolis-Moline. He was employed as a mechanic and traveled throughout central Texas to troubleshoot for dealerships. Oftentimes, he would end up helping salespeople with demonstrations. I went with him on some of those trips during the summers when I was off from school, which was great for me because the demonstrations would sometimes be at a county fair.

Back in San Antonio, where I was in middle school, we were living again on what had been an old military base, near an army airfield called Stinson Field. (No Quonset hut this time, though, thank goodness.) Stinson Field still exists, but during the war the base had been a flight training facility. When we were there, it was a private aviation field. I spent a lot of time hanging around the airport and really fell in love with aviation. For years my dream was to be a pilot—any kind of pilot. (Years later I became licensed to fly.) And hanging around the field, I sometimes got rides from one of the mechanics test-flying an airplane after he had done some work on it. I became well known around there—actually I was probably a pest—but I'd do odd jobs, such as sweeping out a hangar, if I could get a ride.

By the time I was in eighth grade, in 1952, Minneapolis-Moline decided to make Dad a salesman and give him his own sales territory. So, off we moved again—this time to Jacksonville, Texas, where I became very involved in the Boy Scouts and even went on a Boy Scout jamboree. Boy Scouting was a very big influence on my life and the jamboree trip was the epitome. I was only in the ninth grade and the train trip to and from California was spectacular. Although I was with a group, it was the first time that I traveled apart from my family and the trip really taught me self-reliance. Also, the exposure to boys from all over the world and their different cultures opened up new windows and made me realize that there was an enormous universe outside what I had known until then.

I have been a nomad for my entire life. And I couldn't be happier about it. Moving around so much has made me who I am, and nothing could have been better preparation for the FBI. There was a time when I moved every two years and if I put down roots in a city, well, that meant I lived there for four years, tops. When you move, you are constantly pulled out of everything familiar. A whoosh of the U-Haul and suddenly everything's gone. As a result, several things happen.

Moving forces you to learn how to judge people very quickly: the ability to assess whether or not to be friendly with someone is a necessity. When you are constantly thrown into a new environment, you need to know quickly whether the people you meet are the type you want to get mixed up with or not. It isn't as though your families have known each other for generations. As a result, my family and I gained that almost instinctive ability to figure people out quickly and reach a valid conclusion of what makes them tick.

Not only does constant uprooting make you become more self-reliant and introspective, but you grow closer to your family. You have to. That tight little unit is what you rely on. In fact, there was a study done about the social characteristics and development of FBI executives and their families. Like those children of other FBI executives, when my children got ready to go to college, they wanted to stay near their families. The children of more stationary families seem as if they cannot wait to get away and try out their budding wings. In short, thanks to our gypsy lifestyle, both generations of Kennedys have a bond that has shaped all our lives.

• • •

Something else that was critical to my early development was my relationship with my siblings and family. Being the oldest child of four instilled in me a very strong sense of responsibility. Even as a very small boy I was expected to look after Sherry, who was two years younger than I. But, honestly, it made me very proud to do so. My father was a traveling salesman for most of his life and when he left he always told me that I was the "man of the house" while he was gone. I should take care of my mother and sister. I know now that he did not mean that I was literally "in charge," but I took it very seriously.

When my brothers, Dale and Gary, were born I was in high school, but I was very involved in helping to raise them. I didn't have my own car until I was in college, so I used the family car to take them everywhere—school functions such as ball games and the like—they needed to go. We lived in a very small house and I shared a double bed with Dale until I left home to go to college. Gary was still a baby and slept in a crib in my parent's bedroom.

I read about and hear stories of sibling rivalry even escalating to the point of violence, but I cannot even imagine that sort of situation. I was, and still am, close to my sister and cannot remember ever having a serious disagreement with her. Dale and Gary were very little when I left home, and, while I might have been irritated by them being underfoot all the time, I cannot remember ever having an argument with them.

My mother and father never had an argument in my presence and the thought of anyone raising his or her voice in anger at a member of the family was simply unthinkable. To this day if I become angry I do not become vocal; I become very quiet.

• • •

After a year of living in Jacksonville, my father got a big promotion and transfer to Edinburg, Texas, which is in the Rio Grande Valley. I spent the rest of my high school years there. There was a great group of students in my high school and although it was about 90 percent Hispanic and about 2 percent black and Asian, we all got along quite well. There was such total integration in my school that during the 1960s when schools in Mississippi and Arkansas were forced to integrate, I really had a difficult time understanding all the violence. We were so innocent.

In Edinburg, I lucked into meeting a person who helped me enormously. I was assigned to a high school counselor, Mr. Holloman, who convinced me that I should run for president of the student body. "You need to broaden your horizons and you need to get more involved with the students." I wasn't a recluse—that's too strong a term—but I was a bookworm and kind of a nerd. Compared with my classmates, at five feet two inches tall, I was a little bitty guy who seemed to be last in line to hit his growth spurt. I was well liked, though, and friendly with a lot of the football players. I kind of admired them and helped them with their homework.

It took some convincing on Mr. Holloman's part—I think he pushed me because he saw in me himself at my age—but, finally, I did agree to run for office. I didn't do much campaigning, but what I did do was effective. Because my best friend's father was the editor of the local daily newspaper, we were able to go his office at night and make up a campaign poster. The image was very simple and small but the message that Mr. Holloman came up with got attention: "If you want it well done, vote for Weldon." The poster may have been pretty crude, but put enough up of any poster and you'll get attention. We posted these little nine by eleven signs in the shopping center, the classrooms, the gym—anywhere students went. And, out of nowhere, I won by a landslide.

(For my campaign's sake, it's a good thing that I had finally started going by Weldon. As a young kid, my family called me by my middle name, "Lynn," because my father and I had the same name. It was only after I entered school that my teachers started calling me Weldon.)

Though it may sound unimportant, winning the election of student council president—in effect, president of the student body—was one of the pivotal events of my life. For someone who moved around constantly, all of a sudden I had a presence somewhere. I experienced pretty much instantaneous recognition from the whole school. I was now the emcee at weekly student assemblies. Plus I emceed any big half-time programs at the football and basketball games. That meant that I did a lot of public speaking and appeared in front of huge audiences. At a fairly young age I gained experience dealing with both impromptu and planned public appearances, representing the student body of Edinburg High School.

Mr. Holloman was right. Practically overnight I went from an introverted nerd to kind of a "big man on campus." This constant cycle of public speaking engagements was a fast track to maturity. The self-confidence I gained allowed me to eventually apply to the University of Texas, then to the navy Reserve Officer Training Corps (ROTC), . . . and then to the FBI.

## A Couple of Nomads

College wasn't something that I gave much thought to until it was practically time to enroll. Though I did well in high school, I never really thought about my future. Since everyone I knew aspired to go to the University of Texas (UT), it was a no-brainer to take the entrance examination during my senior year in high school.

Good thing. A few months later I opened an envelope inviting me to become a member of UT's "Plan II" program. That meant that my score was high enough not only to admit me to the university but also to a special liberal arts educational program that only accepted one hundred students per year. Program members were permitted to skip all freshman courses and could take graduate-level courses during senior year. Plan II also allowed for several tutorials, one-on-one, with a professor for a semester. In a school with twenty-five thousand students you can imagine how appealing that was.

My parents were pushing me to go to college but at that point I really didn't know what I wanted to do with my life, or what I wanted to be, or practically anything else for that matter. So, the liberal arts program sounded made to order. And, in fact, liberal arts ended up being my major.

I may not have known where I wanted to go, but I learned that to get there I would have to study. Hard. Though I graduated third in my high school class, I had hopes of maybe being salutatorian—if not valedictorian. The difference of three thousandths of a grade point, however, meant that it was not to be. One "B" in my high school career and that was it. (I don't remember what the course was; I must have purposefully dropped that one from my memory.)

UT wasn't that expensive—only $25 a semester when I started in 1956, eventually up to $50 by the time I graduated—but it was still problematic for my father. He had three children at home so he could barely give me anything above that for living expenses. So, when I heard about the naval ROTC I was intrigued. For the first two years I was under no further obligation and received a monthly stipend of $27. Back then $27 was enough to put me on the road to self-sufficiency. Still, my father wasn't happy about my joining. His feeling was that once the military got its hooks into you, you belonged to it.

The naval ROTC requirements at the time were not that taxing. I had to take one course in naval science each semester. All told, there were only twenty-four credit hours in the subject, over the four years, and I didn't have to declare an ROTC major. Of course I had to train some mornings with the navy and was obligated to go on one summer "cruise," but altogether ROTC was a terrific opportunity. Upon graduation I would receive a commission in the navy reserves and serve for a period of two years. After I explained all this to my father, he gave his required parental permission.

I joined and was enthusiastic about it. I was on the drill team and we performed in parades and other events. Every year we went to Mardi

Gras, where we marched in numerous parades, day and night. Being from UT meant that we also marched in the Texas Independence Day parades in San Antonio—it was all kind of fun.

Back at the dorms, the University of Texas exposed me to the first person I ever met from the Middle East, my freshman-year roommate, Hossein Kazemi, who came to UT straight from Tehran, Iran. The Iranian government was paying for him to study petroleum engineering. At the time Iran had a program to subsidize students' U.S. studies in various disciplines, specifically determined through extensive testing. Though the Iranian students studied all over the country, UT had quite a few of them because of its oil and gas focus.

As a devout Muslim, Hossein prayed five times a day, facing east. He had his prayer rug and what appeared to be a prayer rock with some kind of engraving on it. He put that up at the front of his rug and got down on his knees to do his prayers. As you can imagine, a boy from Menlow had never seen anything like this.

Hossein had plenty of money but was very frugal: he only had one pair of pants, two shirts, and something like two sets of underwear. Every night he would wash the clothes he wore that day. And his belt was not to be believed. I'll never forget it—the belt clearly wasn't made for him since it looped around his waist twice!

I assume that whoever taught him the English he learned in school must not have been American because he didn't understand any American idiomatic or slang expressions. His knowledge of the English language was strictly by the book. But he was like a sponge and learned everything about the language he could from me. I taught him so well that he encouraged me to ply my trade overseas.

"You really ought to go to Tehran for a year and teach English," he said. "We could make you very, very rich." Tempting offer, but I passed.

After we got to know each other a little bit, following the first week or so, I think Hossein began to feel comfortable with me. We'd be walking across campus and he'd either want to hold my hand or put his arm around me. Now this was 1956 and I was particularly conscious of preventing anyone from thinking that I was anything other than a he-man heterosexual. (I later learned that in the Middle East Hossein's demonstration of affection is very common. Male friends hold hands and even commonly walk along with their arms around one another.)

"Hossein, I told you not to do that!" seemed to be my mantra that year. He'd keep forgetting though and we'd be going along and he'd just kind of unconsciously try to put his arm around me. I would shrug it off: "Now don't be doing that, Hossein!" He would be kind of embarrassed because I told him to quit touching me, but he didn't really understand why. "I'm your friend," he'd say. I had to keep explaining to him that that's not how two heterosexual men express friendship in the United States, much less at the University of Texas.

In spite of the hand holding, he was making a concerted effort to understand American culture. He tried everything he could but had a hard time even eating the American diet—particularly hamburgers and fries and hot dogs. He literally couldn't eat that kind of food. He occasionally invited me over for dinner at the apartment a few of his Iranian friends had rented. They cooked Iranian food, which I enjoyed: a lot of chicken and rice dishes. But the time Hossein made me a glass of milk was a real eye-opener. I took a swig, not realizing that he prepared it Tehran-style with six spoonfuls of sugar! I think I still have the cavities in my teeth from that experience.

The last time I saw Hossein was during my senior year—after my freshman year I moved into a boarding house and then to an off-campus apartment—and I scarcely recognized him. Dressed like Joe College, he was driving a Ford convertible and had an attractive, very blonde, very American girl in the seat next to him. He had become 100 percent Americanized in his four years at the university and he told me that he had no intention of returning to Iran.

Although we don't talk now, we did keep in contact for a few years after college. Occasionally I'll think about Hossein and the fun times we had together. Recently, I got in touch with him, and, just as I suspected, he had stayed in America. He is working as an adjunct professor in the department of petroleum engineering at the Colorado School of Mines. His kids are all about the same age as mine.

• • •

As if I weren't busy enough during college with classes and the navy, while there I decided to take on a second job as an orderly at the local hospital, Brackenridge, in Austin. I can even remember what I made, $1.12 an hour to be exact, and I worked three to five days per week, usually the 4:00 PM to midnight shift.

Working nights in the emergency room I saw everything. Because this was the general hospital for the city of Austin, and the only one with a twenty-four-hour trauma unit, all the victims from automobile accidents or shootings went there. Besides helping whenever the nurses had an unruly patient or needed to lift something heavy, we orderlies handled the deceased male patients. Preparation to take them down to the morgue often meant removing tubes and cleaning up the bodies. That was not the kind of work I'd recommend to the squeamish.

All of the de-tubing of dead bodies, however, was certainly worth it, because it was at Brackenridge that I met my wife, Kathy. She was a student at Brackenridge's school of nursing, which was located right across the street from the hospital. She took classes during the day at the hospital, and part of her schoolwork required doing on-the-job training. We met one night when Kathy called for an orderly. Thereafter, working with her certainly made all the miserable orderly duties go by much more quickly!

To be fair, though, not all my duties were so bad. In fact, one time I delivered a baby. I was rushing out to the curb to meet the expectant woman's car as she drove up to the emergency room, but by the time I got there with the gurney, she was ready to give birth. A little too ready. When I opened the car door, she was in the front seat, on her knees, as if she was reaching in the back seat for something. She said, "You'd better catch this baby because it's coming right now!" And so, sure enough that's exactly what happened. She gave one more push and out it came. I caught the baby as it came out on the front seat. The baby landed in my arms and I landed in the local newspapers.

Who should see the article but my naval ROTC commanding officer? He recognized my name because of my performance during the previous summer on the mandatory naval cruise for ROTC students between junior and senior years. I had been assigned as a midshipman on the USS *Midway*. On that ship were two hundred and fifty or so midshipmen from colleges and universities all over the country, and we went from San Francisco into the Pacific Ocean for maneuvers over several weeks. As part of our program we took all kinds of courses and were evaluated through written tests. To my surprise, I was ranked as the number one midshipman on board.

"What on earth are you doing working?" asked my commanding officer. I think I responded with something along the lines of "the $27 per month hardly cuts it," but much more politely. Based on my summer performance, he arranged for me to get a $500 scholarship for the last semester of my senior year. For the first time in a long time I didn't have to go to a job. I thoroughly enjoyed those months because I had always wondered what it would be like to have some free time, especially after working practically a forty-hour workweek on top of taking my college courses.

By then Kathy and I were engaged, so the free time was really a luxury for us. We enjoyed the opportunity to spend such a relaxing period getting to know each other better. That was a good thing because our lives soon became a whirlwind, starting with no less than the wedding day itself! June 4, 1960, was—shall we say—very busy: in the morning I received my commission as a naval officer, in the afternoon we got married, and that evening I attended the graduation ceremony for the University of Texas. Thank goodness I was a young man at the time!

Because of timing, we had a "navy" wedding. I was married in my dress white navy uniform and had six of my midshipmen classmates as the honor guards. Kathy and I passed under the swords. I'm a little biased, but it was an amazing ceremony.

We spent our honeymoon driving from Texas to San Diego, where I was assigned for duty. We'd rather have been on a beach somewhere sipping piña coladas, sure, but duty called—literally. I had to report to my new post two weeks later. And Kathy had to rush back to Texas to complete her last month of nursing school. So began our life together as a couple of nomads.

## Reporting for Duty

Considering that it changed my life, I'll always wonder how I drew my assignment: naval intelligence. Or more specifically, how I landed in the Office of Naval Intelligence (ONI) in the Eleventh Naval District in San Diego. With my contemporaries going off to various ships, I expected to be assigned to a destroyer. I was actually looking forward to going out to sea. However, I was to spend my entire naval career in that office.

And it turned out to be a lot of fun. When foreign warships or certain commercial ships visited the United States—via our port—I would board the vessel, take pictures, and record what kind of personnel were on board. If there was something unusual, such as if the ship had recently visited the port of a Communist bloc country, I would make a report after interviewing the captain about things like port security.

My favorite part of the job was conducting criminal investigations. It was through this activity that I got my first exposure to the FBI, which had jurisdiction over items like theft of government property; so many times we had to conduct joint investigations. If a navy person committed a crime against another navy person on board a ship or on a government installation, then the ONI had jurisdiction over the crime. We could arrest and prosecute through the Uniform Code of Military Justice (UCMJ), a statutory criminal code that only applies to people in the military. But if a navy person committed a crime against a civilian then the navy didn't have jurisdiction—it would fall to the FBI or local law enforcement, depending on where the crime was committed. My job was to be the liaison among the police, the navy, and the FBI. For example, if a sailor on leave committed a rape, then the police would have to come to the navy for information about where he was assigned, as well as complete background information. I would also assist them in finding their suspect.

Camp Pendleton, a major Marine Corps base in the Eleventh Naval District (and therefore part of my jurisdiction), was a little more Peyton Place than I was prepared for. Many of the cases that the ONI investigated had to do with homosexuality; there were plenty of allegations that sailors and even officers were involved in homosexual conduct. Any homosexual activity was a career-ender for anyone involved: if someone was found to be homosexual, he was discharged immediately.

Since I was very young looking, more than once was I was dangled as bait. (I'm not sure how much of this I told my friends—or my wife, for that matter.) Throughout my entire career, this was the only time that I could say I operated in an undercover capacity. It worked like this: Let's say we had a case on a given individual who someone reported as a homosexual. Then we surveilled this person, sometimes for weeks. We knew where he went and what he did. If he went into a known homosexual bar, we observed that. And, in a few cases, I would go in to see if this person would hit on me. If he did, and the conversation progressed to where we were allegedly heading someplace for a liaison, that's how we would catch him. Once we were outside I would announce that I was a naval intelligence officer and my colleagues would be there, waiting to make the arrest.

One of the more unusual investigations we had was that of an officer's wife seducing teenage boys—at her home on the base. Her targets were dependents of other navy people, kids she hired to help her around the house. Her husband was one of the many sailors and marines away on a rotating month tour of the western Pacific, making her what we called a "West Pac widow." These "widows," and their children, were all over the place in the married housing section on the base. I can remember one time a three-year-old kid saw me in uniform and thought I was his daddy. Married housing was a family community where everybody looked out for each other. When husbands went to sea, neighbors would help the "widow" in every way possible. For example, the woman who lived next door to us had two or three children and occasionally she would need help of some sort—baby-sitting, fixing her car, and so on—so we would look after her.

In this seduction case, the "widow" certainly took advantage of the situation. Though there were rumors about her, she finally got caught after she went after the wrong kid. He was apparently a little bit too young and kind of taken aback. Rather than complete the whole scenario, he ran home, very distressed. Once his mother heard what was happening she reported it, triggering an investigation. It finally came to light that there were a fairly significant number of teenagers this woman had seduced. Her husband was unaware of this but certainly found out all about it when she was prosecuted by the U.S. Attorney's Office. (It was a crime on a military reservation, but she was a civilian so the FBI handled the case.) As I recall, she was given a probationary sentence.

• • •

"Request permission to conduct a hanging at 1:00 PM."

That was the message that came in one Saturday morning from a Taiwanese Navy destroyer in the harbor. I got that message when I was working my shift as duty officer for the Eleventh Naval District headquarters, which had to be staffed around the clock. During weekdays, regular staff manned it, but on weekends and holidays the shift rotated. I had duty once every month or so, and on that day I was the representative of the Eleventh Naval District. As such, I responded to any inquiries that came in and made the decisions. And what an inquiry that was!

No one on my staff in the command center had ever heard of such a thing. We went scrambling but couldn't find any mention of hanging in any of the reference manuals. So, feeling I didn't have the authorization to approve it, I called the commandant of the Eleventh Naval District.

He asked about my research and then it didn't take him long to say: "Permission denied." We sent that message to the destroyer. Fifteen minutes later we got a message back:

"Getting under way in thirty minutes."

"Wow, this is a new one," I thought. I went up to the control tower so I could see the ship. Sure enough, black smoke was coming from the destroyer as it sailed out to the three-mile-limit, which placed it in international waters. The ship circled there a couple of times and came back. The whole process took several hours but I could see the ship the entire time from the control tower.

On Monday morning, my captain was more than a little shocked to hear about a hanging. I had hardly finished telling him the story when he had me rushing down to the ship to find out exactly what happened. It still boggles my mind: On Saturday morning during breakfast mess in the officers' stateroom, one of the waiters, a Taiwanese enlisted man, became very upset with one of the officers and threw a cup of hot, steaming coffee on him. They arrested him, convened a captain's mast, and had a trial. The man was immediately convicted and the captain sentenced him to hang. That was that, as far as the Taiwanese were concerned. They kept his body in a cold storage locker until they could get him back to Taiwan and return him to his family.

I imagine no one talked back to an officer on the ship after that.

While I was in the navy I became a father for the first time. My son Milton was born at Scripps Hospital in San Diego. To say that I was happy about Milton's birth would be a gross understatement. I was ecstatic!

There is nothing better than being a parent unless it's my somewhat recent experience of being a grandparent! Our children are all separated by four years so by the time the next one came along the older one was potty trained, out of diapers, could talk, pretty much dress unassisted, and did not require the time and attention that babies do. Many of my friends and even family have had several children in quick succession and have had several in diapers at the same time. Wow! I take my hat off to them—I don't know how they manage it.

The downside to the way we did it was that we had small kids around literally for over ten years and then it seemed like forever before they all completed college and we no longer had tuition and college expenses.

I really have enjoyed being a father, however, and wouldn't trade it for anything.

• • •

My navy tour ended up being a little longer than I expected. Originally slated for a two-year tour, I stayed on an extra year because Castro had a different plan. In November 1961—the middle of my second year—the Cuban Missile Crisis occurred. This was to be the first of a few times that Fidel Castro had a direct effect on my life.

The navy in 1961 was prepared for an invasion of Cuba. Officials released a message, called an ALLNAV, from the chief of naval operations to all naval personnel: "Your tours will be extended indefinitely." Unfortunately, I had already been accepted to University of Texas Law School, to begin in September 1962, and I was all set to go.

With this extension, the navy could send you packing at any time. What would I do if, say, the involuntary extension ended in about six months? That would put me out of the navy and on the street in December. Luckily, I had a great relationship with my captain, who was a mentor to me. "Extend for a year," he said. "Since law school only starts in September, you can just start in '63."

My voluntary extension was immediately accepted. The crisis itself lasted twelve days. Six months later, long after the crisis subsided, another ALLNAV came out saying that the previous one was canceled and there would be no involuntary extension. Each officer had the option of designating the date that he would leave. Well, I figured that I could then just withdraw my voluntary extension and enter law school in September 1962 as I had planned.

"Good luck," said my captain as he shook his head. "Give it a try."

The Bureau of Naval Personnel's response? Withdrawal denied. "You voluntarily extended for a year so you are committed," they said. Case closed. So, I had to stay until June 1963. That, however, was a fortuitous thing: it resulted in my recruitment by the FBI.

In those years you had to have a law or accounting degree to become a special agent in the FBI. But, if a military officer, or in some cases, a law enforcement officer had three years of experience, then the FBI had the ability to waive the degree requirement and appoint the officer as a special agent. Thanks to the voluntary extension I had those three years of military service.

In the later part of that extra year some of the FBI agents I knew from working together on cases learned that I was planning on going to law school in the fall of 1963 and started recruiting me. I didn't know anyone in the FBI before meeting these people and certainly had never before thought about the FBI as a career. However, I found the three years of working on naval intelligence investigations to be interesting and I was intrigued that I could make a career out of it.

My application led to quite an interesting meeting (or almost lack thereof) down at the FBI office in San Diego in February 1963. After a morning comprised of a series of tests—written, legal, you name it—the agent doing the processing took me to the special agent in charge (SAC), E. C. "Chuck" Williams. Now, I just thought he was going to introduce me. So, when the SAC stood up, shook my hand, and then sat down and started reading a file, I wasn't sure what to do. I stood there for what seemed like ages and he paid no attention to me. By this time it was after noon and I was hungry. So, I left to get a sandwich.

By the time I got back a few minutes later, the processing agent was in a panic. Turns out, I was supposed to have stayed in Williams's office for an interview and it was my file that the SAC was reading.

"That's it," I figured. "I blew that one."

I returned to my job as I waited to hear. Interestingly enough, during that time—the first part of 1963—the navy made the decision to convert many intelligence positions to civilian posts. One of the positions it converted was mine, the Eleventh Naval District counterintelligence officer, and it offered me the job.

I could take off my uniform and convert to a civilian job at a very good level, in fact, GS-12. In the government, that translates to middle management and financially it meant a lot more money than I had been making in the navy for the same job, even though I had been promoted to lieutenant junior grade. Meanwhile, FBI agents started at GS-10. Even though it took FBI agents seven or eight years to reach GS-12, I was still interested in the FBI job.

Problem was, I still hadn't heard from the FBI. The navy needed me to tell them whether I was staying on in my job and, finally, I had to give notice. So, I departed on June 23, 1963, packing up my wife and Milton, and headed to Texas. I was getting ready to go in the fall to the University of Texas Law School if the FBI job didn't pan out.

So, there I was in west Texas, visiting in my parents' house for a few weeks. It was late June and the Fourth of July was fast approaching. I still hadn't heard anything from the FBI. Things were starting to get more complicated, because I had agreed to take a part-time job while in law school, working for Jim Lozier, a life insurance agent, starting after the Fourth. Jim was (and is) a great guy—he and I have been friends for life. He first contacted me while I was in college—I swear he must have gotten a list of all the people in the naval ROTC—and sold me my first life insurance policy in that conversation. From then on every time I changed my situation or had another kid he was always my life insurance broker.

Nonetheless, the uncertainty was killing me. By July 3 I was really climbing the walls. "Listen," I said when I called the FBI that day, "I already turned down one job. And now I've got a second job that I'm supposed to start on the sixth. I've got a wife and child to support. I need to know within the next forty-eight hours what's going on." To the FBI's credit, they were responsive. The very next day a resident agent in Lubbock, Texas, got back to me: "Your letter is being mailed today. You are appointed to the special agent position and will be entering the new agent training class beginning on July 22."

After all, I guess I didn't blow it like I thought with that SAC. To get hired by the FBI he had to recommend me.

# 2
# Early FBI

## Basic Training

I was selected to be one of the students in new agent training class no. 2 for fiscal year 1964, reporting for duty in Washington, D.C., on July 22, 1963.

My family and I were very excited about what we were going to do. However, we first had to sort out some logistics. Since I was going to be in training, it wouldn't work for my wife and son to go with me. So, during those months they stayed in Texas, first with my parents and then with Kathy's.

In the meantime, I was off to Washington, D.C. My first night was spent at the Hotel Harrington, where generations of agents had also spent their first nights. A block from FBI headquarters, this old warhorse of an inexpensive tourist hotel was ancient then, so I can't imagine what it looks like now. The drill for new agents was to stay the night at the Harrington but bring our bags to class the next day because we were then hauled off immediately for further training at Quantico, Virginia.

When I attended the FBI Academy at Quantico Marine Base things looked a little different. Today the academy is a sprawling complex but back then it was just one building. To give you an idea of our experience, we took classes in the same building where we slept. The top three floors were dormitory floors, where we slept eight or nine to a room on metal-frame cots and kept all our belongings in small metal lockers in the hallway. There was a big, communal, very unprivate bathroom at the end of the hall. When we weren't eating or studying, we were working out in the basement gym. It was all very strict, with lights out at ten. The three meals were served family style at set times. Comparing it to a prison would not be a stretch. When we left the building it was only to be driven in a bus about five miles away to the range facility for our weapons training.

Our training was only sixteen weeks long, but every few weeks we'd hop onto our bus, affectionately named "Old Blue Bessie," to go back to Washington. In those years we alternated between our training site in Quantico and the Old Post Office Building in Washington, D.C., where we did most of our Washington training. It was one block away from the FBI building and was where the Washington Field Office was located; one of the weeks we'd work with an agent from the Washington field and go out in the streets, handling cases. It's also where we took such classes as cryptography and really learned how the labs worked.

Consistent with the behavior I observed throughout my career, the FBI didn't provide us with a place to stay for the times when we were back in Washington. On our first afternoon, we had to go find ourselves an apartment.

Talk about a tough assignment. It wasn't so easy to find a landlord in Washington who would rent to us for sixteen weeks. One option, however, was to stay in one of the number of rooming houses run by widows of FBI agents. I didn't do that, however, and instead rented an apartment in Northern Virginia with four of my classmates. Luckily, one of them had a car.

(The only other agent whom I keep up with from my new agent training class is Don Pettus. He and I got to know each other well, since he was one of the other three with whom I shared the apartment and the one with the car. Later in life we'd work together again after he helped recruit me to Guardsmark, where he currently is working for the company as the group executive handling the middle part of the United States, and we see each other frequently.)

Not only did we have to pay for this housing but we also had to pay for our rooms in Quantico. Our per diem, however, only just about covered the $49 a month that the government charged for staying at the academy. This was my first taste of the personal expense of working for the FBI. At that time I had almost no money but yet had to pay for two residences in the area. On paper, it would appear that I had quite an extravagant lifestyle!

• • •

FBI training was an extremely intense experience but it wasn't competitive, or at least it didn't feel competitive to me. We weren't going for grades, but, in rare cases, people did flunk out. (Not in my class, though—I ended up graduating with all twenty-two of the people I started with.) Failing was quite a feat, considering that since the government had spent so much time and money recruiting and training us, it was not in its interest to have people fail to graduate. If someone failed a particular course, in say firearms, there would be remedial training for that person after hours. If those types of stopgaps didn't work then the FBI had no choice but to kick that person out.

Again, that didn't happen often—for a number of reasons. Before accepting an individual into the academy, the FBI completed a very thorough background and vetting process first, which included a complete review of the applicant's entire life. The FBI talked to former work colleagues, friends, neighbors, and family, among others, for references. We were very carefully screened, but occasionally people decided that after they got there that the FBI wasn't for them. I believe that many of those who flunked out did so deliberately.

Maybe it was the rigorous physical training that they didn't care for. There was a lot of running and hand-to-hand combat. The funny thing is that after we were sent to our field offices, with the exception of more firearms training in conjunction with remedial training on hand-to-hand combat, there was no further effort to do any physical fitness type of work. If you wanted to go to the gym you had to do that on your own time. That situation is much different today; now there are gyms in the FBI field offices.

Of all the physical training, I enjoyed firearms the most. Growing up in Texas I had shot weapons before, but not in combat. On my first day of firearms training I shot so many rounds that the pads on both my index fingers were covered with blisters. In the first few weeks of training we shot thousands of rounds. Back then we shot with the old Thompson .45 caliber machine gun that George "Machine Gun" Kelly used. Those guns are very easy to handle and because they are so heavy there is absolutely no kick whatsoever.

The Thompsons, along with rifles and other kinds of weapons, were kept in the gun vault in each FBI field office. (Nowadays, the Thompsons aren't there, of course; they are a hot collector's item.) The gun that I was issued was a Smith & Wesson model 10, .38 caliber revolver—a plain-Jane police revolver. I didn't carry it all the time; when I was in Florida I bought a small, stainless steel .38 caliber revolver that I could carry and conceal more easily.

Though I kept the weapon at home I never had any problem with the children's curiosity about it. I didn't hide it—my children knew that Daddy carried a gun. I told them that if they ever wanted to see it, all they had to do was ask and Daddy would show it to them. They asked. When each of them was just a toddler I showed them what the gun did. I took them out for a firearms session. They held the weapon and actually pulled the trigger, with a little help from me. This was not very much fun for them at their young age as the kick and the noise actually scared the hell out of them. This hands-on lesson took away their interest because they knew about the gun and what it could do. After that they wouldn't touch it, without my permission.

• • •

With Labor Day approaching I was really missing my wife and three-year-old son, Milton. My class had the long weekend off so I made arrangements for them to visit. They checked into a Virginia hotel on the Thursday night before Labor Day, and the next day they took in the sights in Washington before meeting me for lunch. As they were walking through the FBI building, where my new agent class was training that day, my son came very close to causing what would now be classified as a terror alert.

They entered the FBI building, which, at the time, shared real estate with the Department of Justice, without issue. Though there was security it was a public access building—anyone could just walk in and go anywhere they liked. Back then someone could even walk right into the outer office of Director J. Edgar Hoover.

On both sides of the corridors were offices of FBI agents working away. That day, August 28, 1963, the building was especially full because Martin Luther King Jr. was on the Mall, one block away, making his famous "I Have a Dream" speech. Tens of thousands of people were out there listening. So, even though it was not a very secure building we were all on high alert then. Remember that this was a time of protests and a lot of antigovernment activity.

Young Milton was blissfully unaware of all this. During the sightseeing trip Kathy bought Milt a helium balloon that he carried with him the whole day and right into our building. He merrily walked down the hall carrying his balloon . . . until it caught on something and it popped. Doors flew open all over the floor and FBI agents—armed FBI agents—came charging out of every crevice. For all they knew it was a shot—there were no carpets on the floors in the halls so the echoes were enormous. Crazier things than that were happening all the time in the 1960s. In seconds, the hallways were frenzied.

My wife and son were terribly upset. She, because of the FBI agents, and he, well, because his balloon popped!

● ● ●

Four months after I entered the FBI training I had the honor of graduating. Back then we didn't have much of a ceremony, unlike today where the actual graduations are very elaborate ceremonies, with families invited and the director handing out credentials. Instead, our "graduation" was simply our last class.

Before we left we were each given some ammunition for our weapons, which a truck had to bring in from Quantico since we weren't allowed to carry a gun around Washington until we had graduated. We loaded up, strapped on our guns, and walked out. There certainly wasn't to be any celebrating, at least not locally. We were told, "You cannot spend the night in Washington, D.C." We had to leave that day, because a few years earlier there had been an incident in which a graduate had gone out for a few drinks, had his gun with him, and had gotten into some trouble. From then on, we had to be out of town by noon of graduation day.

When I left that morning, I was on my way to Portland, Oregon. I wasn't too surprised that this was my assignment, considering that I was married, with a child, and a house full of possessions. The rules were that the government paid the cost to transport my household goods from Washington, D.C., to my first office of assignment. They would only pay transportation expenses to cover that distance. So, for example, if I had gotten assigned to, say, Baltimore, then the FBI would only pay for the equivalent cost between Washington and Baltimore. Considering that all my possessions were in Texas—and I would have had to transport them between there and Baltimore—the amount allotted for the tiny distance between Baltimore and Washington would have hardly made a dent. To get around this, the Administrative Services Division had developed a custom called "triangulation." The Special Agent Transfer Unit chief computed the distance from where my household goods were actually located—in this case, Texas—to Washington, D.C. Then he calculated the distance from Washington, D.C., to various possible cities of assignment. The point was to see if the distance was greater from Washington to those locations than from Texas to those locations. If so, then my move would be covered by the government, without me having to pay for it—a much better choice.

I was surprised that I ended up all the way out in Portland, but given the amount of miles needed I figured that it would be in the Midwest or the Northwest. But I couldn't be mad, because that's how things worked out, and, after all, the Transfer Man was trying to look out for us. At that point in my career I had no money and a family to take care of so a cross-country move out of my wallet would have bankrupted me.

In those days we didn't have any sort of per diem allowance once we arrived, only a travel per diem for the trip. That was for us agents, not for family members. We were given $16 a day for however many days the government felt it would take for us to travel from Washington, D.C., to our respective destinations, assuming that we were traveling at a rate of three hundred miles a day. (Sounds like the start of an SAT problem, doesn't it?) In my case, it was eight days.

We weren't entirely without resources, though, once we arrived. As soon as we pulled up we became the responsibility of the last new agent in the office while we searched for housing. That was the custom. Staying with the most recent arrival had its advantages: these men had just looked for housing a few weeks before so they knew the real estate market.

FBI agents take care of each other. Later, when I arrived at my second assignment, an agent said to me, "Come along, we're going to go get your wife and child out of the hotel." This nice agent had arranged for us to "house-sit" for another agent who was on vacation for a month. My rent? Watering the plants.

There is a sense that everyone in the FBI is responsible for everyone else. I knew that soon enough it would be my turn to let the next arrival bunk in with my family and me, and I was happy to take on that responsibility. This kinship is great in noncritical times, such as house hunting when we were completely broke, but it was priceless during times of crisis.

● ● ●

The Portland office was a small one, with only about fifty agents, most of whom were old-timers. There were a handful of new agents who started when I did, and practically all of us were from Texas, thanks to triangulation. We enjoyed the camaraderie. It was a very exciting time and we couldn't wait to get some firsthand experiences.

We were each assigned to a training agent, and mine, Ralph Himmelsbach, later came to national fame investigating the very high-profile case of hijacker D. B. Cooper (more on this later). I was under his wing for the entire time that I was in Portland, and although I was assigned my own cases, he oversaw everything I did. He helped me write my reports, gave me tips on conducting investigations, and let me ride along with him to watch how he handled various kinds of cases. Mostly what I worked in those days were fugitive cases and bringing back military deserters and draft dodgers. Tracking down deserters and draft dodgers is the military's job today, but back then that's what new FBI agents cut their teeth on. The cases weren't difficult but taught me the ropes of how to find people who were trying very hard not to be found.

I also worked a fair number of stolen motor vehicle cases. My big one involved Benjamin John Barber, a man who first came to our attention by buying a new bright yellow Corvette from a Portland dealership with a bad check. From there he traveled all the way around the United States and through Canada, leaving a trail of more bad checks in his wake. My job wasn't easy—early on Barber ditched the Corvette for a series of other cars. A master impersonator, Barber eluded us by portraying military officers, particularly air force, navy, and army personnel—but never a marine. He dressed in uniform and stayed at military bases in the officers' quarters. It was incredibly frustrating for me because I was always a step behind him, not unlike Tom Hanks's character in the movie *Catch Me if You Can*.

However, in this case, we too had a Hollywood ending. Barber was finally caught in Southern California, while trying to enter a military base. A military policeman (MP) guarding the gate noticed that the insignia on his collar was backward, something a real officer would never do. Barber had identification and a story to go along with it but the MP didn't like it. By this time I had Barber's face, name, and all his known aliases posted in every MP station around the country, so when the sentry went back to his post to check if this man was wanted, he took one look at one of my flyers and arrested him.

The Barber case became synonymous with my time in Portland, as I started work on it practically as soon as I arrived and Barber was caught only two weeks prior to when I left the post.

Near the end of my new agent training in Washington, D.C., all my classmates and I took the required language aptitude test. I, however, was dumb enough to seriously study for it. I did my best and scored extremely high, meaning the FBI figured that I had a high aptitude for learning a foreign language. Those who knew better purposely bombed the aptitude test because a high score at that time—in the middle of the Cold War—was a sure ticket to Russian language school. That meant a career akin to working in Siberia. One, you were probably going to be working on Soviet cases exclusively and, second, you were probably going to spend a good part of your life with earphones on, listening to intercepts and translating from Russian. That sounded to me like a very boring, unappealing kind of a job. I didn't know all this when I took the language test, however, and it was too late.

Sure enough, after six months in Portland, I got a transfer to Russian language school. I was surprised, figuring that we'd be in Portland for a year, but, as I learned, when a transfer comes up in the FBI you don't have much choice. My family and I had a very short period of time to move, so we scrambled to load up the car and head to the Washington, D.C., area, where I'd be taking the language class at Anacostia Naval Station, across the river in Maryland.

Good-bye, Portland, and hello, Moscow. Or so I thought.

## Vintage Hoover

There I was, in May 1964, six months into my career with the FBI, crisscrossing the country, family in tow, to start Russian language school in Washington. I had no choice in the matter. And there was certainly no way I could have known that while I was driving—through Tennessee at the time, actually—that a meeting between the special agent in charge of the San Francisco office and Hoover would give me even less of a choice.

A meeting with Hoover was like a game of Russian roulette for an agent. He might well come out of the meeting without a job, if he said or did something that made Mr. Hoover unhappy. Hoover could put out the order, "Transfer this man," or "Demote him," or pretty much whatever he wanted. So, before each meeting the agent did a lot of preparation. Hoover could ask SACs anything and they better know the answer. An SAC also had to figure out what additional resources were needed, because this was the opportunity to make a request. In this case, the San Francisco SAC's request for more agents was met with confusion from Hoover. He couldn't understand the need for more people, since on paper the office was actually overstaffed for the number of cases assigned. "Well, actually, sir," said the SAC, "many of the agents you are including are in language school in Monterey full time and don't work any cases."

"Well, how many are there—a dozen or so?"

"No, sir, at the moment there are ninety agents in language training."

"Ninety!"

That was it. Hoover blew up. Ninety agents at Monterey were clearly too many for him. He summarily ordered the cancellation of all language classes. Yes, there were to be no FBI agents in language school. Period.

I, of course, had no knowledge of this. When I arrived in the Washington Field Office on Saturday morning there was only a note telling me to report to the weekend supervisor. "Damn, what have I done now? I must be in trouble or something." That was all that I kept thinking.

The supervisor greeted me with a sad look. "Well," he said, "this is terrible. I don't have any written order to give you. All I've got is this typed index card: All language schools have been cancelled and Weldon Kennedy is to proceed to Newark, New Jersey, for permanent assignment."

Newark? New Jersey? I scarcely knew where that city was. I'm a Southern boy—and had never been any further north on the East Coast than Washington, D.C. We spent the Fourth of July in Washington and then drove up the New Jersey Turnpike to Newark. I'll never forget pulling off the turnpike on Raymond Boulevard in downtown Newark, which looked like scenes of Berlin after World War II. There were vacant buildings with the glass broken out. It was the worst place I'd ever seen in my life. That night was a very emotional one. I was about ready to leave the FBI since my wife and family were directly impacted. I was going to be working in a place that looked like a war zone.

And that's certainly what my office felt like when I reported in the next day. The SAC at the time, Ralph Bachman, was one tough cookie.

"Weldon," he said, "tell me about yourself." And so I told him about my time in the navy and in Portland.

"Who is the SAC out there?" he asked, skeptically.

"Mr. Williams."

"Oh, do you happen to know his nickname?"

"Yes, sir, his nickname is 'High Pockets.'"

"Do you know how he got that name?"

I didn't. And, with that answer, Bachman demanded to see my credentials. "What's your EOD?" he asked, referring to the term for the month and year of entering duty in the FBI. I answered 7-22-63.

At this point I was about ready to come apart. In those days and, in fact, still in the FBI, an SAC is about the closest thing to God. SACs have total power over everything that goes on in their division and anything that happens. They can make whatever decision they feel is appropriate to run their office. And, of course, these folks can make or break a person's career with the stroke of a pen. So, forgetting for a second that customarily the SAC barely even knew the name of an entry-level agent to begin with, the fact that I was ushered into his office immediately made me extremely nervous.

What I didn't know then was that he thought I was somebody trying to infiltrate the office. He had never gotten a call from FBI headquarters nor was there any paperwork. They weren't expecting another agent to be reporting in for duty. So, I show up and they're wondering, "Well, who is this guy?"

Well, my EOD answer pacified him. I knew I was off the hot seat because of his response. He exploded: "Damn it, the bureau never tells me anything!"

Welcome to Newark.

Why was I assigned to that office of all places? Because of Martin Luther King Jr. I was switched in part because of a statement Dr. King made about the FBI being discriminatory in the South. So, in response, Hoover sent many agents from the North there to work instead and moved the Southerners up North. There were also more vacancies in Newark because many of the agents from the office—one of the FBI's largest offices—were in the South investigating such cases as the deaths of the three civil rights workers in Philadelphia, Mississippi.

My assignment in Newark contained no cases with such a national impact, but I certainly enjoyed the work. My job was to investigate cases of theft from interstate shipments, a federal violation. Generally speaking, though, the FBI would not work a case unless the material stolen was worth more than $5,000. In Newark, New Jersey, there were truckloads of things being stolen.

After six months in Newark I was transferred to the Camden, New Jersey, resident agency—a suboffice of Newark at the time. This was a much more pleasant city than Newark, so I was more than happy to move my family there. In fact, while we were in Camden, we had our second child, Darrell, on March 16, 1965.

• • •

Camden is where I really gained experience on fugitive cases. Although I had a smattering of other types of cases, my primary work was fugitives. It was my experience there that led to my nickname, "the Fugitive Man," in Las Vegas when I was transferred there several years later.

In Camden, I was replaced by an agent named John Otto, only to have our paths cross many times during my career. He later became the assistant director of the Inspection Division, then an associate deputy director, and then the acting director for a short time. Another significant relationship that developed during my time in Camden was with Andy McKean. He was an older agent who worked almost exclusively on stolen car cases. I learned much from him and in the process we became close friends. When I left Camden in 1966 he was still working car cases. But a few years later he would be in a position to give me quite a leg up in the bureau.

The only other notable thing about Camden was the speed with which I had to leave it. After all the FBI language school programs had been canceled in 1964, there was a two-year period during which no agents were in language training. Apparently, this had made it very difficult to work cases requiring language expertise, so suddenly, in mid-1966 Hoover decided to place a large number of agents back into language training. I received a call out of the blue from FBI headquarters (FBIHQ) advising me that I was to be transferred immediately to Monterey, California, to study Spanish.

I was to report there in nine days.

What! I had just purchased my first home in nearby Cherry Hill and my second son, Darrell, was barely a year old. His older brother, Milton, was already five—which I could hardly believe. So, with our two young children, we scurried to move cross-country. We packed and shipped our household goods, put our house on the market, and drove to the West Coast—all in just a little over a week. (Considering that these were the days before the interstate highway was completed, the trip took quite a bit longer than it would today.) We made it in time, but not without a lot of wear and tear. Shortly after we arrived we got a contract for our Cherry Hill house; after Realtors' fees we sold it for little more than what we paid for it. Such was the life of an FBI agent—the moves cost us. Literally.

# 3 Years as a Street Agent

## Pirate Country

My next assignment was a place I couldn't event pinpoint on a map. In six months, I completed the Spanish language course at the Defense Language Institute, in Monterey, where I studied, studied, studied. It worked—I came out first in my class. My prize? A Spanish-English dictionary. Next up was my transfer to Miami, Florida. My family and I left Monterey during the beginning of October 1966, briefly visited Disneyland in Anaheim, California, and then drove cross-country to our new home, arriving in Florida just before Halloween. This was the fourth time in three years that we were driving across the entire United States with the family.

Along the way, my wife had what must have been some sort of vision or premonition. As we descended through Florida she was looking at a map and said, "Look at this—Key West. It's way out there in the middle of the gulf and a long way from Miami. I wonder if anyone is assigned down there."

No need to wonder very long, Kathy. The SAC in Miami greeted me the following way: "Welcome aboard. We're going to assign you to Key West." I nearly fell over.

• • •

When we first arrived in Key West there literally was no rental housing available, either apartments or houses. We lived at a motel for about thirty days, at our own expense since in those days the government did not pay for temporary housing. Eventually, a Realtor notified us that a house had become available: We took it sight unseen. It was a small frame two-bedroom bungalow on stilts with no air-conditioning or heating, but we had little choice, so we stayed there the entire time I was working in Key West—almost two years.

Key West was a colorful, interesting artist community. Hemingway wrote several of his books there. The town was also a mecca for gays, even in the late 1960s when we lived there. But one of the largest presences on the island was the contingent of U.S. Navy personnel and their dependents. In fact, in those days about one-third of the population was year-round residents and the majority was either navy personnel or "snowbirds."

For living, Key West may not have been ideal, but for FBI work, Key West was great because the place was so corrupt. Corruption had been part of Key West's history for a long, long time. In the 1800s Key West was the home of many pirates. A lot of the residents of Key West reportedly became quite wealthy looting ships that had crashed into the reefs surrounding the island. Ships sailed into the shallow waters because residents of Key West purposely moved the buoys and reef markers into shallow water. According to the laws of the sea a wrecked ship is fair game: anyone could loot for booty. In the late 1800s Key West was the richest area per capita in the United States. While there were no eye patch-wearing pirates of yore wandering the island when I was there, their legacy was squarely in place. Besides the abundance of criminals even the rest of the society was very closed and clannish.

My favorite Key West incident—something so quintessentially Key West—was a case that I, unfortunately, didn't work on: a bank robbery over Labor Day weekend 1967. The employees came back on Tuesday to find the place gutted. The perpetrator? The chief of police. He was the head of local crime fighting, and he was the guy who set up the robbery and provided cover for burglars who slipped in through the roof. Stories like that were practically uncountable.

I left Key West in 1970 and in June 1984 the Key West Police Department was declared to be a criminal enterprise under the Racketeer Influenced and Corrupt Organizations Act (RICO), a U.S. law enacted in 1970 to enhance the federal government's ability to investigate and prosecute organizations such as the Mafia. A number of the department's high-ranking officers, including the deputy police chief, Raymond Cassamayor, were arrested on federal charges of running a protection racket for illegal cocaine smugglers.

Only two of us agents worked in the Key West office, and we learned to handle any kind of case that came our way. In New York, for example, there were so many agents that you would only be assigned to handle one type of case. Key West, on the other hand, was a virtual educational buffet for us.

Take the case of a lobster boat vigilante named Vanyo. A former navy diver, Vanyo had an idea to start up his own lobster fishing business in Key West. He bought himself a modern lobster boat, hired a crew, and was off to make a living. Out in the ocean, close to the Bahamas, he found an area teeming with lobsters.

He set up his traps all over the place, but when he returned a few days later to claim his prizes, he couldn't find the line of lobster traps that he'd dropped. After this scenario repeated itself a few times, Vanyo began to realize that someone was sabotaging him.

Not just anyone, but a family of saboteurs. Sort of like an evil Swiss Family Robinson, this gang owned several boats, including the *Bahama Mama,* which was part of a group of four lobster boats that fished in the area routinely.

"What do you think you're doing," Vanyo asked the modern-day pirates when he finally caught up with them. "We're warning you," they told him. "Don't come back. These are our own private fishing grounds. Stay away." Vanyo ignored them and dropped more traps. Those disappeared. He dropped some more. Those disappeared, too. The crew of the

*Bahama Mama* even fished out the line to one of the traps in his presence and cut it. To boot, one of the men in the group flashed a rifle.

Now this got Vanyo pretty mad, especially since he didn't have a gun of his own. So off he went, sailing back the twelve hours to Key West. (Usually it took about fourteen hours but Vanyo was in quite a rush.) As soon as he hit shore he went straight to a gun shop. He purchased a virtual arsenal, with tons of ammunition, and five gallons of gasoline. He and his two people were hell-bent for leather.

When Vanyo got back to the *Bahama Mama* a gunfight erupted. He and his men riddled the *Bahama Mama* gang's boats with bullets—one of which killed someone on the *Bahama Mama.* The poachers radioed the Coast Guard for help. Everyone was taken into custody and taken back to Florida. At this point I was called in because crime aboard a U.S. vessel on the high seas is an FBI matter.

Vanyo couldn't have been more cooperative with our investigation. He told us that before this last incident he went to the Florida Fish and Game board to report the trap cutting. The state of Florida had no jurisdiction, came the response. He even called the FBI. Guess what the response was? No jurisdiction. (He didn't call my office, I can assure you.) He called the Coast Guard and was told that it, too, had no jurisdiction. "That's it," Vanyo finally told himself. "It's like the law of the West. No one is looking after my personal property but me." He decided the only alternative was to hit the gang head on.

On the other hand, the people on the *Bahama Mama* completely lied to us. They refused to acknowledge cutting any traps, denying absolutely everything. The FBI and U.S. Attorney's Office pleaded with them to tell the truth, but no matter. Everyone got on the stand and lied, but people in the court, including the jury, knew it.

So, Vanyo and his two shipmates were acquitted of murder, even though they admitted engaging in a firefight. Once he was released Vanyo came knocking on our door to reclaim his weapons. He was very open and friendly, saying that he knew what we needed to do to get to the bottom of the case. "I didn't mean to kill anyone," he told us, though we never did find out who, whether it was Vanyo or one of his men, actually fired the fatal shot. Whoever it was meant business. The shot that killed the man was copper-tipped, surplus military ammunition. The bullet went completely through the man's body and, since the boat was made of wood, the bullets went all the way through it, too, including puncturing the engine.

The *Bahama Mama* incident wasn't the only lobster boat murder that I had to contend with while I was in Key West. In the Key Largo area several lobster fishermen found that their traps were consistently robbed as well. The final straw for one member of this group was the time when he, a lobster fisherman, was going out to check his traps and saw a boat heading away from the trap. Unfortunately, his lobster boat was too slow for pursuit.

This gave the fisherman an idea. He and his family bought a cigarette boat, which is an extremely fast racing boat, and equipped it with a radio. And they waited.

It didn't take long. A lookout soon spied a diver fooling around with one of their traps. He radioed back to the cigarette boat and a big high-speed chase was on.

There was just one twist: the men on the cigarette boat had a rifle. They opened fire on the fleeing boat, shooting and killing the driver. The remaining passenger was a teenage boy whom the cigarette boat shooters warned about robbing the lobster traps, before they sped off.

Meanwhile, a man was lying dead on the bottom of the boat. The teenager wasn't sure what to do at all, so he took the boat back to Miami and went straight to the authorities, who, in turn, took him straight to the FBI.

Besides an artist's conception of the men driving the cigarette boat we had very little to go on. So, I pounded the pavement, or rather the docks—going to practically every marina and every harbor in the keys—looking for that boat. I never found it. To this day it's my belief that the owners sank it.

The drawings, however, did the trick to help find the culprits. I found someone who said that he could tentatively identify who one of the people might be. When I saw the suspect, I knew immediately that the identification was correct. There was no question that this guy who was said to be working on his father's lobster boat was the right guy. The drawing was a dead ringer.

He was about twenty-five years old and as cool as anybody I'd ever met in my life. "Do you own a firearm?" I asked. He said, "Yes," and he agreed to show it to me.

His calm demeanor made it seem as though he had taken truth serum. When I asked him, "Where did you get this?" he answered with the exact name and location of the store. He had a receipt, too. The date? The day after the murder. No wonder he was acting so cool.

Not so fast. "Did you have a gun like this before?" I asked him.

"Yes."

"And where is that gun?"

"I don't have it anymore. A month before I had this one I saw a guy trying to rob one of our traps and I took a shot at him. I was afraid I hit him and dumped the rifle over the side of the boat."

Mr. Cool was put in a lineup. The young witness refused to identify him, though, apparently for fear of retaliation. Since he was our only witness that was end of my case. Now, I may not remember his name but I remember that interview. Those fishermen—both lobster and shrimp—in the north keys area are a tough bunch.

The payoff from one load of shrimp was equivalent to my annual salary. To make that kind of money, these people lived hard. They were gone for weeks and weeks at a time. Anyone looking for someone on one of those boats would have a tough time. No license was required to work on them and no questions were asked. It's not surprising that many of our hunts for fugitives led us straight to shrimp boats.

Whether I was going after angry men bereft of lobsters or fugitives out on shrimp boats, I was constantly running into Cuban refugees. Key West was full of them, and they were very creative. The homemade things these Cubans used to escape from their island were incredible. There were big, rubber inner tubes held together with ropes that were used to float across from Havana. A lot of people died making the journey, but anyone the Coast Guard rescued was brought to us and to the immigration authorities for interview.

• • •

One of the stories that still makes me laugh from my time in Key West was that of the flying hitchhiker. Our joyriding friend was hitchhiking (via cars, at that point) his way around Florida when one of his rides dropped him off on Route 1 across from an airfield in Marathon, Florida.

After taking a nap under the wing of a twin-engine plane, he let himself inside—easy to do since it required no keys. Once inside, he realized pretty quickly that the plane didn't need any keys to start it up either. Not that he knew how to fly a plane, mind you, but we'll get to that. He flipped, pulled, pushed, and flicked any knob and switch he could see until he got the thing started. Miraculously, he figured out how to taxi down the runway and lift off. He was flying over the ocean in no time. Since he had been a sailor he knew how to read a compass.

He was comfortably flying on a 90-degree heading so he figured it would be okay to experiment a little bit with how to fly. Talk about multitasking: he was reading the manual while operating the aircraft. He lingered a little too long on those pages, though, I guess. By the time he looked up, he realized that he couldn't see land anywhere, only water. So, he turned right around to a bearing of 270 degrees to return to land.

Not so fast. What he didn't realize was that by reentering the United States he crossed our air protective shield, the Air Defense Identification Zone. If you exit the airspace no one pays attention (at least they didn't then), but if you come into U.S. airspace, officials gave you a lot of attention, especially in south Florida. In this case, since there was no flight plan, military jet interceptors were scrambled.

Keep in mind that our hitchhiker had never flown a plane in his life. There he is with two military jets buzzing him and waving at him. He got plenty scared and was trying to get on the radio, pushing buttons, screaming for help.

Finally he struck gold with one of the frequencies and contacted the Miami air traffic center. They told him to follow those jets, which would lead him toward Key West, where I was waiting to apprehend him.

The air traffic control center called my flight instructor (my wife and I were learning to fly around this time), who was up in the sky, and asked him to help out. He established contact with the hitchhiker, rendezvoused with him in the air, and began to give him landing lessons. The hitchhiker made, I think, four passes. He lined up and turned and cut power. Eventually, the instructor got him low enough and he banged onto the runway. It was a pretty hard landing but not enough to even damage the plane. Once he was safely on the ground we took him into custody and charged him with stealing a motor vehicle. (Well, technically it was, of course.)

In Key West something was always going on.

• • •

Since I belonged to a navy flying club I was able to take advantage of their cheap airplane rental rate—$18 an hour!—to practice flying. Kathy and I liked being up in the air so much that we even began taking family vacations by air. One time, we took a flying vacation all the way from Florida to Texas to visit my mom and my brothers. Another time we took a week and meandered around the southern United States. The only problem was that we were flying with our two young boys at the time, and there were many bathroom stops along the way.

I was flying a lot in those days for pleasure and for work. Since I often had to go to the firing range, which was immediately adjacent to the airport in Naples, it was much easier for me to fly over and back in one day, rather than take three days driving. Flying would take me an hour and a half. I'd fly to the Naples airport, park the plane, climb across the fence, and I was there. Then at 4:00 PM I'd fly back to Key West, home in time for supper.

• • •

Besides the excitement of the work, there was no denying that Key West was picturesque and had its moments. However, I can't stress enough how it wasn't the best place to raise a family. The residents had to contend with a lack of housing and horrible public schools. Since my oldest, Milt, was ready to enter school we had no choice except to put him in private school, which, of course, cost quite a bit of money.

This only added to my desire to get out of the place. I was scared of being trapped there, because in the FBI, the third assignment is usually the charm. You are stuck there for your career—and I had no intention of being stuck in Key West for my career.

The only way out, however, was to volunteer for a "hardship assignment," where I'd get placed in an undesirable location for a couple of years and then be permanently assigned to a place that would be a better location. Since I was a Spanish speaker and San Juan was always desperately in need of staff, anyone who volunteered with those qualifications was immediately snapped up for a two-year tour in San Juan. I put in for Puerto Rico. It turned out to be all too easy: after submitting my change of "office of preference," I was there in only a matter of weeks.

## Conflict of Interest

My tour of duty in Puerto Rico was nothing like the idyllic scenes in the travel brochures.

When I was there, from 1968 to 1970, it was a very turbulent time for the island. The "Independistas" (groups who advocated independence of Puerto Rico from the United States) were erupting in violence. We lived in Guaynabo, about twenty minutes away from San Juan, and that area seemed to be a center for angry activity. One block from our house, a grocery supermarket, Pueblo, part of a U.S. chain, was firebombed. One block in the opposite direction, Barkers, another U.S.-owned business, was firebombed as well. American military personnel were forbidden to wear their uniforms off base because several had been gunned down in broad daylight in downtown San Juan.

Needless to say, the FBI wasn't well loved and there were several plots to assassinate the special agent in charge of the office or to kill an FBI agent. This forced us to always work in pairs and to always be extremely cautious. It was nerve-racking at times but we learned to live with it. I was always most concerned about my family. They, too, had to be very careful. Fortunately, we never had a violent incident, but we dealt with constant discrimination. For example, when entering a restaurant we would be the last to be served and in stores we would be ignored. As "gringos," we were not welcome on the island during those years.

• • •

When we weren't dodging firebombs we were doing more of the typical FBI work. In those days Puerto Rico was a haven for stolen cars. Ships would constantly arrive filled with four hundred or more cars and we knew that many of them were hot. The island wasn't the only place for trafficking in stolen vehicles, of course—thefts were happening all over the country. In the late 1960s the FBI began putting stolen car Vehicle Identification Numbers (VINs) in a database for the National Crime Information Center (NCIC). (As fate would have it, the database would eventually be a key part in solving perhaps my biggest case, the Oklahoma City bombing.)

The system worked great for the rest of the country—reducing the number of stolen cars—but not in our little backwater. The office in Puerto Rico was not set up with an NCIC terminal. So, we took matters into our own hands, entering the twenty-five-digit VIN for each of the cars and sending them by Teletype to Washington, where they were run through the NCIC system. Surprise, surprise: about one hundred of those four hundred cars per shipload were stolen; you can guess that it only took a couple more of these identifications before the number of stolen cars came to fifty or fewer. The sad thing is that the buyers didn't realize that the cars were stolen. Vehicles were shipped for a song and sold to customers at great discounts.

On many of these cases I worked with Howard McCook, the FBI's principal man assigned to tackling the stolen car problem. McCook was the one who came up with the idea of putting the VINs in the database. In one case I remember, we got a big break on a car thief we had been hunting forever. The office had been at it so long that I thought that we might never catch him. Then one night an informant contacted us out of the blue: our guy was drinking in a bar in San Juan. "Could we respond?"

"Are you kidding? Sure!" McCook said.

I was always happy to go on an apprehension. They were usually a lot of fun and this one was shaping up to be no exception. We went right over to the bar and found someone who looked like he fit the description of the suspect, based only on what he was wearing. But he produced an ID with a different name. Because he didn't look like the right guy, we were all set to dismiss him. To do so, however, we'd have to take him downtown to clear up his identity.

"No problem," he said. "I'll go with you."

Since we weren't arresting him, we didn't use cuffs. Howard drove and I sat in the back with him. En route back to the office Howard called the San Juan office by radio and asked them to get started—it was 4:00 AM at that point—by doing a reverse directory check on his address. By the time the dispatcher called back a few minutes later, we were going about forty miles an hour on a street heading toward the office. It was late and we wanted to wrap things up for the night since it looked as if we'd be going home empty-handed, again. The dispatcher came back on the radio, but before he said anything our suspect was out the car door. Howard slammed on the brakes and then we were out the doors, too. The chase was on. And then off—almost immediately we lost him. Every now and then we heard him, but he picked quite a neighborhood to run away from us, a slum right by the river.

Howard and I communicated with each other by yelling since we knew that our would-be arrestee was in between us. We were triangulating the guy. Suddenly, I heard him crawling along a concrete block wall. I jumped on top of it. I saw him. He saw me.

"Stop or I'll shoot," I said.

He froze. But who knew whether he was armed or not? We had not searched the man because we had not arrested him.

Before I could weigh that any further, Howard was reaching over the wall, grabbing him, and cuffing him (finally!). The whole thing was odd because he was this dapper guy who had just crawled around in the mud, and he still looked perfectly dressed.

Considering the neighborhood, that was nothing short of remarkable. Called the *Barrio Fangito* ("Mud Neighborhood"), it was one of the filthiest areas you can imagine. Not to mention one of the meanest. This was a place where you'd think people would cut your throat just to see you bleed. The houses were built on stilts, literally on mud flats. We're talking wood planks laid on mud in lieu of streets. The alleys between the houses were so narrow that if you were walking on the planks with your arms folded, your elbows would hit the back walls of the houses. You can guess that there was no electricity or running water or garbage removal. The residents threw trash and chamber pots onto the mud flats. It stunk like you would not believe.

I learned that many of the residents were as honest as they were poor. They often helped us in finding fugitives, which was great since their neighborhood was extraordinarily confusing. The first time I went into the area, I did not think that I was going to come out alive. Everything was built so helter-skelter that you could wander around for years and still be lost. The residents would have to lead me through what looked like a maze. Whether they realized it or not, they were an essential part of our work in the area.

I still get the shivers when I think about the time I was on a stakeout watching the back of a particular house. If anyone left the house I was supposed to arrest him. I had been in position for barely five minutes, with my flashlight off, when I began to hear all kinds of uncanny noises. I turned my light back on and stood there for more than a minute in disbelief. In the tiny backyard area there must have been a dozen rats about the size of small cats. They had scattered the moment my light went on but sure enough when my light was off again I could hear those noises once more. I figured out that the sounds were their claws scratching.

That was it, my cue. I'd had enough of rat scratching. I'd prefer to take my chances in the house. Adrenaline pumping, I went inside after a radio call to my team. Searching the whole place, we couldn't find a soul. Finally, at the back of one of the bedrooms I spotted a group of old school lockers that looked as if they had been probably ripped from the wall of the local high school. I knew something good had to be in there. So, I opened the lockers one by one. Bingo! When I opened the third one there was a guy in there all scrunched up. So, I yanked him out and put the cuffs on him, and we took him downtown.

Another fun time in the barrio happened when I was again looking through a house, trying to find a fugitive. I'm in the house, which was filthy, by the way, talking to the fugitive's girlfriend. She says she hasn't seen him. She says her boyfriend's not there but seems awfully distracted. Twice I see her eyes glance at a pile of clothes in the corner. When I go over to the pile and kick it, I just about lose an eardrum amid all the yelping. There was certainly more than dirty shirts and socks in that pile. The whole thing still makes me laugh. If only the girlfriend hadn't been looking his way, I would have completely missed him and had one less fugitive in custody.

• • •

It wasn't all fugitives and dirty houses while we were in Puerto Rico, however. I continued to take the flying lessons that I started in Florida. I got my commercial pilot's license and instrument rating in San Juan. In fact, flying led to my first and only matchmaking attempt.

My instructor, Paul Raker, was always saying that he couldn't find anyone to date. The Puerto Rican girls didn't want to date an American and there were very few single American girls down there. Or so we thought, until I remembered that I knew one very well: my secretary, June.

One afternoon as June was doing some typing for me, it hit me. Why not set them up? So, Kathy and I invited the pair to dinner at our house. They hit it off very well, in fact. Soon thereafter, they got married, are still together, and remain good friends of ours to this day.

By far the most important event that took place in Puerto Rico, however, was the birth of our third child, Karen, on October 20, 1969. The hospital care was not that of the continental United States—it was much better. In Puerto Rico the mother is totally taken care of, completely pampered. The hospital staff hardly let the mother hold the baby for fear that it would tire her out. Nurses insisted that Kathy was to recuperate and not do anything. Her getting out of bed would have started an argument. She had a completely normal pregnancy, but the hospital insisted on keeping her there for days. Can you imagine anything like that here with today's health care market?

But good medical service alone was not enough to keep us in Puerto Rico. Not by a long shot.

## Spies Like Us

Nothing about one of my San Juan colleagues, Richard Miller, indicated that he would go on to become the first member of the FBI to be indicted for espionage. He was a bumbling idiot. There's always that one person in every FBI office about whom everyone tells a lot of stories and asks, "Did you hear what so-and-so did? Have you heard the latest?" In our office that person was Richard Miller.

I was continually amazed by what he'd do. He was singularly the sloppiest person I have ever known. He just was dirty, physically dirty. He constantly wore the same outfit, a sport coat and a pair of pants that seemed to be made of canvas. The pants were always soiled and spotted. I highly doubt they ever saw the inside of a washing machine. He could have stood them up in a corner! There were so many complaints about Miller—he constantly smelled sweaty, for example—that the supervisor finally had to have a session with him and order him to wash his pants and to take a bath.

Miller and I were in a carpool together. In those days you couldn't take an FBI car home. You had to get to work and then get your FBI car and go about your business. Another agent in the carpool was a man who was the exact opposite of Miller; let's call him "Mr. Neatnik." He was always just as neat as a pin. Even at the close of the day he looked as if he had just put his shirt on—it was freshly pressed, without a wrinkle on him anywhere. I've never met anyone who looked as if he had just stepped off the pages of *Gentlemen's Quarterly* magazine more than Neatnik did. Sharp as a tack.

The way we operated our car pool was that one guy would drive a whole week and then it was rotation time and somebody else would drive the next week. You can imagine how much we would look forward to being picked up by Miller, who had a beat-up old car that was as dirty as he was. One morning, after he made the rounds picking everyone up and we were exiting the car, walking to work, I noticed something that I knew would not sit so well with Neatnik. On the back of his coat was stuck a partially eaten peanut butter and jelly sandwich. When I pointed this out to him I thought that he was going to explode, literally. I think he would have physically assaulted Miller right then and there if we weren't around: "You slovenly, dirty, low-down. . . !" Miller was scared out of his wits—so was I, for that matter. I thought Miller was about to be killed since we were all armed. As you can imagine, that was the end of the carpool as far as Richard Miller was concerned.

Then there was the time our office worked a special case over in St. Thomas to complete a comprehensive background investigation on a judicial appointee very quickly and, lucky me, I got to be Miller's roommate. For the several days while we were there I am pretty sure that he never bathed. In fact, I don't believe that he ever took off his underwear.

In the middle of the trip his wife showed up with their children, depositing the kids with him while she went shopping. (St. Thomas is a free port and things from Europe are very cheap there.) Keep in mind that we were there on official FBI business, not a duty-free vacation. Not so for Mrs. Miller, who purchased a complete set of china. But it ended up costing enough so that a duty would have to be paid to bring the set into the United States. So, what did she do? Turned the set over to Miller and returned to San Juan with the kids.

Miller approached each of us working in St. Thomas on the special case and asked if we would pack some of the china in our suitcases and bring it to San Juan. Was he kidding? Of course, we all refused. Funny enough, I later learned that Miller had approached the agent who was permanently assigned to St. Thomas and asked him if he would put the china in the FBI mail, two or three pieces at a time. Now this was the man whose job it was to prevent incidents like this! He, too, refused. I supposed that Miller finally paid the duty on the china because I don't know of any other way that he could have smuggled it into San Juan. Regrettably, we didn't report him for this activity—we just regarded it as another of his goofy behaviors.

Years later—in 1984—when I was watching the news one night, I was stunned. Miller was being arrested, along with two Russian émigrés, for spying for the Soviets. While I was shocked that he was being charged with being a spy, I can't say that I was totally surprised that Miller's behavior had become so bizarre that it got him into serious trouble.

While I don't know a lot about the case, I do know that the Soviets did approach him while he was in Los Angeles. As bait they used a woman, Svetlana Ogorodnikov, who would eventually become his lover, in order to get him attracted. Miller's story, however, was that he was, in fact, trying to recruit her as a double agent. That, he said, was the reason why he was clandestinely meeting with her. The problem was that nothing of that nature was substantiated in files anywhere. There were no reports made, nothing. Now I'm not sure how the whole situation came to the attention of the Los Angeles office, but it did. Miller, who was working in the office at the time, was placed under surveillance. His phones were tapped, he was followed, and everything was done that you would normally do in a very complex investigation until Miller was ultimately caught red-handed. He was in the act of passing Svetlana some information, in exchange for money and gold, whereupon he was arrested, along with the woman and her husband, Nikolai.

Miller was so goofy that I think there was probably some grain of truth to his recruitment defense. None of us who worked with him would have ever thought that he was a danger to society or a potential spy. However, his behavior was inexcusable and he deserved the prison sentence that he (eventually) received. After a first mistrial, he was found guilty of espionage and bribery at the second trial, but that was later dismissed on a technicality. After the third trial and conviction, he was sentenced to twenty years, later reduced to thirteen, and he was released early.

## Sin City

"Guess the location," said Nick Stames, the assistant special agent in charge (ASAC) in San Juan, when he called with the news that he had my transfer in hand.

"San Antonio?" I asked, thinking that though I wanted Dallas, I knew I wouldn't be so lucky. Maybe I'd get the next best thing.

"No, try farther west."

"El Paso?"

"Nope. Keep Going"

"Albuquerque?"

"No."

Now by this time I was, shall we say, rather tense. Nick could tell—and decided to let me off the hook.

"Las Vegas."

"Las Vegas?"

"Las Vegas."

Serendipity!!

Besides the gamblers and the soon-to-be-marrieds, I was probably the happiest person ever to show up in that city. Why? No better reason than that Las Vegas wasn't Puerto Rico. And though Las Vegas wasn't my ideal city, this move got me closer to my top choice, Dallas.

It wasn't until years later—when I became the FBI agent in charge of assigning transfers—that I learned how this transfer came about. (But even though I didn't understand it when it happened, you can be sure that I didn't mind.)

An assignment to San Juan was for a two-year tour, unlike most FBI assignments, which are indefinite, because of the hardship nature. So, about ninety days before my time there would be finished, the transfer agent called me with a request.

"Would you mind voluntarily extending your assignment for a year?" he asked.

Was he joking? Now, of, course, it was completely routine for him to be asking the question, but there was no way that meant that I would have to entertain it. The choice was strictly optional, but an option which I declined.

It just so happened that on the same day that the Transfer Man had my file on his desk for consideration of my new assignment, he received a request from the special agent in charge of the Las Vegas office.

"Do you have a Spanish-speaking special agent?"

Did he ever.

Las Vegas needed one Spanish-speaking agent following Castro's takeover in Cuba. A large number of Cubans involved in the gaming industry there had fled the island for Las Vegas, where they went to work for various casinos. Once again Fidel Castro would have an effect on my life. Thank you, Fidel.

• • •

I left Puerto Rico in July 1970. It was quite a trip. We first had to ship our car to Miami from San Juan about two weeks before actually leaving. This shipment was just one of many, many moving expenses to come, throughout my career, for which the bureau did not reimburse me. Though it galled me quite a bit, there was no option but to get used to it. In this case, the shipment cost about $500—quite a lot of money then.

After said expensive shipment, we flew to Miami, where we picked up our car for the drive westward. My daughter, Karen, was an infant, making the cross-country trip an especially tough one. En route we stopped to visit my family in Texas, where we collected our dog, Benji, who had been shipped there from Puerto Rico (no reimbursement, either). Finally, we arrived in Las Vegas during a searing heat wave—the middle of the summer was not the best time to acclimate—but we were thrilled to be there, nonetheless.

Since we now had three kids and a dog, it made sense to make a house purchase. (Though this would be our second, the idea was still exciting.) We bought a three-bedroom ranch on the west side of town, which was about a fifteen-minute commute from the office. This was one of the happiest living experiences for our family—lots of barbecues and dirt bike riding for the kids. It was a very nice, middle-class community whose neighbors included a local high school chemistry teacher, a minister, and a person who worked at the Nevada Test Site, where nuclear weapons were tested. I bought myself a 1957 GMC pickup truck for $500. I had wanted a truck to commute in and this one fit the bill: thirteen-years old, beat up, and with over 100,000 miles on it.

• • •

During my time there, the Mafia was still very much alive in Las Vegas, though it was a far cry from the power it was during the Rat Pack era. The Nevada Gaming Commission had been established for many years by the early 1970s and was trying desperately to crack down on Mafia ownership and influence in the casinos. The FBI worked very closely with the commission and would furnish information routinely concerning any mob activity relating to the casinos. The bureau had its work laid out for it, since the mob and attendant attorneys were very clever at using straw men and corporations to hide ownership.

Not that I was personally involved in any organized crime cases. During those years there were only two squads in the office—one handled only organized crime cases (Mafia, etc.) and the other handled everything else. I was on the "everything else" squad. I worked primarily fugitive cases. I also handled a number of general criminal cases such as bank robberies, theft from interstate shipments, interstate transportation of stolen motor vehicles, and so on. There was a friendly rivalry between the two groups.

In those days a lot of the FBI organized crime cases were essentially gambling cases involving rings operating throughout the United States. Because Las Vegas was a "free" territory for the mob—that is, no single family had control—any family was free to operate in Las Vegas. Consequently, the organized crime squad in our office had investigations involving mobsters from Chicago and Philadelphia as well as New York. As a result they rarely got credit for convictions, since they were usually assisting another field office elsewhere. My squad never got tired of goading them on this issue.

We also had fun reminding the organized crime squad that gambling in Nevada was legal. "Maybe your time would be better spent investigating something that was illegal?" That almost always got a rise out of them.

In Las Vegas one always had to be especially careful of acting in any way that carried a whiff of impropriety. To that end I didn't go near the casinos really, except on business and when guests were in town. I could not afford to gamble very much, anyway, but I had my share of luck on the slot machines. Many times I would go to the grocery or pharmacy to pick up something and would put a dollar or two in the nickel slots. (Remember, this was Las Vegas and the slot machines were *everywhere*.) I won a lot, hitting $25 jackpots and once hit for $200 on a single nickel.

My work hunting fugitives required me to contact officials in casinos often because Las Vegas was a powerful attraction for those who had hit it big robbing a bank or successfully completing a scam of some sort. During the three years that I was there I made hundreds of arrests and a good number of them took place in the casinos or hotels within the casinos. This meant that I was in the casinos frequently enough to be recognized by the staff. Therefore, if I went into a casino after hours with family or friends it wouldn't exactly be an anonymous trip.

Once, when my sister and her husband were in town, we went out one evening to see Sammy Davis Jr. perform. I had personally made the reservations in my name—a mistake as it turned out. We had a great evening at a dinner show, but when it came time for the bill the waiter informed me that it had been taken care of.

"Pardon me?" I asked the waiter, who was not used to seeing people question free evenings out. He wouldn't, or couldn't, tell me any information.

I got up from the table to find the captain. As an agent for the FBI, I couldn't have my bill taken care of.

"I can only tell you that there was no bill for your party since someone else had taken care of it," he said.

"But who?" I asked.

With that question came silence. Neither the captain nor any member of the staff would give me the bill, even though I made quite a show. To this day I don't know who picked up the tab, but I believe it was someone on the casino staff. At least I hope that was the case. Since they wouldn't let me pay, I made sure to leave a huge tip.

When I went back the next day and talked to some of my contacts there at the casino, they were adamant that I should drop the matter. Their position was that I would be insulting the management person who authorized payment of my bill since it would imply that my dinner bill was a bribe or something unusual. They pointed out that at every dinner show are were a large number of people "comped" by the casino (comped as in "complimentary"). After that I rarely went to the casinos in the evening, and if I did, reservations were made under another name.

## Unrest—Civil and Otherwise

When I was working in Nevada, the country was experiencing a period of great unrest. With all the turbulence surrounding the civil rights movement, the late 1960s and 1970s were particularly difficult times for the FBI. Americans were very distrustful and many stood against any authority.

Between Jane Fonda running around and the activities of people like the Black Panthers, who were as violent as anybody you ever would want to find, mayhem ruled. These radicals were darlings of the liberal left. Any law enforcement intrusion or investigation into their activities was looked upon by the media, and society for that matter, as very oppressive.

"Off the Pigs" was practically the motto of these groups, especially the Black Panthers. They could say things like that—that was fine—but you couldn't investigate any of these people. If you did then you were trampling on their civil liberties, oppressing their political viewpoints. That atmosphere was highly frustrating for us.

Not only that, but it was dangerous. There were a number of sniper killings of police officers. The furor got to such a point that the FBI office in Berkeley was blown up. Anarchists planted a bomb in a public area that shared a common wall with the office. (This happened on a Sunday morning so, luckily, no one was there working, but considerable damage was done.) After the bomb exploded they came in and sprayed graffiti all over the remaining walls of the office.

Berkeley was the center of everything that was happening in these times. I happened to see a picture taken from a police helicopter of a truly disturbing scene there. Knowing that the authorities would be looking down, radical teachers had lined up the first, second, third, and fourth graders to spell out "Fuck You" in a Berkeley schoolyard.

That was the kind of sentiment that existed at the time. It was very, very difficult to be a law enforcement officer of any type during those days, because there were very strong feelings against the establishment represented by the government. In many ways it was like war. And the FBI definitely got some black eyes.

The biggest black eye of all was the Counter Intelligence Program, otherwise known as COINTELPRO. That was the moniker for all plans to counter the activities of these radical groups in any way that we could. The program was designed to disrupt these cells so they were not able to function.

The movie *Mississippi Burning* shows some good illustrations of how COINTELPRO worked. In the movie Gene Hackman plays an FBI agent investigating the Ku Klux Klan's murder of the three civil rights workers mentioned in chapter 2. In one scene he and his colleague pick up an individual at his place of work and act very friendly to him. They say such things as, "We haven't talked to you in a long time." They get the man in a car and drive him through town, making it appear as though he is cooperating with the FBI.

This, of course, is all a surprise to the man they picked up. But to the outsiders looking in, they see the situation and think, "Boy, he is really chummy with the FBI. He must be one of their informants."

It wasn't too much longer before the KKK was taking him out into the woods to teach him a "lesson." Incidents like this one happened many times.

In COINTELPRO, you destroy a person's ability to function within the organization. As a result, he either has to leave or else gets thrown out of the organization. Sometimes he gets murdered, if it's a fairly radical group.

Another common example of COINTELPRO strategy was document forgeries. Mysteriously a report written to the FBI, as if written by a particular group member, would find its way to the headquarters of the group.

One of the most famous COINTELPRO targets was Martin Luther King Jr. He and Hoover were very much at odds with one another and so Hoover had the FBI investigating some of his activities. And, at one point, allegedly—I never saw this and I'm recounting from other things that I've heard and read—a letter was sent to Coretta King, Dr. King's wife, about some alleged illicit sexual activities of her husband's. The goal was to cause him all kinds of grief and lessen his ability to be a leader.

Why did Hoover hate Dr. King? Communism. Some of Dr. King's key advisers and key members were believed by Hoover to be Communist sympathizers. So, Hoover, who was fervently anti-Communist, felt that Dr. King was influenced, if not controlled, by the Communist Party.

COINTELPRO was exposed in the aftermath of a break-in at the office of the Media, Pennsylvania, resident agency FBI office in March 1971. An extremely radical group, "Citizens Committee to Investigate the FBI," stole documents, case reports, and all kinds of stuff and gave it to the media. Some of those documents were related to COINTELPRO. After that events just snowballed. There were lawsuits and even a Senate investigation.

This was one of the FBI's darkest hours. The media painted the FBI as the most horrible, wicked organization you could possibly imagine. Their take was that here we were willy-nilly destroying the reputations of these wonderfully innocent people. That's all crap. These were not wonderfully innocent people. With very few exceptions, these were some really bad people who were doing terrible things, many of them quite violent.

• • •

As you can imagine, this was an era that created folk heroes out of antiestablishment figures. One such hero whom America was cheering on was "D. B. Cooper."

On the eve of Thanksgiving 1971, one of America's most infamous hijackers made his name, although no one really knows what his name really was. Cooper was on a flight from Portland to Seattle for only a few minutes, when he handed a note to one of the stewardesses: "I have a bomb in my briefcase."

He demanded $200,000 in twenty-dollar bills, four parachutes, and "no funny stuff." During a refueling stop in Seattle he got everything he requested. From there, Cooper ordered the plane to fly to Mexico City via Reno. The plane was to fly at a low altitude because he was planning to jump. Since passengers were evacuated in Seattle and the one remaining stewardess was ordered into the cockpit, no one knows exactly where Cooper made his exit. He lowered the rear stairway somewhere over the Lewis River in southwest Washington.

He was never found. However, in 1980 an eight-year-old boy discovered $6,000 along the banks of the Columbia River near Vancouver. The (frustrated) FBI agent on the case was Ralph Himmelsbach, who had been the senior agent assigned to help me, the new agent, learn the ropes when I first joined the FBI in Portland. Himmelsbach, who wrote a book about the case, thinks that Cooper died in the jump, although he admits that we never will know what really happened.

In keeping with the times, Cooper instantly became *the* folk hero. Why? He had tricked the establishment out of money, all the while was polite to the aircrew, and his "bomb" consisted of nothing more than a briefcase filled with road flares and wire held together with clay. There was even a song written about him, and every year in Washington State there is a party and look-a-like contest as a tribute.

As with any successful operation there are copycats and D. B. Cooper's was no exception. In the wake of his hijacking, the first one pulled off just for money instead of political reasons, there were scores of emulators.

We had our own D. B. Cooper in Nevada. This hijacker took control of a plane flying out of Oakland. He commandeered the aircraft while it was on the ground. Like Cooper, he demanded, and got, a large amount of money and several parachutes (one of which was rigged, unbeknownst to him, with a radio beacon). Once he got all the goods he kicked the passengers off. Airborne again and headed toward Denver, he set up his grand exit over Nevada. When the rear door opened, two parachutes went out, one of which was the rigged one.

The spot he chose was about fifty miles out in the middle of absolutely nowhere. A long way from Las Vegas, it would take hours to drive out there. So, we decided to fly the distance since the trip would be quicker and searches by air, rather than ground, would be more fruitful. FBI headquarters agreed (remember that we had to run everything by HQ) but insisted that we hire a contract pilot rather than have me, an FBI person, fly the plane.

When we did finally get everything together and reached the area, we realized that the coordinates that had been given to us were way, way off. The parachute with the beacon had opened and drifted in the wind, but once we flew over a nearby mountain range we could see it immediately.

We never found the second chute.

When the ground units later arrived we directed them to the site. They couldn't even see the parachute until they were within ten feet of it—despite the fact that there were no trees and the brush was barely a foot high. The parachute, however, turned out to be a decoy.

The hijacker merely sent the parachutes out over Nevada to confuse things and buy some time. Instead he bailed out over his own property—as I recall he sprained or broke his leg when he landed—near Denver, the destination he had demanded for the plane. A neighbor saw him floating from the sky and turned him in. The money was found in an abandoned toolshed on the property.

● ● ●

One of the events that stands out most in my mind during these times was the huge civil rights demonstration in Las Vegas after Dr. King was killed.

As the planning got under way, and thousands were getting ready to show up, casino owners became increasingly panicked. Would their properties get trashed? Would customers get scared off? Would millions of dollars be lost? To prevent any such outcome, they hired just about every security officer in the state of Nevada. Think about the monumental task this kind of protection would be, considering that most casinos didn't have front doors since they were open twenty-four hours a day. Oh, and throw into the mix that Jane Fonda was involved in this thing, too. It's not as though this rally would need any more help to get people's emotions stirred up.

And I was one of two street agents assigned to be out in front of the rally.

The demonstration was to take place on the steps before Caesar's Palace. And so, on that morning, ten thousand people were marching up the main driveway toward the front of the casino. Since Caesar's was one of the few casinos with doors—glass doors in this case—it begged the question: "Should I close them?" If I did, what effect would that have? I thought about these things as I hurried inside, trying to beat the crowd. I ultimately decided against closing the doors. That, as it turned out, was exactly the right move.

The leader of the march gave his speech and then without much ado led the masses, all ten thousand of them, through the casino. There was no stopping them, megaphones in hand and singing "We Shall Overcome." The crowd went in and went out, and it was over. Nothing was damaged. Amazing. All of that worrying for absolutely nothing.

But the part that I'll never forget was the reaction of the gamblers inside the casino. Or, more accurately, the lack thereof. The people inside playing the slots couldn't have cared less. They momentarily stopped what they were doing, looked up at the sea of marchers going by, and that was it. Seconds later they were pulling away again on the levers.

No one can say that Las Vegas wasn't without its charms.

• • •

During my time in that city I began to get cocky about my ability to arrest fugitives. I would compete with myself to see how many I could arrest in one day: three was my best score. I was the smuggest agent ever. I had become overconfident and had made several arrests of dangerous fugitives by myself.

This was all fine and good until one day I had an epiphany, when I was about to make the arrest of a heavily armed and dangerous man. Other people were busy so I figured that I'd take this guy by myself instead of waiting around for help. Then just as I had him in my sights it dawned on me that this was stupid. Really stupid. I realized that I was exposing myself unnecessarily and that unless I changed my ways I was going to get my head blown off one day.

And after ten years chasing down fugitives I began to wonder whether I wanted to spend another twenty years on the street, especially since I was getting so reckless. Ten years as a street agent is quite a bit longer than many other FBI managers put in before starting up the career ladder. Did I even want to try to move up?

Around same time as I was weighing all this, a colleague was doing some weighing of his own. "I'm sorry that I never had the initiative to advance," an old-timer in the office counseled me one afternoon, out of the blue.

Although this man frequently complained about management—and I agreed that some FBI managers were sadly lacking—he admitted that he had no right to complain, since he had not taken the initiative and made the sacrifices to go up the career ladder.

"You, however, should do it. You should try to go higher," he said. "You have the experience and personality that street agents like to see in management."

Flattering doesn't even begin to describe this statement. Maybe I had been thinking about this kind of move all along, but hearing him say it really lit a fire under me to do something.

So, I took his advice and started up the ladder. And out of Las Vegas.

# 4 Washington and Boston

## Getting into Uniform

That I spent ten years on the street before being promoted to FBIHQ was somewhat unusual. Most agents who were interested in advancement began seeking promotion very early in their careers.

I was very fortunate because the ten years of experience I did have were extremely varied. I had worked in a small field office (Portland), a large field office (Newark), in a large resident agency (Camden), and in a small resident agency (Key West). In terms of geography, I had worked in the Pacific Northwest (Portland), the Northeast (Newark) and the Southeast (Miami and Key West), outside the continental United States (San Juan), and the West (Las Vegas).

During those ten years and these various assignments, I had worked almost every type of case imaginable within the FBI's jurisdiction and in every program area. The broad experience I had gained proved invaluable as I moved up the career advancement ladder. It gave me a leg up over other candidates in the promotion process. And it gave me enormous credibility with those who worked for me because I had actually done the work that I was asking them to do.

As hesitant as I had been about going for that first promotion, it turned out to be pretty easy. In this case, it was a perfect example of "ask and ye shall receive." I made the request—asked for consideration for promotion to a supervisory assignment—and I got it. However, it unquestionably made a difference that I knew the right people.

The unwritten rule in the FBI back then was that if you wanted a promotion, you had better be connected. Luckily, thanks to relationships I had formed while in previous posts, I was. When I was thinking about my next move I called Andy McKean, with whom I had worked closely in Camden, for advice. By that time he was working at headquarters as the assistant section chief of the Uniform Crime Reporting (UCR) Section. I was interested in advancement, I told him, and I was up for anything that was available. It just so happened that his group was receiving applications. "We're adding five agents," he told me, and offered to put my name in the hopper. Based on his recommendation I was selected to be one of those people. It was 1973 and I was headed to headquarters in Washington for what was my eighth assignment in ten years.

A footnote: Now, of course, there were some people who didn't want to get promoted. In the FBI, a promotion almost always spelled transfer, which was usually costly, involving a family move. Many agents would effectively say, "No, I don't want to be considered for advancement, thank you very much, but I'll stay where I am." In so doing, many agents could stay virtually their entire careers in two assignments.

That, however, was not for me.

• • •

I was off to my new assignment, as a supervisor in the Uniform Crime Reporting Section, which came complete with quite a history.

Back in the early 1900s there was no standard way that crime information and data were reported in the United States. One police department would have some data about how many crimes were committed in its jurisdiction, but it was completely uncoordinated with other departments. A report, for example, in the New York Police Department bore little resemblance to a report made by the Chicago Police Department. That meant that there was no way to keep track of the number—and types—of crimes occurring. Plus, because different states had different definitions and penalties for the same crimes, one crime could be called a felony or a misdemeanor, depending on the criminal's location.

It wasn't until the late 1920s that the International Association of Chiefs of Police (IACP) recognized that this was a major problem. To fix it, the IACP put together a committee for all the police departments to figure out how to report crime data uniformly. With that they could properly gauge fluctuations in the overall volume and rate of crime. What resulted was a crime index, which included and defined seven crimes: murder or non-negligent manslaughter, forcible rape, robbery, aggravated assault, burglary, larceny-theft, and motor-vehicle theft. Arson was added as the eighth index offense in 1979.

Unfortunately, for the IACP it worked too well. Starting in 1930, the reporting began, with monthly data coming in from four hundred cities, representing twenty million people in forty-three states. The IACP needed to turn over the task of collecting to a government agency that had better funding and a better ability to administer a nationwide system. The IACP lobbied successfully for legislation to designate the FBI as the agency to do just that.

From then on, individual police agencies reported their crime data monthly to the FBI, which processed and compiled the reports. From there, the FBI published the information annually. The number of agencies reporting grew to such a point that by the early 1970s the number was around sixteen thousand.

Considering the overwhelming volume of paper, the FBI decided to streamline the system. When I arrived the bureau was trying to convince every state that it should collect all data within its state—instead of having the individual departments within each state reporting directly to the FBI. The FBI proposed that the agency handling the state's data collection would then report its data monthly to the FBI by computer tape, using a tape that was compatible with the FBI's national database. Sounds easy now—sort of—but back then this just seemed like a Herculean task. It involved many states—ideally all fifty—all using the same reporting system. This required increased staff and money.

There were five of us assigned to beef up and convert as many states as fast as we could to this new reporting system. That's what I did for over three years, traveling all over the country, speaking to various police departments and legislators. It required an incredible amount of police training because the reporting standards were very different for many police agencies. In the UCR reporting system, if a person breaks into and enters an apartment and then rapes the occupant, then that crime is reported as a rape, because that is the more serious crime. For Uniform Crime Reporting, the incident is counted as one crime (rape), not two (rape and breaking and entering). The UCR system requires that multiple offenses committed during one incident be counted as one crime classified under the highest offense category.

The system is very complex and requires constant monitoring to ensure accuracy and uniformity. Today, the program encompasses seventeen thousand city, county, and state law enforcement agencies, representing about 282 million U.S. inhabitants—about 94 percent of the total population.

But as with anything well intentioned, this system has been the subject of controversy and criticism over the years. There have been various efforts to improve the system and how it works—the years I spent there in the 1970s were just part of one of these many efforts. However, what this system offers, essentially, is what the police departments report and there are inherently going to be problems with this data. For example, it's happened that the mayor or police chief decides that he or she doesn't want any more adverse publicity about the crime in the community so the mayor or chief underreports or misreports crime. While the FBI has an auditing system to catch those kinds of discrepancies, it was, and is still, a hassle. It's happened that we'd have to take a city out of the report because its data was unreliable. Criminologists and researchers worldwide rely on the data, so every effort was made to ensure its accuracy.

All told, it was a very fun job that I enjoyed tremendously. It gave me very valuable exposure and experience in teaching and public speaking. I was continuously standing before groups of police or legislators, trying to convince them that they needed to go along with this new plan. Initially, I was nervous, because I had never done anything like this before, but it was all very worthwhile, especially for me later in my career, particularly when I was on the firing line and facing the press during the Atlanta Penitentiary riot and during the investigation of the Oklahoma bombing. Those audiences were often less hostile and easier to sell to than these local police agencies! I couldn't have bought this kind of training.

But after a few years, not only did I become frustrated waiting for the next promotion, but also I began to miss doing investigations. That was what I loved. As much as I liked what I was doing I was not in the mainstream of what the FBI was all about.

● ● ●

I started off in the Uniform Crime Reporting Section in supervisory level grade 14, which was considered entry level for supervisory status. I had served in that unit for nearly four years when Andy McKean, who had been the assistant section chief, was moved up to the section's top job after the longtime previous chief retired. Andy liked all of us working in the department very much and encouraged us to stay on and work with him after his promotion. "We really need to keep you people around because we need the experience here in the group."

That was a nice sentiment but I still hadn't decided what I was going to do. Granted, I had been frustrated waiting for my next promotion but that didn't mean that I was thrilled when I got it. Andy wanted me to accept a two-year commitment to move up in the Uniform Crime Reporting Section to the assistant section chief job—Andy's old job—and I wasn't sure if I wanted to accept that. Part of my concern was that I didn't want to be locked in. Even though I enjoyed the work in the Uniform Crime Reporting Section, I felt that spending two more years specializing in a unique talent that no other department in the FBI could really use wasn't practical. In addition the promotion offer was extraordinary, but a little unusual. I would be leapfrogging over other people in the section; the people I was working for would now be working for me if I took the job. This, I felt, would make it sort of awkward.

What to do? To answer that, I went to get some advice my from my old assistant special agent in charge (ASAC) in Puerto Rico, Nick Stames, who at that point was the SAC of the Washington Field Office. I considered him to be my mentor. "Don't turn down a promotion," is what he told me, when I went across the street to drop by his office. "I've been in the bureau for a long time, and if I've learned anything else it's that you should never turn down a promotion. Not only will you be passed over then for the next promotion, but also in the meantime things can change if you accept it."

This was in early 1977 and I had been in the FBI for almost fourteen years. My career in the bureau was fairly young, so given that, I took the gamble. I told my wife and family that I was committed to working there for two more years.

After only two months into the job my group felt the effects of a massive reorganization within FBI headquarters. Clarence Kelley was the director and he was reacting to criticism that headquarters was bloated with too many agents. He initiated a review of the bureau to analyze staff needs. Several teams were formed to conduct the analysis and one of the teams, headed by Bud Feeney, became known as "Feeney's Ferrets." His team was assigned to evaluate the Uniform Crime Reporting Section and it quickly determined that the number of special agents assigned should be cut by three agents. At the time there were only five of us: two grade 14s, two grade 15s, and one grade 16. Feeney's Ferrets reported that the section needed only one grade 16 and one grade 15, which meant that one grade 15 and two grade 14s would have to go.

When we got the order to reduce, our boss, Andy McKean, said, "I will leave it up to you as a group to decide who wants to go and who wants to stay." The four of us met and only person wanted to stay, whereas the rest of us were ready to go. I was one of the three volunteering to go. How right Nick Stames was!

One week after this meeting I was given a transfer to the inspector's staff, also based in Washington, D.C., as an inspector's aide. On the surface it would seem like a move backward because the Uniform Crime Reporting Section assistant section chief was now going to be only one of many aides.

But besides the appearance of a demotion, I must admit that I had a great deal. Although I had a made a two-year commitment to be further pigeonholed in the Uniform Crime Reporting Section, after a few months I was suddenly in a different job, at a grade 15 level on the inspection staff. Normally, you'd go onto the inspection staff as a grade 14 level, then when you left from the staff you'd be a grade 15. The fact that I went on as a grade 15 was highly unusual. I was the only grade 15 inspector's aide on the staff. That meant better pay and more seniority for the same work.

And the work *was* great. The skills acquired as an inspector's aide proved immensely valuable to the rest of my career. We conducted audits of all the field divisions. We did analyses of all the programs, reviewing the pending and, in some cases, closed files; interviewed support staff and supervisory staffs; and even did interviews outside the bureau, such as with police executives.

Are offices in compliance with all of the rules of the inspection? Are they doing a good job? And, if not, we'd make recommendations to correct those deficiencies. To make all of this happen the inspector in charge of an inspection would travel with anywhere from ten to twenty inspector's aides to review the office in question for two or three weeks. In the case of the New York office it would be four weeks, for example. The aides assigned would have to learn in a hurry about the investigative program they were assigned to evaluate. If it was the violent crime program then the aides had better be up on how to inspect an office handling a lot of violent crime cases.

With all the various inspection trips the agents were getting broad exposure. During the time I was there—ten months—I went to ten different field offices and reviewed ten programs. The entire process was not only calculated to improve FBI efficiency but was an invaluable learning vehicle for aides on what worked and what didn't work and who was effective and who wasn't. While you were learning yourself, you were looking at the agents to see how good they were.

In addition to the skill set that I was picking up, I was adding a few new names to my list of lifetime friends. You become close to people when you're traveling with them, and considering there was much movement of agents rotating in and out of the inspection staff, I met so many new people. As you travel together and do the inspection you are forging bonds. That can have enormous benefit later with people down the road, since most aides go on to become SACs and leaders in various other FBI positions. A group of contemporaries, who have moved through the ranks together, form a kind of loosely knit alumni group or cohort.

Because of this, when I became an ASAC I knew many of my counterparts. And, later, because of this same system, the ranking agent in charge was someone I would likely know from personal experience. The ones I didn't know I became acquainted with during SAC conferences.

If you look at the FBI as a pyramid then it works out like this: in the field there are four hundred supervisors, eighty-five to ninety ASACs, then seventy or so SACs, and—during my era—ten assistant directors. Each step up the career ladder narrows down the number of people at the next level. As a result, people at the top all know each other very well. That, I think, is one of the great strengths of the organization. When I encountered a new situation with which I wasn't familiar, I could easily call on a colleague who was. That person could do the same of me. The expert in organized crime could seek advice from someone like me who was experienced in chasing fugitives or public corruption and vice versa.

I think this is a good way to organize things but it does have its detractors. They say that it's an "old boy's network." That may be true but I think it's a benefit.

● ● ●

After ten months of constant travel, in 1977 I was ready for a different job.

My timing was good. "When you return from the San Francisco inspection," the chief inspector told me as I was preparing to leave for my latest inspection assignment, "you report to Bob Cahill. He is the transfer unit chief and you'll be assigned to the transfer unit." I was completely surprised—Cahill's was a one-man show. He was the person who controlled all the transfers of all FBI special agents in the system. I had no idea what I would do there or how I could help him, but I knew that soon I'd have thousands of new "friends." Every agent in the FBI knew who occupied the transfer office.

The transfer unit reported directly to the assistant director of the Administrative Services Division, the most powerful and feared of the FBI headquarters' divisions. Why? Because the division controlled all personnel, financial, and budget matters for the FBI. Whether it was special agent staffing, support personnel staffing, travel budgets, or even the number of automobiles or equipment purchased for and assigned to a field office, it was controlled by the Administrative Services Division.

## The Transformation

As head of the Special Agent Transfer Unit of the Personnel Section I was simultaneously the most loved and feared person in the FBI. It's not surprising that of all the positions that I held this was the most stressful, on a daily basis, of my whole career.

After running the unit by himself for years, Bob Cahill had finally convinced the powers in charge that he needed an assistant. The job was too much for one person, he told them. Indeed. But I never learned why *I* was selected. I had been expecting a transfer because I had completed my time as an inspector's aide but who knew to where? I did not know Bob Cahill, the unit chief, or his boss, Dick Long, assistant director of the Administrative Services Division, and in the FBI who you know counts for a lot.

When I arrived Cahill was smoking constantly, shaking, and generally a nervous wreck. The reason for such behavior—pressure—couldn't have been made any clearer than when he suffered a serious heart attack during my second week on the job. He was literally carried out of the building. After he recovered from the heart attack he never came back to work.

Welcome to your new post, Weldon!

I had very, very little training to be in such a position. It was never planned for me to wind up solely responsible for the special agent transfers throughout the whole FBI system. At that time there were roughly ten thousand agents and I was the one, the only one, responsible for staffing the fifty-six field offices.

Bob Cahill had run that unit solo for years and knew everything there was to know about the transfer program. He and the position had taken on an almost mythical quality. His office was thought of as a kind of inner sanctum. Everyone I knew was amazed that I had been transferred there at all, much less now running the show.

There had been theories and jokes galore about how the transfer operation ran. One of the most popular was that it was a blind monkey throwing darts at a map of the United States. As an agent I had always been intimidated by the transfer process. As much as I was terrified of it, I was always trying to figure out how the transfer person was going to place me. I knew people who kept lists going back ten years of where people had been moved in the hopes of finding out the logic of it. However, what it came down to, in large part, was pure chance.

Take how I was transferred from San Juan to Las Vegas. Ninety days before my two-year tour was up in San Juan I got a call from Bob Cahill, who asked if I wanted to volunteer to extend by one year in San Juan. I replied, "No way." Two months later I received my transfer to Las Vegas. The only Spanish-speaking agent in that office was being transferred out to Reno, despite the high numbers of Cubans, and other Hispanics, living in Las Vegas. Upon learning that his only Spanish-speaking agent was being moved to Reno, the SAC immediately called Cahill and sent documentation that the work in Las Vegas could not be effectively done without a Spanish-speaking agent. The Las Vegas request happened to hit his desk the same day that he was cutting my transfer letter. Bingo! If luck had it that my transfer came up to Cahill the previous day, who knows where I would have been sent?

It was these kinds of "mysteries" that I didn't fully realize until I arrived at the transfer unit. Transfers happened quite often because of a directive from on high—on high being the SAC of a particular office. As the Transfer Man, I was always scrambling to fulfill those requests with whatever warm bodies were available for transfer.

Before this job I had been a little bit in awe of SACs and other high-ranking people in FBI. My plan had always been to go about my business, giving them a wide berth. Now as transfer unit chief I was talking to SACs numerous times a day, and they would try as hard as they could to impress upon me how important their vacancies were. Each person's vacancies *needed* to be filled first! On average, I personally spoke to the agents in charge of all fifty-six field offices two or three times a month.

However, filling a vacancy wasn't a simple transaction. I compare it more to a treadmill or, better yet, a chess game. Everything was always in a state of flux. Each transfer required multiple moves and, invariably, a lot of people would be left unhappy. In every case where I transferred an agent out, the SAC would call and scream at me that the office there was already understaffed. Peter was always getting robbed to pay Paul.

The transfer office used information received from the inspectors, who made evaluations of the various offices and made recommendations about how many special agents were needed to staff a given field office. However, the Transfer Man could not rely only on the inspectors' evaluations. The reason was quite simple, really. The FBI was seriously understaffed during those years. The inspectors evaluated the caseload, unaddressed work, and so on and arrived at a specific staffing number for that particular office. That number *always* exceeded the number of special agents on board in that office. If you added up the recommended number of agents for each office, the number was about fifteen thousand. This created a huge problem since there were only about ten thousand special agents on duty.

The inspectors gave an ideal number for how many agents should staff a particular office. And then the SAC took that number, no matter how unrealistic, as if it were gospel—as in "the inspector said that we should have eleven zillion agents here to have an office running perfectly; therefore, give them to us now! The inspector suggested it!" Even if you were to magically come up with the extra agents, no sooner than the ink dried would the SAC be on the phone asking for more agents.

If the SACs weren't on the phone to me, then they were on the phone with the assistant director or the director to complain. Then I would get a phone call from the assistant director or the director, "Weldon, what's happening with this?" Explaining every situation to these other people was a time-consuming part of my job.

As hectic as my job was, I did catch one very lucky break. My boss, Dick Long, who was the assistant director of the Administrative Services Division, had total confidence in me. He would always back up my decisions, no matter who was applying the pressure. His only stipulation was that I couldn't play favorites. That meant that I was free to tell the SACs to go pound sand.

But telling off the SACs wouldn't solve the long-term problem. I had an indefinable, and unattainable, goal for my job. According to the inspectors, the bureau was understaffed by thousands of agents, and since I couldn't clone people, I needed to get realistic, or more important, make the bureau get realistic.

During the time that I was in the position, William Webster became the director. In an effort to understand special agent staffing needs he called a meeting with Long and Will DeBruler, the assistant director of the Inspection and Planning Division. I attended the meeting in my capacity as Special Agent Transfer Unit chief and a subordinate of Long's. Two subordinates of DeBruler's, Terry Dinan and Dick Sonnichsen, also attended.

At this meeting Webster came up with the directive that the Office of Planning and Evaluation should work with the Administrative Services Division (i.e., the Transfer Man) and with both the Criminal Investigative Division and the Intelligence Division to establish *realistic* target staffing levels (TSLs) for all fifty-six field offices. The total TSL could not exceed the exact number of special agents on board.

It seems hard to believe but this was the first time that we would be factoring in real numbers when filling staffing requirements. Now when an SAC complained about a transfer of one of his people I had the ammo. I came back to him with the official number of how many agents should be staffed in his office. If he had a further complaint about staffing levels, I gladly told him, and all the others, that it was out of my hands. I didn't have the authority to raise the staffing levels of a particular office. As it was, I had enough trouble working to fill the vacancies of the system that existed!

• • •

The SACs, who were very powerful men, watched the staffing levels like hawks. While I was indeed free to tell them to go away their scrutiny did make my life more stressful.

Every day my phone rang off the hook. If their actual staffing levels fell below their TSLs, the SACs were, invariably, the first people on the line. "When can I expect this staffing situation to be resolved? I need a Spanish speaker, a sound technician, etc. Immediately! When are you going to get these positions filled?"

Some SACs made my life more stressful than others. These were the ones who would scream bloody murder. They needed agents on a particular assignment, immediately! It was an emergency! A unique situation!

But watch out if you ever tried to transfer someone *out* of an office. The SAC of the office the agent was leaving invariably said that the designated person could not be let go. He's working the biggest, most important case there. Funny, the ones you want to transfer out are *always working the biggest, most important case there.*

The Washington Field Office, however, always seemed to have the *most unique* situations that required agents to be transferred in and also the *biggest, most important* cases, which meant, they said, that no one could leave! The SAC there was my old friend and mentor, Nick Stames. Unfortunately, since the Washington Field Office was so close—across the street from our offices, actually—the agents there assumed that we'd think of them more often when we needed to transfer people out. But we didn't think too long about that—Nick was a lot like a mama bear protecting her cubs, albeit a Greek mama bear. (Nick was very proud of his Greek heritage and had a Greek flag in his office as well as on a lapel pin.) With any little thing he wanted to complain about, Nick was in our offices. I'd look up from my desk and there he was. Yet, despite all this, we managed to maintain a good working relationship.

• • •

During my tenure one thing I tried to do was to get all the offices up to their target staffing levels. Even as the new TSL system was becoming more organized and streamlined, I was still struggling with my biggest headache, New York City. It was the driver of the entire transfer system. It was the largest field office, accounting for about 15 percent of the total staff of the FBI. However, nobody wanted to go there.

I'm guessing that 20 to 30 percent of the agents who were transferred to New York quit before going. Agents assigned there were paid less than garbage truck drivers. When a young married agent was sent to New York it was a huge blow to the couple. In those cases very often the family lived in New Jersey or even Pennsylvania because they couldn't afford to live in New York. Very often the agents who did go barely lasted two years. Typically, the agents who wanted to go to New York were the ones who had been born and raised there. But there weren't enough of those. There was an insatiable need to fill positions in New York.

Before I arrived in the transfer office a Band-Aid approach was arranged, called the "five-year plan." If an agent who didn't have New York as his office of preference was sent there, then we would set up a "light at the end of the tunnel." His next transfer, after five years, would be to his office of preference or an office in an area near that office.

However, when I arrived it didn't take too long to see that this five-year plan wasn't working. There were agents who had been in the New York office for ten years. No one even knew how many there were—as I found out when I asked for a list, which no one had previously requested. It wasn't even being tracked appropriately!

Remember, this was long before laptops. The headquarters' IBM computer filled up a room and those were the days of punch cards. But that could have worked out fine if the Transfer Man had access to the computer, but he didn't. So, everything was done by index card. It worked like this: the clerk who typed up a transfer letter made two index cards for each letter—each with the agent's name, office of assignment, and date of transfer. One was filed alphabetically and the other one was filed geographically, by office, and then those were then further filed by chronology. The person most recently transferred into a particular office was at the back of that section.

This was our sophisticated system—thousands of index cards manually filed.

After an agent had been in an office for one year he or she was eligible for rotation, but it wasn't automatic that he or she be moved. Perhaps that office was understaffed. Or perhaps the SAC was working on a huge monster case and needed everyone to stay put. In that case it made no sense to move anyone from that office. So, a hold was placed on transferring anyone out of that location. These kinds of decisions were at the sole discretion of the Transfer Man.

I cannot stress enough how everything that I did was completely monitored and scrutinized, and not just by the SACs. If an agent who was awaiting a transfer to his or her office of preference was overlooked for that post, my phone rang immediately. "Why did this person who was tenth on the list get it over me when I was first? What the hell's going on here? Why did this person get transferred?" The first person didn't much care that the open spot was for someone with a specialty, say a Hungarian speaker, which number ten was.

Then there were situations in which the transfer that the agent requested in writing wasn't the transfer the agent wanted. Sometimes he put down the office of preference that his wife really wanted, figuring that he'd never get it. When his lucky number finally came up, I'd let him know the "good news" only to have him plead with me not to transfer him there. Unfortunately, in those situations there was nothing I could do. If someone put down an office of preference and the opening came up it would look odd if I didn't do the transfer. I ran an honest ship and wasn't about to bend the rules.

If an agent refused a transfer, it wouldn't be a good thing for his or her career. Once an agent refused then that agent got a letter of censure from the director. A letter of censure meant that the agent would not be eligible for an office of preference transfer for five years.

● ● ●

And then there were the scam artists.

Another problem that I sought to correct during my time on the job were the undeserved hardship transfers. It was common knowledge among the agent staff that there were agents who played hardship transfer games and won. That made me very, very angry. I wanted to restore the credibility of the system.

When the hardship transfer requests were real, it was still a very difficult thing to juggle assignments to grant the requests, but having to navigate the undeserved ones made things a nightmare. Agents could make a plea for a transfer based on hardship, such as a sick wife or child. The temporary requests were easy to take care of. We'd review their application for a temporary hardship assignment—requesting a time anywhere from two to six months—and they were done. What was harder to deal with were the permanent hardship situations. These were usually based on the health of various family members, including elderly parents who needed care. Unfortunately, unless it was a unique and severe medical situation, and even then it would be tough to accommodate, I usually turned these down. Almost every agent had elderly parents.

The situation that seems to sum up all of the shenanigans was the time when two very coincidental requests arrived on my desk simultaneously. One was a medical request, with a supporting letter from a doctor, stating that an agent's daughter had a medical condition made worse by living in the Miami climate. For this condition she had to be moved up to Philadelphia, where the climate was perfect for her condition. (Never mind the fact that this Miami-based agent had been raised in Philadelphia and that's where his family lived.) At the same time, another request came in, from an agent in Philadelphia whose child had exactly the same medical condition. Only in this case the child had to leave Philadelphia and move to Miami, where the climate was perfect for the child's condition. Go figure!

I turned them both down.

As Transfer Man I always seemed to be getting sued and filing affidavits. One particularly annoying case involved an agent in Savannah whom I transferred to the Washington office. Since I was determined to clean up the hardship transfer debacle, I pulled the files of all agents on a hardship transfer and carefully reviewed them. I found a glaring abuse in the case of an agent who, with only a couple years of service, had received a hardship transfer to Savannah (his hometown), jumping over dozens of senior agents on the office of preference list.

His file showed that shortly after arriving in his first office assignment in Albany, New York, the agent submitted a hardship transfer request for Savannah, citing the needs of elderly parents. The transfer was denied since the file reflected that several of his siblings lived in Savannah and were perfectly capable of caring for the parents. Scarcely had he received the denial letter when he submitted another request, along with a supporting letter from a doctor, stating that he had a medical condition that could be relieved only by living in Savannah. Somehow my predecessor fell for that one and granted the transfer.

Within sixty days of arriving in Savannah the agent submitted a letter from a local doctor stating that the agent was cured and could resume full duties. (Agents on hardship with personal medical conditions were placed on limited duty and were not eligible for any overtime pay.)

I was outraged. This was a textbook case of an agent gaming the system. I contacted the National Institutes of Health. I described the medical condition of the agent (allergic reaction to certain flora present in

Albany and not in Savannah) and requested information on environments similar to Savannah. The closest, they said in writing, was Washington, D.C. So, that's where I decided to transfer him. According to his EOD (entering on duty) date he still was about number twenty-five or so on the Savannah list, so it would take about fifteen to twenty years before he was the number one agent on the list and could go back there.

This started World War III. He fought the transfer tooth and nail, filing affidavits by the crate-load. He even filed suit to get an injunction against the bureau. He lost.

In the end? He moved to Washington, D.C. I imagine that Nick was pleased. He got another agent—right?

## Epiphanies

Two things happened to me while transfer unit chief that caused particularly unbelievable amounts of pressure. But together they added up to quite an epiphany.

When I held that job, I constantly took work home with me because I couldn't keep up with it all during the traditional workweek. One Sunday afternoon shortly after becoming the Transfer Man, as I was working at my kitchen table, I studied the information sheet prepared about the latest new agent training class. On it was biographical information, such as date of birth, marital status, education level, as well as background information. Based on the biographical information shown, balanced with the needs of the various field offices, I chose the agents' destinations. On the far right side of the sheet was a column with a blank space that I filled in with the name of the field office where the person would be headed. I went through the whole class of nearly forty members and put down their destinations.

When I finished and was looking over the document, I realized that I had sent four new agents from the training class to Pittsburgh. That was too many for one class. So, I took out my eraser—I was smart enough to fill in that very fluid right-hand column with pencil—and as I erased one of the names and assigned that person to another field office, something struck me: with a simple swipe of the eraser I was changing someone's life. Actually, *lives*. The experience of an entire family would change.

There I was, almost like a divine being, deciding where this person was going to go. I was altering the entire course of this person's life by erasing Pittsburgh simply because I had put too many people in that office. I had never met this person but his friendships, career, and family life—everything—would be changed in one moment by my erasing Pittsburgh and substituting in another field division.

From that moment forward I really had a different attitude, at least internally, about my job, what I was there to do, and how critical it was that I make the right decision. Of course, I *knew* all that from the beginning—going about my work on a daily basis, but not really giving the implications a whole lot of thought—but it didn't really hit me until that Sunday afternoon. I certainly should have deeply considered all of this earlier, especially since I was no stranger to the process. I knew, firsthand, how each particular office and city could affect your life differently. However, just in that moment, that act of erasing the name made everything become crystal clear.

My second epiphany actually occurred after I left the job.

Bob Porter, an agent with whom I had worked in San Juan, had kept in contact with me after I left Puerto Rico and a lot more so after I became the Transfer Man. By that point, Bob had been in the San Francisco office for about eight years, working as a street agent mostly out of Oakland. He moved to the Bay Area right after leaving Puerto Rico and was now eligible for a transfer. He really wanted to go to Phoenix, which was relatively close to where many of his relatives lived. He called me to ask, "What are the chances of being transferred there?"

Unfortunately, the odds weren't so great. He was number twenty-five on the list. Phoenix has always been a very desirable office.

"What about Spanish," he asked. "I'm a fluent Spanish speaker." Porter was a Mormon who had been on a two-year mission to South America.

"Doesn't help," I told him. "It will maybe bump you up a name or two, but that's it. You're still way down the list—it will be a number of years before you'll be considered for Phoenix."

Then he said something that I always think about to this day. "Well, whatever you can do. Something in the Southwest would be fine. If anything comes up there I'd appreciate it because I'd really like to get back down closer to my family."

About a month later a vacancy in the Southwest came up. It was for El Centro, California, a two-agent resident agency located one hundred miles east of San Diego and a part of that FBI office. Considered a hardship post, the desert town was such a difficult place to live and work that the agents were assigned there on a tour basis, just like in San Juan. El Centro wasn't really considered a dangerous place but a poor little town near the border with Mexico with a tremendous amount of illegal traffic—both of narcotics and aliens. Primarily agricultural, it's very hot and dusty and there are many crop-dusting chemicals in the air. You went there with the understanding that you would be in El Centro for only two years and then be moved to San Diego. Typically someone who listed San Diego as their office of preference was offered this opportunity, but after so many of them turned it down this time, I extended it to Bob.

"Can I think about it?" he asked. "Can you give me a week because I'd like to make a trip there?" Sure.

He took his family for a scouting trip and they were fine with the move. So, I filled out the paperwork for him to fill the vacancy, everyone was pleased, and they were on their way. I didn't give it another thought.

Until nine months later, that is, when I was working in Boston.

Word reached me that the two agents working at the El Centro resident agency had been shot dead. One agent was Bob Porter, forty-four, and though I didn't personally know the other agent, Charles W. Elmore, thirty-two, I had transferred him there, too.

On the morning of August 9, 1979, a former social worker by the name of James Maloney came in to the El Centro office for his 9:00 AM appointment, ostensibly to discuss getting a copy of his FBI files under the Freedom of Information Act. Maloney was a pacifist involved in various causes including supporting the United Farm Workers labor group, at the time a very hot topic in California. He indeed had been under investigation earlier in the decade for his ties to radical groups and for a case involving the misuse of public funds.

Since it was a small office, without a secretary, when Maloney started knocking Bob went to open the door. There wasn't a peephole—this wasn't a very secure office—so Bob couldn't see that Maloney was armed. As soon as the door opened Maloney opened fire. The agents didn't have a chance, although Charles did get off a couple of shots. After he killed them, Maloney killed himself. It was a real disaster.

The agents had no way of knowing that before he arrived at the agency Maloney had left two suicide notes with his estranged wife saying that he planned to take his own life and "take others with him." He also wrote about how he hated the government and capitalism. A warning came to the agents but by the time their phones rang they were already dead.

That slaughter had a profound effect on me. I had been responsible for their transfer to El Centro. If it hadn't been for me the men wouldn't have been there. Although I realized that I was not to blame for the incident, it was my decision that caused people to wind up being killed in the line of duty. I often thought about the five children whom Bob Porter left behind.

It was tough. For the longest time I had difficulty getting over that. As I went on to work in various crisis situations I did a lot of thinking about it and realized, in many instances, I would be making a decision that, perhaps, was going to put people in harm's way. Someone might die if I made the wrong decision—or even the right decision.

One thing that did offer me some solace was how the FBI treated Bob's family. Director Webster attended the funeral, along with 650 mourners, many of whom were FBI agents and law enforcement officers. Webster also eulogized him at a separate memorial service and gave Bob's credentials to his widow, Flora.

I kept in touch with the family over the years, as J. Robert Porter was never far from my mind. At the ceremony for the FBI Memorial Star Award, for agents killed in the line of duty, I presented the honor to Flora and the rest of the Porter family. I was also there when Flora came back to El Centro—Flora and her family moved to Arizona not long after Bob's death—for the opening ceremony of the new office there. We had a very nice tribute to Bob, complete with a picture of him and Charles Elmore in the lobby.

Today, Bob Porter's son, Kenneth, is an agent and a very good one. He was sixteen at the time of his father's death and decided then to follow in his father's footsteps. A Spanish speaker, like his father, he also learned the language from a Mormon mission to South America. Kenneth worked in the San Juan office and when it was time for his next move he, too, put Phoenix as his office of preference.

The general policy in 1994, however, was that if a person was relatively new to the FBI and therefore way down on the list, he wouldn't get his office of preference coming out of San Juan. Only the top person on the list should get that, was the theory; others would maybe get assigned to the desired area somewhere but not to their top choice.

I felt differently and told the Transfer Man exactly that when he contacted me. "Wait a minute, first of all, his mother is living here in Phoenix," I said. "Obviously, her husband is deceased and she needs the assistance. We've got a martyr who died in the line of duty, and this is his son. Can't we do something to bring his son back to his family?" I argued that we shouldn't let our policy prevail in this situation.

The Transfer Man came through and Kenneth was transferred to Phoenix, where I was serving as SAC at the time. I enjoyed a nice relationship with him. Since leaving that post I've written to him to check up on how he's doing. The last time we were in touch Kenneth was the legal attaché in the U.S. embassy in Johannesburg, so I'm pleased that he's doing well.

In an odd postscript, years later my son Milt worked for seven years as a Border Patrol agent in El Centro, California. My only concern about his living there was that his son Cody, my first grandchild, was born during that period. I was concerned that all the chemicals used in agriculture might be very unhealthy for small children, not to mention adults.

## In the Driver's Seat

As Transfer Man I couldn't promote anyone to SAC, ASAC, or supervisor. Career Boards handled those decisions and subsequent transfers.

Since leaving Las Vegas I had been on the career advancement ladder. The next step on that ladder for me was an ASAC position—one to which I couldn't promote myself, of course. So, I was delighted when, in October 1978 and after about eighteen months as the Transfer Man, the career board selected me for Boston—and Webster approved!

I had long wanted to go there and was thrilled when the ASAC position there opened up. Boston was a terrific experience. I had never lived in such an exotic climate—that of the cold Northeast—considering that I was a Texan.

As a city, Boston was a great place to live. The family really enjoyed it. We traveled extensively on weekends, and every moment we could get off we went up into Maine and all throughout New England. I don't think there was one historical site we missed. What an unbelievable educational experience. To go to Plymouth Rock, visit Paul Revere's home, and see all those places that I had read about as a schoolboy were really amazing. We were like tourists for the entire two years.

My transfer there meant that I became one of two ASACs in the office and I took on more of a supervisory role than I had in the past. My work consisted of a lot of public corruption and organized crime cases. I don't think I ever realized how much the Mafia could really permeate a city until I went to Boston. Part of my responsibility was to target the notorious Providence-based Raymond Patriarca crime family and make cases against as many members as possible. Mr. Patriarca was still alive at the time but living in Rhode Island. The principal figure of the crime family in Boston itself, though, was a fellow by the name of Gennaro "Gerry" Angiulo.

Ironically, looking out the windows of our office we could see into the North End of Boston, a little Italy, where the Mafia conducted most of its business. The area seemed so much like Italy that it was uncanny. The ubiquitous markets, for example, even had dead chickens hanging in the windows. It was an incredible place with great food, great restaurants, and . . . great mobsters.

It was a very close-knit community, too, so it was extremely difficult to do any kind of surveillance activity that we normally would. We did the best we could, though, and narrowed it down to where Gerry was operating on a daily basis. The problem was that while we wanted to be able to actively surveil him, we couldn't put just anybody on the street. It was an almost impossible task since this was an area where everybody seemed to know everybody.

Then it hit us. Bingo! About a block away on the same street there was a public building—I can't recall exactly what agency it was—but the important thing was that it was owned by the state of Massachusetts, not by the Mafia or Mafia sympathizers. At five or so stories high it was the right height for our purposes.

The building faced onto the street where Gerry's place of business was located. Now it was time to get to work. We decided that we were going to get our monitoring devices into this building by embedding them in a window air-conditioning unit. So, we got our lab to put one together. They constructed a very elaborate surveillance camera that would look through the louvers of the unit. It was angled precisely from an upper floor of the building to point right at the front door of Gerry's "office."

The lab labeled a lot of the inner workings of the machine as "EPA" (Environmental Protection Agency), with different things inside the machine supposedly measuring air quality and so forth. So if anyone were to inspect it inside, he or she would quickly dismiss it as scientific research. To complete the whole ruse we had agents pose as EPA people to complete the installation. Once in place we were microwaving the signal from that camera to our office in Boston.

Although we couldn't actually see down onto the street, because of the height of our building, we did have that great view of Gerry's front door. This was important since many times, particularly during the summer months, he would come outside and hold court right in front of his building.

We were excited because we knew we were going to get all kinds of good information about who he was meeting with and when and for how long. Yes, we couldn't hear what was going on, but we could certainly see what was happening.

The elation was brief. The second day the unit was up we caught Gerry out in front of his place, talking to several people gathered around him. Looks good, except that the talk apparently centers on our building. He's pointing at the "air conditioner" and there's more talk. He points at it again and some more people show up. Finally, a young guy arrives. There's talk for a while with him and then he walks off, out of our sight. About fifteen minutes later, the camera that was looking through the louvers of the air conditioner suddenly had a screwdriver in its lens. Up close. Very close.

We don't know exactly what Gerry knew before he sent the guy up there except that this air conditioner was something different in the neighborhood. He had sent somebody up to scale the building and find out. No more air-conditioner camera. So, we had to come up with another method to surveil. The technical people from the lab and the people in the office came up with an idea to park a car with a hidden camera on the street.

We decided to use a certain Chevrolet model—about nine years old with a straight-six engine—the only car with enough room in the engine compartment to install the equipment needed. The hurdle with this plan was bureaucracy: FBI cars were bought through the General Services Administration and it's a lengthy process to get one. Plus, this car was kind of like a clunker. This led us to come up with an inventive way to buy this car without calling it a car. Solution? We purchased ourselves two "movable camera installations."

Two were needed because of parking regulations. You can't park a car and leave it forever. So, we painted the clunky Chevys different colors and kept moving them around. We were able to record for four hours at a time and, with any luck, get at least four hours of Gerry Angiulo out on the street doing his business.

It worked. We pulled the car up there and parked it. The camera was shooting through the grill directly at where Gerry was standing in front of his building. The car would record for four hours at which point we would drive the other car up there and one of our agents would act like he was the car owner coming back to get the first car. Then the second car would pull in.

No one noticed this handoff for quite a long period of time—several weeks—during which we got a lot of good information. We stopped using the cars after a few weeks because after realizing how adept Gerry was at noticing subtle neighborhood changes—for example, the air conditioner—we figured we shouldn't push our luck. If he caught on it might get him all hyped up and suspicious about what we were doing. Not soon after though we were able to up the surveillance ante: a judge granted permission to install listening devices in Gerry's place of business.

Gerry could be quite a colorful and entertaining guy. During the time that we had the microphone installed, one of Gerry's brothers, unbeknownst to him, was running a gambling operation. When he found out about it there was a big scene in his office, with him literally pounding on the desk, saying, "You idiot, don't you know that gambling is one of the predicate offenses for the RICO statute?" Gerry Angiulo was talking like an attorney. But you know what? He was absolutely right.

"You're setting yourself up," he told his brother. "They catch you doing it we're in deep trouble." (Keep in mind that I'm cleaning the language up considerably.)

I can only assume that after that the only gambling Gerry's brother did was on the other side of the wagers. And, yes, Gerry was ultimately prosecuted, but that was years after I left. The Boston agents worked those Mafia cases for years and years and years.

But sometimes we got lucky.

One of those times took place on a freezing winter night in Providence, when agents were surveilling a couple of members of the Patriarca family. At about midnight these two wise guys drove up to the home of a third Mafioso to pick him up. He naively got into the back, never expecting where this ride would take him. The car drove around for several minutes, seemingly en route to the airport.

Just as they approached the airport the agents trailing them lost the car; they were stuck at a red light while the mobsters went through the intersection and underneath an overpass. By the time the agents were rolling again they had lost sight of the mob vehicle. They drove around for a few minutes but didn't spot the car again until one of the agents happened to look into the parking lot of a rental car agency. The windows of one of the cars were all fogged up, and that car happened to be the exact make, color, and model of the mobsters' vehicle. The agents approached the car only to find the bloody corpse of the third mobster, freshly shot to death in the back seat.

After calling for backup units to secure the vehicle, they raced to a local bar where the wise guys were known to hang out. Sure enough, the two were seated at a table there having a drink. One still had blood spatters all over the sleeve of his gun arm! Nonetheless, their drinking brothers swore that the two had been there all evening. The agents figured that there might be a different story, however, and took them into custody. They were both convicted for murder, in violation of the RICO statute, and given lengthy sentences.

• • •

I had been in Boston for about a year and a half and was the senior ASAC (based on time worked in that office) when the SAC, Jim Dunn, retired. This left me in charge for about four months until a new SAC, Larry Sarhatt, came on board.

What four months they were! I can remember looking out my office window—in the JFK Building—in downtown Boston, just staring at the planes taking off and landing from Logan Airport. In those days there were a lot of hijackings, but until September 11, 2001, no hijackings had ever occurred in Boston, as far as I know, and it dawned on me that if one were to take place I would be in charge. I suddenly realized that if there were to be a hijacking or if a major event happened here, I was going to be the person responsible.

It was scary. "I don't have an SAC here anymore," I thought. Before that, I always had a buffer. The other guy's in charge. Kick the problem up to the boss. That was a comforting feeling, but then I realized, it's like the old Harry Truman thing: "The buck stops here." If anything bad happens, I'm going to have to handle it. That was a sobering thought to realize after those many years of working my way up through the ranks.

Now I suddenly had a completely different perspective on what it was to be an agent in charge of a field operation instead of being any other agent. When I used to be a street agent I can remember thinking, "Boy, those supervisors—they've got kind of a cushy job. They sit there and don't have to go out on the street very much. All they do is read my reports and nitpick my cases. And the ASAC doesn't even really have a squad. He doesn't really have anything to do!"

How wrong I was. Beyond having to take over for the SAC, in the regular course of the job, the ASAC has to carry out the SAC's order, which doesn't always make everybody happy. And as the ASAC you do this day in and day out and you're thinking, "Boy, I tell you, I'm dealing with all these problems. The SAC, all he does is sit up there. He issues a fiat and I'm the guy who's got to carry the water. I've got to do the work."

That, of course, was before I landed in the SAC chair, now responsible for all of the FBI's activities and for everything that the FBI did in Boston. And ultimately, I was the person responsible for anything that happened in our investigations. That's a heavy burden.

This may sound trite, but I learned that it really is kind of lonely at the top when you get into leadership positions. In many instances you really can't be totally candid with, or bare your soul or doubts or misgivings to, your troops. You've got to make decisions based on all the information that you have and to the best of your ability, keeping reservations to yourself. If you don't, it can create all kinds of problems.

What a moment to realize that no longer do I have the one desk between me and the ultimate authority, the boss. Now I'm in that chair. What will I do? How can I effectively discharge my responsibilities as the leader of this organization here in this place?

Though nothing happened in Boston, it wouldn't be long before I would get answers to those questions.

## Inspection Time

For years and years, FBI inspectors were plucked mainly from the ranks of ASACs. These people would not be permanently transferred to the inspection staff. Rather, they would be tapped to serve as an inspector in Washington only on temporary duty, until an appropriate SAC position opened up and they could be promoted. The length of time served as an inspector varied; it might be only a couple of months or maybe a year or more. It all depended on when and how many open positions in the SAC ranks there were. It was thought of as a quick purgatory. The experience, however, was invaluable. In conducting a thorough review of a field office, the inspector got an up close and personal experience of how a field office functioned, where its successes and failures were, and, most important, what were the strengths and weaknesses of the SAC.

This system worked fine until the late 1970s, when there was a huge turnover in the bureau. The SAC ranks were turning over so rapidly that there were cases where someone was tapped as an inspector but promoted to SAC before doing an inspection!

Given all this it should come as no surprise that the inspection process became dysfunctional. There weren't enough inspectors with the training and background to do proper inspections. This generated much concern internally because the inspector position is a critical one and one that must be performed effectively. After many, many meetings—this was the FBI, after all—they decided how to "fix" the inspection process. The inspector position would become a little more stable. There were to be four "permanent" inspector positions at any one time. These people would transfer to Washington, D.C., and serve a minimum of two years in the job.

I was among the first four chosen to fill one of the four permanent slots. (There was no particular reason that I was in the group, except that I was an ASAC on the cusp of getting the promotion to SAC.) I really had no idea what I was in for, but it sounded like an exciting opportunity when I got the call about it from the transfer office. We met with Director Webster, who explained that we were, in effect, the sacrifice to fix the inspection process. We were to be serving for two years. "It will happen that people who are junior to you will be named to be SACs and you won't—because you'll be serving for two years," said the director. "That's the situation. However, as compensation for that, at the end of your tour we will make sure that you are given priority consideration for the office where you want to go as SAC. Secondly, we will not force you to go to a small field office—as we would have done in the past—and then get promoted to a larger one, and then to an even larger one yet. You will go straight out to a very large office to be SAC."

That sounded very good to me.

Although I enjoyed my work as an inspector, part of my enjoyment came from knowing that this would be a temporary job, with a very nice light at the end of the tunnel. In the meantime, I learned a lot about the various offices, but I can safely state that I wasn't very popular. In this job, absolutely no one is excited to see you show up at his or her office.

The inspections were generally surprises, although, FBI agents, being so interconnected as they were, had ways of finding out a few days before that an inspection was upcoming. During that time it was a rush of cleaning up desk areas, washing cars, and updating any files that needed it. That last-minute scrambling, however, didn't do much if things were really out of shape. These audits were so very comprehensive that they took a minimum of two weeks for one field office, no matter the size.

During the inspection, the inspectors pull virtually every file and look at every case that's ongoing, look at closed cases, and look at pending prosecutions. They also interview other federal heads and state agency heads to determine how their cooperative effort is working with the FBI and if they know of any deficiencies or problems. This is all part of an effort to assess the performance of the field office.

During my travels and inspections I became very impressed with the Houston and the San Antonio offices. These visits just confirmed how much I wanted my next position to be that of an SAC in either of those offices, if not somewhere else in Texas. And pretty much everyone in the bureau knew that.

I figured that my ticket out was taken care of when I received the news that the San Antonio office SAC position was open. I had been an inspector for two years and according to the promises we were given when we signed on, I was in line for a promotion. Although the Jackson, Mississippi, job was also open, I didn't think much about it since it was a very small office with only forty or so agents assigned.

The Career Board met and considered their candidates, and, though I wasn't supposed to know it, I was tipped off that they recommended me as their number one candidate for San Antonio. Another man, Bill Dalseg, was recommended as number one for Mississippi. Cases closed, SACs delivered.

Those two packages went to Director Webster's office for his consideration. A few days went by before the official news came out. I was to be assigned to Jackson and Dalseg to San Antonio.

Pardon me?

I was in a total state of shock. I didn't know what hit me. When I recovered, one of the first things I did was to talk to the number two person in the bureau, John Otto, who looked me in the eye and reminded me of the importance of this transfer, in case I was debating accepting it. "Any SAC job in the bureau is the best job there is, no matter where it is. That doesn't make any difference," he told me. "You've been selected as SAC for Jackson and I would recommend very strongly that you go to Jackson and make the best of it. Or, you have an alternative. You can always step down—you don't have to be an SAC at all."

Point taken.

Having been assigned to a field office before, I knew that if word got out that I was upset and didn't want to go to Jackson that would not bode well for my tenure there: I would start out on the wrong foot. So, I decided to play good soldier. But in Washington my first choice wasn't exactly a secret. For example, at an SAC conference I attended after I took the Mississippi position, the emcee at one of the big events, Bill Gavin (who later worked at Guardsmark with me), made a not-so-veiled reference to it. There was a slide with a picture of me standing in what looked like a swamp. The caption above my head read: "But this doesn't look like San Antonio." The entire room cracked up, with the exception of Webster, who didn't get it.

Was I unhappy with the decision? Initially, yes. But there was no appeal process for me. In fact, in the FBI that's tantamount to instant death. The director made his decision and that was the end of it. Mr. Otto informed me that I could go to Jackson and do my job or I could do something else. And, by something else, I figured that going back to the street was the best possible scenario.

I would be going to Jackson, thank you very much.

The reason I was given for the decision to send me to Mississippi was that the Jackson office was in a tremendous state of turmoil. The SAC had died suddenly of a heart attack, but prior to that there had been a long series of serious allegations made against him by the ASAC in the office, Johnny Wendt. He had written a long affidavit that the SAC was aspiring to run for governor in Mississippi and to further those aims he had become closely aligned with people who were very questionable, if not actually corrupt. Wendt alleged that in situations where it might benefit him politically in the future, the SAC informed subjects that the FBI was investigating them, thereby thwarting those investigations.

Based on Wendt's allegations, a huge inquiry was launched. However, its result was probably not what Wendt had in mind. Since his charges were unsubstantiated—a lot of rumors and innuendo—the FBI could not prove any misconduct on the SAC's part. But there was no way that Wendt and the SAC could work together after that, so Wendt was sent to Washington and another ASAC replaced him in Mississippi. The SAC was cleared of all charges before he died.

Keep in mind that all this had happened within a few months of my transfer to Jackson, so the wounds were still fresh. It wasn't until many, many years later that I learned the real story of what actually happened with my transfer. When the packages for the San Antonio and the Jackson promotions arrived simultaneously at the director's desk, he called a trusted Texan resident to advise him on which of the two prospects he should really send there.

"I've got two candidates for the FBI vacancy in San Antonio," Webster said to Jim Adams, who was serving as commissioner of the Texas Department of Public Safety but had previously been an assistant director in the FBI. "One is Weldon Kennedy and the other is Bill Dalseg." Bill Dalseg had worked in Jim Adams's office when he was at the bureau; Adams knew Dalseg but he didn't know me.

Up next on Webster's phone call list was Jim Ingram, who had been the SAC in Chicago before he retired to Jackson, where he was the director of security for a major bank. "I've got two candidates here for Jackson," Webster told Ingram, giving him our names. Although Ingram didn't know either of us too well he still offered the director his opinion. "I think Weldon will be much of a better fit here because he is a Texan, a Southerner, and considering the Mississippi mind-set that will make him much more successful here than Dalseg."

The director took the advice of the retired FBI executives. He must have respected their judgment, clearly more than he respected that of the Career Board, considering that he reversed its decision.

# 5 MISSISSIPPI

## Taking Old Dixie Down

When I walked into the Jackson office on that first day in 1982, I had no idea how divided it was. The allegations floating around that the former SAC was corrupt had poisoned the office. While there was a camp in the office aligned with former ASAC Wendt, there was another group who felt just as strongly about the SAC's innocence. None of this mattered to me. And it was my job to make sure that it didn't matter to them.

I knew that in order to get anything done that this division had to end. I wasn't sure how I could make that happen but I did know that I had a very short window of time to gain the agents' respect and attention to do so. If it didn't happen in the beginning it wasn't going to happen at all.

Fueled by adrenaline, I barely sat down at my new desk before I introduced myself to the office. And, although I hadn't planned on what I was going to say, I've been told that the agents there never forgot that speech. People in the office, like Keith Bell (who we'll talk a lot about later), tell me that they can still recite it.

"Look, I'm the new kid on the block," I told the group after I sat them down.

"This office is terribly dysfunctional. Reputation-wise, this has been the worst FBI field office of all fifty-six. I don't care what happened yesterday or the day before. I don't want to hear about what happened yesterday or the day before. We're starting today with a brand-new slate. We're starting from scratch and we're on the bottom. And we're going to get off of the bottom and become a functioning, respected field office of the FBI. We can't do that if we focus on who did what to whom in the past. That's gone. That's history. I don't even want to know about it."

Looking back, I feel that the speech seemed to help them focus on the job at hand and not office politics. In the year before I arrived, the office, which covered the entire state of Mississippi, had eighteen felony convictions in cases that it was investigating. That is abysmal. To put it in context, most years when I was a street agent I personally had more than eighteen convictions. There were forty-five agents in this office. Mississippi was fertile ground and it was about time we cleaned things up.

The following year after I arrived, we had 130 convictions. And as things would turn out, the first case we tackled, and the entire office tackled it together, was a grand slam. Our success was written up on the front pages of all the state papers.

I guess we kind of owe thanks to a certain corrupt individual, whom I'll never forget, by the name of Howard Leroy Hobbs.

What occupied much of my time as SAC of the Mississippi office, and the time of the agents working at the office long before I arrived, was something called the Dixie Mafia. Composed of loosely tied groups spanning the South, the Dixie Mafia boasted diverse talents. Besides contract murders, armed robbery, and extortion, they were very proficient in the smuggling of narcotics.

The Mafiosi from the East Coast, the likes of which I encountered in Boston, were nothing compared to their Southern counterparts. The Southerners were much more dangerous. They didn't have to ask anyone for permission to murder, and there was no massive hierarchy and no ruling family structures to keep balance. It was said that in the 1970s they killed five times as many people as La Cosa Nostra. And these were no ordinary crimes; theirs were of the most violent nature imaginable.

It wasn't uncommon for public officials to be closely associated with the Dixie Mafia, either. With "law enforcement" on their side, the Dixie Mafia would brazenly commit crimes without fear of jail time. One such law enforcement officer, who fell under my jurisdiction, was the Harrison County sheriff, Leroy Hobbs.

The funny thing was that Hobbs, who had been so distinguished as the Gulfport police chief that Hoover once wrote him a commendation letter, campaigned for the job as someone who stood for something. It was quite apparent soon thereafter what he stood for. He took kickbacks, openly associated with mobsters, visited hookers, facilitated gambling joints, and so on. That was just the start of it.

His jurisdiction proudly became one of lawlessness, at least in the traditional sense. The people knew it but didn't seem to care; they just kept reelecting him.

One vintage example of the way the sheriff conducted his business was how he handled Dixie Mafia crony and strip joint owner Dewey D'Angelo, who had a hand in botching a mob drug deal. Friendship meant nothing—D'Angelo would have to pay. And he would pay locally: Hobbs had given his word that the killers wouldn't have to worry about justice catching up with them if the men got rid of D'Angelo in the area under Hobbs's jurisdiction.

Poor D'Angelo had no idea what was about to hit him. The Dixie Mafia was brutal and Hobbs let it flourish. In this case the payback would be particularly personal. The hit man who was approached to do the deed, James Edward Creamer, had an issue with the intended victim. D'Angelo was selling drugs to Creamer's wife, despite repeated warnings by Creamer to stop.

Creamer was so incensed at D'Angelo that before he slashed his throat and stabbed him, he chopped off his ear and made him bite it. After the killing, he brought the ear home to scare his wife. That's how things went in Mississippi then, especially Hobbs's Mississippi.

Sheriff Hobbs didn't always just offer protection. He had also ordered at least one hit that we knew of. The hit was on Larkin Smith, Gulfport's then-chief of police; Hobbs thought he was going to run against him in the next election. Though the assassination plan was leaked, and Larkin was saved in time, this was not what took down Hobbs. But it was another building block for our case against him. What ultimately brought him down? It was something far less sinister.

• • •

Since the agents in my office working the Dixie Mafia cases weren't having much luck taking them down for the more violent crimes—which we'd been chasing our tails on for years—they began to figure out that narcotics was the area they would have better luck targeting. But how best to start developing a narcotics case from scratch?

Bring in the Drug Enforcement Administration (DEA). The FBI was brand new to narcotics cases, but these cases were, of course, the DEA's primary jurisdiction. So, I called in the DEA to work together on this; they couldn't have been more helpful. They immediately furnished us with a couple of undercover agents to pose as South American drug dealers and approach local Dixie Mafia honcho, DJ Venus III, looking to make a deal.

DJ was all ears. He quickly met with these men at a farm where he and the Dixie Mafia did a lot of their dirty work—a kind of local HQ for them. The men told DJ that they could bring in a lot of cocaine, the likes of which he had never seen, but the load was so big that it would have to be delivered by air. How about right here on this farm? The catch, however, they said, was that they would need protection from the sheriff. That way, the whole thing would be covered and protected by the sheriff's office, and there would be no outside intervention by law enforcement.

Great idea! DJ loved it.

It all seemed to be working out pretty well, with many more meetings to follow. All the while, the agents kept pressing the point about wanting the sheriff's direct involvement. What they wanted most of all, they said, was to speak with the sheriff personally.

DJ, however, kept putting them off. "Don't worry about it. It's all taken care of." That was his standard response. No matter how well the meetings seemed to go, the agents couldn't get to that next step of actually having a face-to-face meeting with the sheriff.

But in the midst of our frustration we caught a break. A big one. Around the same time—and quite by accident—we found out that an FBI agent from Georgia had an informant who had been part of the Dixie

Mafia. He had spent a lot of time on the Gulf Coast and not only had he dealt with DJ, but the informant supposedly owed him money.

Perfect! We enlisted the willing informant immediately, using him to introduce another federal agent—an FBI agent, Al Millard—to DJ. I should stop here to say that the things Al did on this case were absolutely incredible. I can't praise him enough, and I must say that I was thrilled when later I was assigned to Atlanta, Georgia, and had a chance to work with Al again.

With the informant's stamp of approval, the Dixie Mafia had no reason to suspect its newest friend. Al passed himself off as an old Georgia cracker, a role he played to the hilt. His act came complete with the "can't hardly talk English very good" kind of phrases, in a deep, deep drawl.

He offered up his criminal history—just as dogs sniff each other to prove that their new friends are OK—telling the Mafiosi that he had been a crook for a long, long time. He said that he grew marijuana. A lot of marijuana.

The informant had brought Al out there on the pretext of giving the Dixie Mafia advice on their growing drug business. And here the Dixie Mafia was, faced with a real "expert"! At this meeting at the farm HQ, it was like a Q&A with the Dear Abby of pot! The Mafia talked to him at length about how they were growing pot and he gave them "tips."

That went on for a while and then he took a gamble.

"Can you show me some of your stuff that you're growing here?" he asked. Not one of us knew this at the time—this was a new piece of information—that the Dixie Mafia was actually growing marijuana on the farm's surrounding lands. And it wasn't exactly on private property.

"Actually, it's state forest lands," they said. "We got a lot of plots back there."

"Well, can I see this?" he asked. "Can you show it to me?"

"Well, sure," they said. No problem. They were eager to show it off.

The Mafia and their guests all jumped on three-wheeler and four-wheeler ATVs and went off into the middle of this state forest. There, Al was greeted with a whole mess of small marijuana plots—one acre or less, to avoid discovery—all around the forest. The Mafiosi were just as proud of their crop as they could be, but Al was there to throw them off. "This marijuana plant here is kind of small," he told them.

"Look," Al said, "you can really make these produce a lot more. Do you know about how to pinch off this top bud here and make it bushy and spread? It's more or less the same thing you do to a tomato plant to make it produce more." The Mafiosi weren't aware of this technique. "No, we hadn't heard about that. How do you do it?"

It should come as no surprise that they hadn't heard about the technique, considering that Al completely made it up. Well, Al certainly showed them. Walking out into the marijuana field, he started plucking off about two or three inches of the top growth off the plants. Keep in mind that he was wearing overalls because he's playing his "Georgia good ol' boy" character, but these were one smart pair of overalls. They had a handy little pocket up on the front, which was particularly helpful for storing evidence. While plucking away, Al also plucked a few things for himself. "Hell," Al said later, "I don't know how they believed it." Not only did the Mafiosi not question or later check anything, but they didn't even blink!

Once the "Marijuana Growth 101" talk was finished, he said, "You know boys, this is a nice location here. It's really wonderful. Could I get a picture with you?"

"Great idea!" The pot growers were all for it. Though no one had a camera on hand, the Mafiosi were so eager to take the picture that one guy jumped on his ATV and went back to the farmhouse to get one.

Once back, Polaroid camera in hand, he led some kind of photo shoot. With all their enthusiasm, you'd think it was a spread for *High Times* magazine. Al stood in the middle of the field posed with his arms around two of the Mafia members. Just as they do on cruise ships and theme parks, the photographer gave Al a snapshot—as a souvenir!

"Thanks," said Al. "I'm going to take it to Georgia to show my boys how it's done in Gulfport, Mississippi." He tucked the picture in his little pocket, alongside the hidden marijuana plant leaves that he picked. So, to put things in perspective, on his first visit to meet with these guys he came out with evidence of marijuana growing—including the actual plants, or, rather, part of them at least—and he's tied the suspects to it with a photograph of two subjects standing in the middle of the marijuana field.

Bull's-eye! That's pretty hard evidence.

Incredibly, this one visit by Al established enough credibility with DJ and his crew—keep in mind that he had been personally introduced to

DJ, and vouched for, by a known criminal associate of DJ's—that they decided to seek his advice on a big cocaine load. This required that Al be introduced to two new associates—the "South American drug dealers."

Meanwhile, we still had the problem with the DEA agents not getting a meeting with the sheriff. It was "high" time, we decided, so all three of the undercover Feds—the two DEA agents and one FBI agent, Al—started bearing down even more. They made it quite clear that it was necessary to meet the sheriff soon . . . or the deal was off.

Progress was slow, though, but with this threat things seemed to be finally moving along. At the next meeting a sheriff's deputy was there. (Sounds official, doesn't it?) However, the federal agents said they still wouldn't feel secure with the airdrop until the sheriff himself was directly involved.

Either way, though, we knew that what we needed was to get DJ taped on video and audio. Even though we had two undercover DEA agents and an FBI undercover agent who could testify, we knew that to really have a slam dunk we had to back up their testimony with a recording.

This was, oddly, one of the easiest parts of the investigation. The DEA agents asked for a location change for their next meeting—to a New Orleans hotel room—and the Mafiosi agreed! What was going on here? The New Orleans room was as wired for sound and video as a movie set. We weren't going to miss a thing. What we really needed was to record them talking about a payoff. However, in the FBI, payoffs are never easy—particularly payoffs to public officials.

To make a payoff of a public figure we had to get various approvals, depending on the amount of money we wanted to pay. For example, if we were going to pay, say, $5,000 to a public official, a person at the section chief's level at FBI headquarters could approve that. If we were going to pay the official, say, $10,000, then the next level up could approve that. Up to $15,000, an assistant director could approve it. If we wanted to pay $25,000 or more, it required that the director of the FBI personally approve it.

We didn't feel it was necessary in this case to go that high. The DEA, however, did. "We really ought to offer this guy $25,000," the DEA agents kept saying. But I really didn't want to do that, simply because I didn't want to go to the director, with all that that entailed. Anytime an approval is required from the director on a public corruption case, it becomes a major issue. "We think $15,000 would work just as well, and we can get that money more quickly! Plus, since we're the ones furnishing the money and this is our case, we insist." After a lot of back-and-forth arguments, we finally got them to agree to the $15,000 figure.

That settled, the two DEA undercover agents went to the meeting, payoff plan in place. We were back in the New Orleans FBI office, ready to monitor. But there was a surprise. No sheriff was there but since the wheels were already in place, we had to keep going. Plus, we knew that the payoff talk would still be helpful to us.

The two DEA guys began to talk to DJ about how they're going to bribe the sheriff and how much they wanted to pay him directly.

"How much you're thinking?" asks DJ.

"Oh, we thought about $25,000," responds one of the DEA men.

Well, I nearly died.

I'm sitting there, listening in at the New Orleans FBI office with Bob Bryden, the DEA SAC. In shock. "Goddammit," I said, "What's going on here? Doesn't he know that we don't have the authority to go that high? What in the hell's the matter with him?"

Well, almost before I got those words out of my mouth, DJ said, "No, that's too much. I've been dealing with this guy all my life. I think $15,000 is a better figure."

And we just all broke out laughing. In fact, Bob turned to me and said, "Who's he working for? You, Weldon? Is DJ an FBI guy or what?"

That was the best. We couldn't believe this ridiculous scenario. I mean here's the principal criminal and he thought that Hobbs was only worth a payoff of $15,000. $25,000? Nah, that would be too much. It was all a comedy of errors that provided some necessary comic relief.

Now for us this was more or less betting the farm. The DEA agents told DJ, "If there's no meeting with the sheriff then there's no deal. We're not bringing the cocaine in, none of it. We need to have assurance that we're safe."

DJ tried to wriggle out of the meeting once again, saying that he would take care of the payment to the sheriff personally and that the undercover agents need not be there. No way. Again, they told him that since it was such a big shipment they had to personally meet with the sheriff. No meeting, deal's off. Period.

“Okay, okay,” DJ finally agreed. “We’ll set up another meeting about the drop,” he said, “and the sheriff will be there.” He promised Hobbs would be at the farm to receive his $15,000 in cash.

We would be there, too, listening in.

On the appointed day the sheriff showed up. It was well worth the wait.

FBI agent/cracker Al didn’t waste any time. He started questioning the sheriff about how exactly he was going to protect the deal. I couldn’t believe his gall. It was great. Even better, it was being taped.

“Where are you going to put your people?” Al asked. Remarkably, in response, the sheriff began to tell him the exact roads where the deputy and his officers would be in order to secure the place. “No, wait a minute,” said our guy. “You got a map where you can show me this?”

The sheriff didn’t have one but our man persisted. “Well, I’m from Georgia and I don’t know anything about your roads and streets and all that around here. Somebody’s got to show me a map.” The seconds seemed forever while we were listening in. We just couldn’t believe what we were hearing. Before the sheriff could say that nobody’s got a map, the quick-thinking agent took out a brown grocery sack, tore it, and flattened it out on the table and said, “We’ll just make a map, okay?”

And so he did. Drawing the road around the farm, he was careful with his detail, even putting cars on the route. One he labeled “Sheriff Hobbs here” and another was labeled with where the deputy was going to be and so forth. When he finished, Al asked him to sign the map.

I’m not joking.

Al said, “Yep, I’m going to take this to our people and convince them that this is the real McCoy. We met with you, we paid you, and you designed and helped this security plan. You’re giving it your personal endorsement.”

And sign it he did. I could hardly believe it; the prosecutors were practically turning flips of joy. That map, of course, became key evidence in the trial.

Everything was set: We paid the sheriff the $15,000 in cash—all hundreds with their serial numbers documented—and we had a map that he drew and signed describing how he was going to provide protection for us on the day of the drop. In the sheriff’s eyes we were all ready to go, and our documentation was all set!

Now that the sheriff had done his part it was our turn to do ours. We put together an elaborate plan, getting the DEA, the FBI, and necessary Special Weapons and Tactics (SWAT) and special operations people in place in the county ready to cover all of this—without anybody in the Mafia knowing that we were bringing down a major operation.

At a rural farm owned by one of the agents, located about fifteen miles away from the sheriff's location, we got everybody suited up, geared up, and ready to go. Right before the appointed drop time, our group headed out, in convoy, to set up to make the arrests. The plan was to apprehend the sheriff at his location, the deputy at his location, and then surround the farm, apprehending everybody else who was there participating in the plot.

In this case, Bryden and I were jointly running the show. He and I were stationed in a mobile command post—more like a mobile home, actually—in which we had all kinds of communications equipment. Think Mission Control. We positioned ourselves on a dirt road just off the highway—but weren't visible from there—and were able to communicate with the rest of our troops.

It was among the tensest times I can remember. As I said, these Dixie Mafia people were very dangerous. They were armed, and, of course, the sheriff and his officers were obviously armed. To that end, we had a very elaborate and careful plan about exactly who was going to be responsible for apprehending which people to make sure that this situation didn't escalate.

This was the first major operation where I was responsible for sending a large number of FBI agents in harm's way. We had spent countless hours planning down to the smallest detail, but in these highly charged situations anything can happen. The benefit of 20/20 hindsight will detect flaws in the plan or its execution, but, of course, we didn't have that. The thought that one of my people could be hurt or killed because of some mistake or oversight on my part could never be completely put in the back of my mind.

Despite all that, I became intensely focused, aware of everything taking place, to the point that time seemed to pass in slow motion. A few seconds sometimes seemed like hours as my mind processed the incoming information, adapted or altered the plan as necessary, and issued instructions. The experience that I gained from this operation was extremely important and the lessons learned enabled me to handle larger and even more dangerous situations.

As the drop time neared, we took to the convoy once again. Everyone quickly took his place. In rapid succession we heard by radio that the sheriff was in custody and that the deputy was in custody. And there were no shots fired. The only casualty was that the deputy wet his pants.

But no plan goes exactly perfectly. The group that had headed into the farm had arrived there to find nobody around. Apparently our approach to the farm had been heard or observed in some way and these people had cut and run. They took off in a pickup so full that people were barely hanging on off the back as it sped along the dirt back roads trying to get away. However, since the DEA had an airplane up, we were able to keep track of them.

Barely minutes later the DEA plane was radioing to let us know that the pickup was heading along the dirt road . . . right toward our command post! Immediately, we ordered several units to come to our location, but we knew that there was no way they could reach us in time. It was just Bob; the driver, who was an unarmed radio technician; and me. Bob and I got out with our handguns, and the driver pulled the command vehicle crosswise to block the narrow road.

During the course of my career I had made hundreds, possibly thousands, of arrests. Though many of these people were armed and very dangerous, I had never had shots fired at me, nor had I ever fired a shot at anyone. This time it certainly looked as if that record would change. It was shaping up to be quite a shootout.

We, the commanders, had been deliberately placed away from the action so that we could direct all the activities without interruption. But all of a sudden, according to the radio from the DEA aircraft, there were several heavily armed tough guys barreling toward us, the two SACs. That wasn't supposed to happen!

Suddenly, we saw the truck round a curve about twenty-five yards away from us. Bob and I drew our weapons, he on one side of the road, and me on the other side. We ordered them to stop. If I were a betting man I would have put my money on them not stopping, among other things. The world, however, is a strange place, and the Dixie Mafia members were not too smart. I could not believe me eyes, but they stopped! They stopped the truck, laid down their weapons, and surrendered to us without incident. It didn't take long before we had them disarmed, apprehended, and spread-eagled on the ground, awaiting our backup.

And what about the trial? Let's just say that our documentation became important. Paying a large amount of cash to a public official is extremely sensitive. Since this payoff was on audio we had good evidence that he was paid, but how could we prove the amount, other than the agents' testimony?

We had our ways. For one, the bills were all $100 denominations of circulated money. We had made photocopies of each and every bill. This is pretty much routine, but in this case it turned out to be the bonanza.

After he was arrested, Hobbs's defense was that he was secretly investigating a major drug case. Although he had accepted the cash, he said, it was actually evidence in his case, locked in a safe for future presentation at trial. The prosecutors—the U.S. Attorney's Office, Southern District of Mississippi—sent Hobbs and his attorney a letter demanding that the money be returned to its rightful owner, the U.S. government.

Shortly thereafter a total of $15,000 in cash was delivered. However, only some of it was the original money we had photocopied. The remainder was not the actual money that he had received.

So much for the defense that he was working a case! All were convicted, and most received a twenty-year sentence.

## Culvert Operation

In the middle of the Howard Leroy Hobbs case we were hit with even more allegations of corruption in our state. Information came in from other parts of the United States—namely from the Memphis, Tennessee, office of the FBI and from the Dallas, Texas, office of the FBI—indicating even more high-profile illegal activities in Mississippi. Agents in these other FBI offices were reporting that people who had tried to do business in Mississippi were finding it difficult to do so honestly. Upon trying to sell products or services to a given county, the seller would be rudely informed that they had to pay a substantial bribe to do so.

What was particularly interesting was that these businesspeople had gone separately to their respective local FBI offices to detail their experiences, yet they all had the same story: there were demands for bribes to be paid before they would be allowed to do business in the state of Mississippi. Since these businesspeople didn't pay a bribe—in fact, they were so upset about even being asked to do so that they cut off contact with those who had solicited a bribe—the information could only be filed away as intelligence. What was invaluable to us, however, was that these instances told us that the problem was systemic, or throughout the state. It was the way these Mississippi county governments operated—wide-open-door inviting and sometimes demanding bribery and corruption. While we couldn't quite put our finger on why that was, these various reports coming in showed us that it was undoubtedly happening all over, and it had been going on for quite some time. So, we were looking for a way to attack the corruption at its root.

The answer came to us finally as one agent was interviewing a preacher who had been in the business of selling culverts. A culvert is a round pipe, usually cement or metal, that comes in all various sizes, from a few inches to several feet in diameter. Culverts are used in roadwork—from building a highway to building a driveway to a private residence. When there's a water problem, you need to put down a culvert so that the water can pass under the roadway. For example, if you're maintaining a driveway from a person's residence that joins up to the country road, and there's a ditch along the side of the road where the driveway meets it, then you need a culvert to allow the water to drain through properly so it doesn't back up and flood. There's a fairly substantial need for culverts along the major highways in Mississippi.

The preacher was being forced to pay bribes in order to sell his culverts in the state. A very religious man, he felt that these bribes were a violation of a whole lot of things, not to mention the law. He wouldn't continue to do business like that, so instead he closed up shop. However, he had been so successful that he had become very well known. It was a big deal when he called it quits.

This was just the kind of opening our office had been looking for. Here was a way to attack this system-wide bribery and corruption in Mississippi. After doing our research and confirming that he was indeed who he said he was—a well-respected businessman, with good connections, who had been in business for years—we knew that we were ready to go.

We came up with a plan: the preacher would go back into business, but this time it would be with the FBI. We would set up the company selling culverts and he would be our CEO. It was called Operation Pretense. His old clients couldn't wait for him to come back.

As with all big undercover operations in the FBI, this wasn't going to get easily approved. We had to submit the project details to FBI headquarters and then go to Washington to appear before the Undercover Review Board, who would review the proposal from a number of standpoints. There's the financial standpoint: How much is this going to cost? What kind of funding has to go into this operation? And there's also the legal standpoint: What waivers needed to be obtained? What laws might possibly be violated if we're operating in an undercover capacity doing, perhaps, illegal things like bribery?

This board's job is to very particularly and carefully review the proposal to determine whether it is a viable, justifiable project. If the proposal earns the board's approval then the necessary waivers that have to be obtained from the Department of Justice are sought. For example, for the FBI just to place money in a bank account under an assumed name, the Department of Justice must issue a specific waiver. This is because it is a violation of federal law to take federal funds and deposit them into a bank account under an assumed name. And in order to open our business we had to have a bank account so that we could buy and sell our culverts. All of those kinds of things are reviewed very, very carefully. And once the approval is given then periodic reports have to be made to the board concerning the progress of the undercover project.

Well, even in spite of all the complications, we were finally given the go-ahead. We began to set up shop, and since this was an FBI business, our first task was picking our two undercover agents. One would cover southern Mississippi and the other would cover the northern half of the state. The rest of the business setup fell into place and it didn't take long for us to begin our business of selling culverts to county supervisors. Considering that they wanted bribes and we were willing to dole them out, right away, it was phenomenally successful. All the preacher had to do was let his prior customers know that he was back in business and had hired two new salesmen.

During all of these conversations with county supervisors, these undercover agents were wearing a wire. Everything was recorded. These supervisors wasted no time, by the way. Almost at the very outset the agents found themselves recording conversations in which the supervisors were demanding bribes, or kickbacks, a certain percentage of any sales. Usually, they wanted 10 percent, but sometimes they'd go higher, demanding 20 percent of whatever the agents sold to the county. It was all shockingly overt. It was almost as if bribery was just a normal way of doing business and that's what was expected. Everybody just seemed to know that this was the way that it worked and that was just the way you had to do it. Period.

After our men had completed a few transactions, some of the county officials got even greedier. They demanded phony invoices when there was actually no sale. In these cases, the culvert salesman prepared an invoice to the county stating that so many of these culverts had been sold to the county, and the county would pay that bill. Then the arrangement—and mind you, we had all of this on tape—was to split the money between the salesperson and the county supervisor. Considering that this kind of behavior was rampant, and each county had five supervisors, this meant that in the state there were some 405 county supervisors to keep an eye on. With only two salespeople/agents—one agent in the northern federal judicial district and one agent operating in the southern judicial district—we were busy. We racked up supervisor after supervisor after supervisor who bribed us.

Now granted, these were fairly small amounts for the culvert sales. The numbers were in the hundreds of dollars, maybe sometimes in the low thousands. So the kickbacks—some of them were as low as $50 or $100—didn't amount to huge money either, at least on an individual transaction. However, over time, with enough phony invoices, the culvert—and the kickback—totals mounted. Finally, it became apparent that it was time to stop the undercover phase: it seemed as though we could go on forever, building up current accounts and adding new individuals from time to time. We agreed that we had made the case and it was sufficiently strong enough to warrant some change in the counties' and the state laws to close the loopholes that existed for these county supervisors. We had well over a hundred county supervisors involved in this case, which amounted to a large portion of the supervisors in the state.

We took the case down and started making arrests, presenting to grand juries, and obtaining indictments. The majority of the supervisors—in fact, possibly all of them—decided not to go to trial. After being presented with videotapes of their meetings and audiotapes of their conversations, they pled guilty. They were devastated to learn that they had been dealing with an undercover agent and been caught with their hands in the cookie jar. To boot, they were now charged with a federal felony.

Considering the outcome, who knew that a culvert could be so pricey?

• • •

These kinds of FBI successes helped boost the morale in the office. Agents were enthusiastic about their work and eager to develop good cases.

Virtually everybody in the state knew in his or her bones that the system was corrupt. They may not have had any information about it, or if they did, it was so general that nobody could have done anything about it anyway, but if you were living there, you just knew it.

And, quite often, citizens benefited too from the corruption so no one rocked the boat. If you lived in a very rural area in a county, and let's say, for example, you needed your driveway to be redone—maybe it had been washed out by rain or deteriorated by weather—well, then, you contacted your county supervisor to have it done. While the law was very specific that the county could only pave and improve within a few feet of a roadway, the county supervisors routinely ignored that. For a very strong supporter they would put in the new culvert and pave the driveway all the way up to his residence. The supervisors took care of the people who took care of them.

These recipients of the largesse knew that the county ought not to be paying for their driveway but probably figured that this is what they got in return for their taxes and supporting the supervisors. A driveway maintained in good, paved condition was their due!

Back then, if you drove into any county and asked who the county supervisors were, you'd be directed to the nicer homes. While they didn't have the Rockefeller kind of money, they did very well, especially in Mississippi, where the extra income went a long way.

But of course, one didn't know the history. To play devil's advocate, maybe they inherited money and came from a wealthy family. Some of them did come from prominent families and those supervisors chose their careers because they felt that they owed it to the county or state to do some public service. However, those people were, sadly, the minority.

One thing to keep in mind is that most of these corrupt supervisors were not criminals in the traditional sense of the word. They weren't violent people robbing banks and committing murders. They were just public officials behaving in a very corrupt way, which meant that they were draining resources away from the county in which they held their responsibility.

However, this was, sadly, the county supervisors' tradition in Mississippi. Business had gone on like this so long that some of the supervisors didn't even realize it was illegal. While a county supervisor was paid almost nothing—it was an elected position, and the county assumed supervisors had some other means of support—this was quite an interesting way to augment the salary.

As a result of this mess, the state law was actually changed, and the job of the county supervisor was radically changed. Up until 1985, when the laws were changed, each of the five supervisors in each county had a budget for public works and repairing that he or she alone controlled. Not after our case. The county supervisor no longer had sole and complete discretion over how those funds were spent. The laws, in fact, changed so much that those funds were assigned an oversight that was practically as tough as that of the most bureaucratic government office.

This wasn't immediate, of course. Our whole investigation began in 1982 and these changes weren't enacted for three years. But it was a busy three years, with our office getting even more corruption-busting experience.

## A Corrupt Nixon

It got to the point where I began to wonder if corruption was something of an epidemic in Mississippi.

As if I didn't have my hands full with enough high-profile cases, in this state it seemed as though there was always room for one more. It certainly felt that way one afternoon in 1984 when I received a call from an agent assigned to the Pascagoula, Mississippi, resident agency.

He said that he had received a call from a friend, an agent assigned to the Washington Field Office, who had gotten quite an anonymous complaint phone call. Phoning from the southern part of Mississippi, the caller stated that he believed corruption was so rampant in Mississippi that he couldn't trust the local FBI or law enforcement with his information. He felt he had to call Washington to furnish information about a bad U.S. district judge in southern Mississippi.

Finally, the agent in Washington convinced the informant to call an agent in the Pascagoula, Mississippi, FBI resident agency with his information. When the informant finally phoned, he had quite a tale to relay about U.S. District Court judge Walter Nixon. He gave specific information about three oil leases, shares of which had been given to Judge Nixon by a wealthy Mississippi businessman, Wiley Fairchild.

Almost from the time of my arrival in Mississippi, numerous law enforcement people and businessmen had told me that Judge Nixon was corrupt. However, when I closely questioned them I couldn't get any specific information—they just clammed up. In addition, members of the Mississippi Bar Association had told me flat out that Judge Nixon was corrupt. None of them would cooperate, however, because for them to do so would be tantamount to professional suicide.

You can imagine how frustrated I became with these responses. Federal judges should be above reproach and yet the community was telling me that Judge Nixon was otherwise. Even more infuriating was the unwillingness of anyone to provide any specific information that could be the basis for opening up an investigation. Just to open up an investigation on a federal judge would be quite a step, requiring highly specific and verifiable information. However, it seemed as though Judge Nixon was so powerful that I'd never get anyone to volunteer it.

I asked the Pascagoula agent to document the information that the caller had given so that I could open up a case on Nixon. However, the bad news was that the source was still anonymous, but there was good news: he continued to be in touch with the agent.

It seemed that no matter how hard the agent tried to convince the source to reveal his identity, nothing worked, but along the way the source did, however, reveal more details. Among them: Fairchild had lent the money to Judge Nixon to purchase oil well shares at a greatly reduced price that would guarantee a profit. Not only that but he told us that Fairchild never intended to collect on the loans. In return, the source alleged that Judge Nixon intervened in a local drug smuggling case against Fairchild's son, Drew, to convince the prosecutor to drop the charges. The paperwork for the leases was backdated to well before Drew had even been arrested so that it would never appear there was any connection.

Eventually, the agent had gained the source's trust enough to convince him to come to Jackson. There, he was told, he would meet with FBI agents and with an attorney from the Department of Justice. We really pulled out the heavy artillery for the meeting. Reid Weingarten, probably the best attorney I have ever known, came down from the Department of Justice Public Integrity Section just for the occasion.

The big question that remained, however, was would the source show up? We were on pins and needles on the day of the meeting. But he showed—thank goodness—and the meeting went better than expected. He agreed to continue working with us and ultimately agreed to testify if we needed him. Our caller also revealed his identity. It turned out that he was Fairchild's grandnephew by marriage, Robert L. "Skip" Jarvis. He worked in Fairchild's office, handling oil lease matters.

Right away we established that the caller was who he claimed to be and that he knew what he was talking about. After doing research and pulling the public document records pertaining to those leases, we did, in fact, find that Judge Nixon was one of the people receiving royalty payments—a portion of which was from the production of a particular oil well. There was no legitimate reason that we knew of for the judge to be receiving royalties from oil wells. Given that, it appeared that we had established a very good reason to open an investigation. The Public Integrity Section agreed, so we opened the case officially.

It didn't take very long before it became apparent that we were going to have to have a grand jury to subpoena certain items of evidence—phone records and such things. However, in a federal judicial district, the chief U.S. district judge is the supervising official for all grand juries convened in that jurisdiction. Considering that Judge Nixon was the chief U.S. district judge he would technically be the person who would convene a grand jury to hear and seek evidence against himself. We would have to find another way. Until then, we were at an impasse.

To solve the problem we had numerous conversations back and forth with headquarters and the Public Integrity Section before a decision was made to have Reid Weingarten go to Judge Clark, chief judge of the Fifth Circuit Court of Appeals, and brief him on the allegations concerning Judge Nixon. Reid requested that Clark appoint another federal judge from another district to convene and supervise a grand jury in Mississippi for the purpose of hearing evidence, issuing subpoenas, and other matters concerning Judge Nixon. This was an unprecedented step. I can only image what Judge Nixon thought when he heard.

Eventually, Judge Nixon personally appeared before the grand jury and testified—which was ultimately his downfall. While he was under oath, he denied discussing the drug case with Wiley Fairchild and with the Mississippi prosecutor who had dropped the charges against Drew Fairchild. Unfortunately, for him, there was credible testimony to the contrary. Although he was acquitted of accepting illegal gratuities, he was convicted of perjury by a federal court.

Nixon's appeals up to and including the Supreme Court were denied. He was sent to jail but since a federal judgeship is a lifetime appointment he had to be impeached by Congress before he could be removed from the bench. Not a problem. Congress impeached him and, following the trial, convicted and removed him from the federal bench. Judge Nixon was part of an exclusive club: since 1789 only thirteen federal judges have been impeached—seven were convicted.

Mississippi had racked up another black mark for corruption to add to its collection. The FBI, meanwhile, was on a high, as we kept making these major cases against the bad guys.

A few years later Judge Nixon's name was brought up again in Congress—but not for new crimes. During President Bill Clinton's impeachment proceedings, both his defenders and his opponents referenced aspects of Nixon's trial, albeit different ones, and pointed out the similarities as a reason to either impeach or acquit.

And Reid Weingarten? He's now one of the country's top defense attorneys and the man to call if you are a corporate officer with a fall from grace. His client list has included former WorldCom CEO Bernie Ebbers, former Enron chief accountant Richard Causey, and former Tyco attorney Mark Belnick. I know one thing: if I ever have any criminal allegations made against me, the first person I will call will be Reid Weingarten. He is the best.

## Horsing Around

I picked up my phone one afternoon in my Jackson office to hear a tale that would have shocked me before my assignment to Mississippi. However, a few years in the state had a good desensitizing effect. On the line was a man claiming to be a businessman from northern Mississippi who was involved in horse racing. He had been trying, unsuccessfully, for some time to have a statute passed in the state to allow horse racing to be legalized on a county-by-county basis. Now, this being Mississippi in the early 1980s, he was asked by various officials—county and state—to pay some substantial bribes. When he said no he was rebuffed. No one would help him.

Here we go again. By this point I knew just who to call in for this case.

Royce Hignight and Keith Bell did such an outstanding job in the Sheriff Hobbs case that the choice was obvious for me. At the time they were still working on the Hobbs case, and prosecutions were pending. They had pretty much achieved their objectives and all the people involved were under indictment.

I called the two of them in from the coast to meet with the horse-racing man. The finer points of the story he told them were even more incredible than the quick version I got on the phone. Apparently, he had been sent from northern Mississippi down to Jackson, the capital, and been instructed to get in touch with various people to pay off. One person he told us about was an aide to state senator Tommy Brooks, the second in command in the Mississippi Senate.

This was no ordinary bribe. Mr. Horse Racer had been told to pay off these officials with shares. He'd have to pay big time for getting the statute passed to permit horse racing in the state. Hignight and Bell interviewed him at some length to get the details, all the while convincing him to continue cooperating with the federal government. He agreed, and they all put a plan together for him to reestablish contact with the aide to Senator Brooks.

After a number of back-and-forths, Mr. Horse Racer finally met with the aide, who made it quite clear what it would take to get the statute passed. He finally relented on the request for shares, saying that Mr. Horse Racer could pay in cash—better for us, since it makes a much stronger case—but it was going to cost him a bundle: $15,000.

Why so high? The aide replied that there were a number of people who had to receive payment but he would coordinate it all through the senator. The payees, he said, would have to be paid, but the aide declined to name them. However, he insisted it would be absolutely necessary for the statute to be passed.

Here we were again. A $15,000 bribe meant one thing to us: we had to get FBI headquarters to authorize that kind of payment. It was a public corruption payment and we'd been through this before in the Hobbs case. We had to obtain the required approvals from FBI headquarters. Nonetheless, we labored through it, in the end getting it okayed.

Meanwhile, we made the decision that to bribe the aide wasn't going to accomplish what we wanted. Busting him wasn't going to be sufficient for us, because, after all, he could just be a very, very corrupt individual, acting alone; the senator could be totally honest. Maybe he wouldn't even know this aide was demanding bribes and receiving bribes on his behalf? Unlikely, but possible.

We agonized over this dilemma. Finally, we decided to approach the aide. Would he roll? We didn't know, but we were hoping. What we did know was that we weren't going to lose anything because we had a case on him—a pretty tight one, in fact. But if there were bigger fish involved we wanted them, too. However, if the aide refused to cooperate with us that would end the case. That was the gamble. Yet, in the end the fact was that we didn't have anything on them anyway. It boiled down to a calculated risk. But, really, I had enough confidence in Hignight and Bell that I believed that they could convince anybody to do anything.

Just as I had hoped, he rolled! Jackpot! He agreed to wear a wire and record his conversations. It got even better. He made it clear for us that the actual bribe being paid was going to Tommy Brooks.

You can't afford to slip up on these kinds of cases. Not only that but you can't even open up one unless you've got substantial information indicating that there is illegal activity going on and that the person in question is believed to be very much involved. The fact that the FBI opens a case on a given public official—regardless of whether the individual is eventually found guilty of any crime—could very well ruin their reputation, ruin their chances for election, and ruin them financially. It could ruin their lives, when there just may be nothing there at all. That's why every public corruption case must be airtight.

Considering all that, getting this aide to roll was one thing but getting him to help us effectively, and appropriately, in this very delicate investigation was another. Remember, he was not an experienced member of the FBI, but rather a cooperating witness. All of our i's had to be dotted and t's crossed. There could be no ambiguity. If it was a bribe, then the words "cash" or "money" had better be mentioned as well as the amount. These public corruption cases also get reviewed very, very carefully and not just locally. They are reviewed at FBI headquarters when they involve a high-ranking public official. And, for our investigation, FBI headquarters told us that we had to have a specific reference to money or we would not have a case.

How were we going to do this? How were we going to set it up so that this cooperating person could have a very specific discussion mentioning cash? "Headquarters just shot us in the foot," I thought. "The minute we mention money to this guy he's going to run. He's not going to cooperate in that kind of conversation." The bribery conversations that people like the senator and his staff were used to were likely subtle, more along the lines of "Well, if you want the senator's support, you're going to have to recognize that certain contributions will have to be made to charitable causes [or whatever] in order for him to favorably consider your piece of legislation."

It wasn't surprising when the senator's aide got really upset after we told him that he was going to have to throw the ambiguities out the window. This isn't the way that he and the senator spoke to each other, he reasoned. "I would never have that kind of conversation with the senator. Never did and never would."

That made sense, of course, but no matter. His conversation would have to be crystal clear—mentioning not only cash but also the exact $15,000 amount. We worked on him for hours, finally convincing him that he could do it.

Before he lost his nerve, he placed that phone call. The senator was on the floor of the Mississippi Senate at the time, but he pulled himself away to take the call, which he was expecting.

The aide told him that he had met with the principals, who were interested in the legislation. "And they've agreed, Senator, to pay you $15,000 in cash."

The senator was furious. "I told you never to mention anything like that! I'll talk to you later." Boom! He slammed down the phone. We figured, "Oh, man, we've blown it. It's gone." Who knew if he'd go through with the regular arrangement that he and the aide had for dropping off the money?

We had no choice, however, but to hope that he would. So, we had the aide go to the local bar at the Holiday Inn to meet the senator right after the Senate adjourned. We thought that there was no way that the senator would show. But, lo and behold, when the aide walked into the bar, wearing the wire, the senator was there waiting on him—wanting his $15,000. But since he didn't speak in such direct terms, he never asked for the $15,000. "You got it?" is what he said instead.

"Yes," the aide replied, holding up the brown bag.

"Fine. My car's outside," said the senator. "Drop it on the passenger's seat. The windows are down."

With that the aide went outside, walked by the car, and dropped the $15,000 in cash on the front seat and walked away. The senator came out a few minutes later, and once he reached over and opened the bag, Hignight and Bell arrested him.

When he tried to mount his defense later, he, of course, said he didn't know how the sack got there. He only saw it when he got in the car and didn't know what it was or how it got there. He was merely opening it up to find out what it was. No one bought his story. The senator was convicted and sentenced to twenty years.

The citizens of Mississippi were simply shocked. While many suspected that this senator was corrupt, it was crazy to see him actually charged and convicted. Up until then, no one had ever really seriously investigated this powerful man.

The times were changing. Swiftly.

# 6
# ATLANTA

## Atlanta Calling

When in 1985 Director Webster's associate director, Lee Colwell, called me out of the blue, I hadn't the slightest inkling of what was to come. I was back in the squad room talking to one of the agents when my secretary found me. "Mr. Colwell's on the line," she said. What in the world? As I walked back to my office to take it, I figured that he was probably going to transfer my ASAC, Earl Whaley, who had been there during my entire three-year stint and had done a great job. "Oh, man, this is a bad time to be replacing an ASAC, with everything we've got going on," was all that I could think.

But I needn't have worried. Colwell had no such intention. "Weldon," he said, "the director's really been pleased with the job you've done there in Jackson, and he wants to reward you." OK. "There's a vacancy in Atlanta and you've been promoted to be SAC in charge of the Atlanta Field Office."

I was blown away!

This was totally, totally out of the blue. I didn't expect it for several reasons. For one, my office of preference was Dallas. It had been my choice for a long, long time but Dallas was a popular choice, so I knew that it would be quite a wait. However, I was happy to wait right there in Jackson until the Dallas SAC either was promoted or retired.

But Atlanta was a promotion. It was a major field office, much larger than Jackson, and I wasn't in a position to be turning down promotions. My response? "I really appreciate the director's confidence. Thank you very much."

After I hung up, the realization of the move hit me. What would happen to all of these cases that I have going here? Not wanting to cause any disruption or panic in the office, I kept the news quiet for the time being. However, there were a few people I had to tell about it because I was concerned that they might oppose my transfer entirely.

One of the people I told, Department of Justice attorney Reid Weingarten, who was very involved in the Judge Nixon case, was extremely unhappy when I let him know about the transfer. "I don't think that we can let you leave in the middle of this case," Reid responded to my announcement. He did have a valid argument: the case was still being investigated and people were still being brought before the federal grand jury. We were heading for an indictment but one had not yet been returned. Reid felt that it was quite important that I should stay there as long as the case was pending.

Okay, next phone call.

When I reached George Phillips, the U.S. attorney for the Southern District of Mississippi, with whom I had worked on several cases, including Operation Pretense and that of Howard Leroy Hobbs, his (initial) response was not much different than Reid's. He was not very pleased that I would be leaving so soon, but we managed to work through it for the next few weeks. He came around to the fact that I was just one person. The cases would survive. There were very good agents working on the cases and everything was on track, with no major upsets on the horizon. After all, I wasn't going off the face of the earth. I would be in another field division but I would still be available for whatever might be needed.

Finally, Reid understood, too, that the cases would survive without me. Both he and George agreed not to pose any interference with my transfer. What a relief. Had there been an issue or if I had to request a delay or reconsideration by the director, that would not have been very well received. It wasn't too difficult for me to remember the chilly reception I had received, when, only three years before, I had gone to the second in command of the FBI, John Otto, to question my assignment. I didn't intend on having a repeat performance.

## Tensions, Teamwork

As SAC in Atlanta beginning in 1985, I had to deal with my fair share of racial tensions. The worst of those occurred in 1987 in the town of Cumming, in Forsyth County, about an hour's drive north of Atlanta.

Way back in the 1920s there had been a terrible incident in the county in which a young white girl had been found dead after being sexually molested. The crime was—as so often crimes there were—blamed on a black male. The punishment was horrible: the lynching of that individual.

The result was that the few black people living in that county then left the area and never returned. Even when I was there, in 1987, there were no black people living anywhere in Forsyth County. Zero. And quite frankly they were not welcome there in any way, shape, or form. But tensions were particularly high in 1987, after a local man organized a march to honor Martin Luther King Jr. He cancelled the event because of death threats but others took up the cause and went through with the march. It was not surprising that the march met with protests.

As news of the incident spread, leadership of the black community in Atlanta and, as it turned out, national leaders decided that a big demonstration should be held, including a march on Cumming.

This turned into the first really large civil rights march in the United States in more than a decade: twenty-five thousand people strong. National leadership of the black community showed up in force to participate. As you can imagine, there was a great deal of concern over the safety of the marchers and how this was going to be ensured, because quite a number of the Forsyth County citizens were still overtly racist. They were quite upset about this march and felt that they should not be subjected to this kind of "mistreatment" and "unlawful focus on their beliefs." Given all this, there was a great deal of concern that there would be a clash, perhaps a very violent one.

In cases like this, the FBI had no jurisdiction over anything to do with the march itself, although it could have jurisdiction if there were a violation of someone's civil rights. So, for example, if a person attacked a marcher, let's say, with the intent of physically harming him or her, then we would step in. Physical harm could be construed to be a violation of the marcher's constitutional right to free speech and that would, therefore, be under the FBI's jurisdiction. So while the FBI was ordered to be physically present in Cumming, ready to respond to any eventuality, we weren't to be actively participating in crowd control. Instead, we were to be as unobtrusive as we could but just present enough to intervene should there be a huge disturbance, a breakdown in law and order, or some massive assault on the marchers.

That said, we had a number of planning sessions. We met with every possible law enforcement group imaginable: the Georgia Bureau of Investigation, Georgia State Patrol, Forsyth County Sheriff's Office, Cumming Police Department, and all others responsible in any way for this march. A lot of meetings—but all were necessary.

Since the march was going to terminate at the courthouse in downtown Cumming, we decided to place our FBI SWAT team in the basement of that building. It was centrally located. Our concern was that if we had the SWAT team or the FBI resources positioned outside the town and something happened in the town, we would not be physically able to respond. None of our vehicles would have been able to reach the scene to conduct any investigation or actively intervene in the situation in any way.

We planned that a couple of my people and I would be in the courthouse's command post, which was jointly manned by all the law enforcement agencies mentioned. We were all in communication with each other and cooperated with each other to make sure that the march took place peaceably.

But nothing ever goes as planned.

The march started south of Cumming, on the highway from Atlanta, and was proceeding seemingly without incident. But as the march got into town the crowds grew even larger and the route was totally lined with people, many of who were carrying the Confederate battle flag, known as the "Stars and Bars." While many people fly this flag as a point of

Southern pride, it's commonly associated with the KKK and other racist groups that have adopted it.

In the meantime, my SWAT leader, Leon Blakeney, came up to the command post and said, "Boss, we feel like we're in a position where we're not able to do anything and won't be able to respond. I need to put some eyes and ears outside this building to report back to me, so that I can be in communication with them about what's going on. I need better intelligence and the only way I can get that is to have a man outside the building, roaming around unobstructed." I considered his proposal and gave the go-ahead. Leon put out a man who was wearing an FBI raid jacket—the blue jacket with the big yellow FBI letters on the back. But there were a lot of Georgia Bureau of Investigation people there, too, and they had practically an identical jacket, except theirs said GBI.

Keep in mind that I had been given orders that we were to be practically invisible. We were not to be involved directly in any way in the activities of the day. Jackets like that are hardly invisible. Now CNN and a whole host of networks and media were covering this march. Within thirty minutes after I had authorized this person to be outside in Cumming to gather information and report back to my SWAT commander, the phone rang. It was FBI headquarters and on the line was Buck Revell, the associate deputy director, and he was irate. The FBI was not keeping a low profile, as instructed. I told him that's exactly what we were doing—we were not directly involved in any activity. He wasn't buying it. "I am watching CNN and just saw an FBI raid jacket," he said. I countered that the GBI's raid jackets were identical to ours except that they had "GBI" on the back. Perhaps that's what he had seen?

"I know what I saw!" he exploded. "Get him out of there!"

To me this whole thing really illustrated how someone who was sitting back watching a bank of televisions with coverage from all of the networks could actually be better informed than those of us who were standing in the command post and allegedly knew what was going on. The TV networks, of course, had news teams all over the town of Cumming covering this march and everything that related to it, and they were documenting interviews with people on the sidelines and the marchers. But we in the command post were not plugged into all that information since live network feeds could not be installed in a command post on short notice. While we had our own intelligence, it was very different.

The bottom line was I withdrew our guy, with the FBI logo on his raid jacket, from the field temporarily. (He went back out immediately with my approval and without the jacket.) As it happened, the march was conducted without incident, essentially, except for an unidentified individual throwing a brick that hit one of the marchers on the head. (The injury wasn't serious.) No one saw who threw it since the brick was thrown from behind the crowd. This brick throwing led to something of a standoff, with people yelling at each other. The shouting groups were separated only by a very few feet, and the shouting could have degenerated into a riot very easily. But, thank goodness, the state police, in conjunction with the local law enforcement, had very, very efficiently controlled the crowds with barricades and so forth, so that opposing groups were not able to intermingle.

So, it got all very tense and very close to an explosive incident, but nothing major happened. The brick caused the only injury in the event. And the march went on from there. It continued on to the courthouse and a platform was set up where a number of speakers made speeches. The end was very peaceful.

One might think we were lucky, but it was more than that. A lot of very close planning and coordination among all of the law enforcement agencies ensured that a full exchange of information took place. We had full cooperation with each other and a generous exchange of resources. It helped that the director of the GBI was Robbie Hamrick because not only were we professionally associated, we were also currently enrolled together at Georgia State University and taking graduate courses in criminal justice. Though I hadn't known him previously, I also got along particularly well with the new head of the Highway Patrol, Col. Curtis D. Earp, a descendant of Wyatt Earp of O.K. Corral fame. The heads of law enforcement agencies all had good working relationships, which filtered down to the troops who were actually involved in carrying out our instructions.

This was somewhat unusual, because many times the various agencies that need to work together during an event or crisis are at odds with each other. In my opinion things always boil down to a personality issue between the agency heads. If the heads of agencies are at odds with one another, because of jealousy or what have you, it filters down to all the people involved. If the subordinates know that there is dissension between the leaders, there will be dissension at their level as well. It is incredible to see how this takes place, but I have seen it many, many times. On the other hand, if the leaders are in complete accord with one another, that sort of nonsense gets stopped right at the source. The conflict rarely starts at the lower level, but if it does and it bubbles up to the top, the leaders put an end to it quickly. In short, the attitude, preferences, and prejudices of the leaders filter down to the entire organization.

The head of a law enforcement agency also sets the tone for how that agency conducts its business. This is particularly true in the FBI. For example, in the bureau there were people who were very, very knowledgeable and had a lot of expertise in organized crime. In an office where such a person was the SAC, you would find the office to be very effective in conducting organized crime investigations because that's what the boss was interested in doing. But, on the other hand, if the boss was really focused on a particular program, other kinds of investigations didn't get needed resources. Those investigations and programs would be less effective than those favored by the SAC.

However, no matter what their particular expertise or interest may be, all SACs know that terrorism is today the number one priority and their offices should be fully utilizing all resources allocated for the program. I have no doubt that this is true throughout the FBI. But that raises a concern.

Immediately following 9/11 massive amounts of resources were shifted from other programs into the terrorism program. If those resources have not been replaced, and I do not believe they have been, then all programs other than terrorism will suffer. There will be less focus on organized crime, white-collar crime, public corruption, reactive crimes (kidnapping, bank robbery), foreign counterintelligence, and other important areas. This lack of focus will be detrimental to the nation in general and to the FBI in particular.

Take Jackson and the state of Mississippi, when I was the SAC. I had a very strong interest in public corruption and I was very aggressive in going after anything that had to do with public corruption in the state. Consequently, we did a lot in that area. No doubt some critics would say, "Well, you did that and while that perhaps deserves recognition, who knows what you ignored by really focusing on public corruption? What about other programs? You didn't do a strong enough job there." And they would be right. That would be an accurate criticism.

The truth is that you cannot focus on everything at once. But the point of the illustration is that the personality, the focus, the expertise, and the interests of the leader all trickle down to the people who work for the leader. What's important to the leader becomes very, very important to subordinates.

My experience in Jackson taught me that as the leader I had to constantly monitor myself to ensure that all my subordinates received my attention and felt important. Even those working mundane cases needed support and encouragement. While this might sound difficult, I found it to be quite simple. All I had to do was to walk around the office and stop to talk to people about their work. By listening to concerns and asking a few questions I could show my care and concern about their work and make them really proud of themselves. I recall that when I was a street agent and an SAC noticed my work, it had a very positive effect on me.

As with every organization, the performance of the leader, in this case the SAC, is measured by the performance of the organization. In general, the performance of an FBI field division is gauged by success in its investigations.

At FBI headquarters each of the program managers (white-collar crime, organized crime, foreign counterintelligence, terrorism, etc.) are closely monitoring the overall performance of the program and the individual performance of each field office in that particular program. The field office performance is considered when the program manager allocates resources obtained by the program during the budget process. Believe me, resource allocations are extremely important to the SAC.

In addition, the annual performance rating given to the SAC is based on the performance of his or her field office. Measures of success vary somewhat from program to program, but in criminal programs the major factor in performance appraisal is the number of criminal convictions obtained by the field office.

Upon receiving allegations of a criminal violation in its territory, an FBI field office opens a criminal investigation and retains responsibility as the office of origin for that particular case. If a conviction is ultimately obtained, the office of origin receives credit and other offices that may have worked on the case are not credited.

Let me illustrate. If two people traveled from Dallas and robbed a bank in Atlanta then Atlanta would be the office of origin. Atlanta would work the crime scene for evidence and interview witnesses. When information developed to indicate the robbers were from Dallas, then Dallas would become an auxiliary office and open a case to handle leads. This could involve an extensive commitment of resources for the Dallas portion of the investigation, yet Dallas would receive no credit for the case since the convictions were obtained in Atlanta where the case was prosecuted.

With this arrangement, some offices and some SACs would not commit sufficient resources to auxiliary office matters since they would receive no credit for the case. This was all very frustrating to me and something that seems to counter what I thought the FBI was all about. While the FBI is not a national police agency, it operates on a national level and is able to do things that a state or city police agency or a sheriff's office can't do. By setting out a lead from Jackson, Mississippi, we could, for example, have an investigation conducted anywhere in the United States by an FBI agent. And I would expect that investigation to be completed with a very high level of professionalism. But occasionally one encountered some field offices that were really only interested in pursuing cases to generate statistical accomplishments for their own division. Covering an auxiliary office lead would not. Now, while that was rare, it did happen. When encountered, the attitude was always frustrating.

Coming from the small office at Jackson and going to the large office of Atlanta I had a very different perspective. Jackson was a small office and it was very difficult for us to undertake a large investigative effort because we simply didn't have sufficient people.

For example, I didn't have a SWAT team all together in Jackson. Instead, I had a SWAT team that served the state, but members were scattered throughout various resident agencies in the state. To get a SWAT team together took four to five hours because I'd have to call members of the team to drive the two or three hours to Jackson before I could have a team ready to go to work. In situations like these we had to learn to cooperate and share resources. By contrast, in Atlanta I had an extremely effective SWAT team of about fifteen to twenty people. They may have been on different squads but they were all in the city and could be assembled at once.

One thing I did do in Atlanta was to make sure that my division would be cooperative and supportive of the smaller FBI field offices surrounding it. When I first arrived in Atlanta, there was a Birmingham office in Alabama, which was a small field division; a Mobile field office, a very small division; a Jacksonville, Florida, office, again a small division; and similarly small offices existed in Columbia, South Carolina, and Savannah, Georgia. Atlanta was the big magilla in the southeastern part of the United States. We were a very large field office, with a lot of resources available to us, unlike those other offices. So, we made sure that the Atlanta office was operating, in effect, on a regional basis. We provided aviation support, SWAT team support, technical support, and any support that we could offer to the smaller field offices surrounding us that weren't as well staffed or equipped.

It was a departure from the norm, but it paid off. The 1987 riot at the Atlanta Federal Penitentiary, which I'll get into later in this chapter, was the biggest crisis in the state arguably since the Civil War, but we got help from all sides. From everyone. Helping out the Atlanta SWAT team was Birmingham, Mobile, Savannah, and Columbia—no matter how small their SWAT teams might have been. Even the Jackson office SWAT team got involved, although they went to the concurrent riot, taking place in Oakdale, Louisiana.

In my mind no office was too far away for us to lend a hand. If, say, the Savannah office wanted some investigation conducted in the Atlanta Field Office then we would do it with dispatch and professionalism, just as if it were a case that we had originated. That was the first principle that I set forth. Another principle was that if Jackson needed some kind of assistance from Atlanta, for example, then all they had to do was ask. Need my SWAT team from Atlanta to help in an arrest you're not staffed to handle? Just ask. Our office in Atlanta had two polygraph operators; several of the small offices didn't even have one. So, the polygrapher from Atlanta would go to one of the small offices to conduct polygraph tests. Also, our office had airplanes, a twin engine and a single engine, available. The Jackson office, and most small offices, didn't have any airplanes. So, if a small office asked for some sort of aerial surveillance or some sort of aviation support from Atlanta, then I made sure it was delivered.

We even helped out the office in Anchorage, Alaska—one area that some may have considered just a little bit out of our territory. The Anchorage office was planning a rather significant raid to bring down a motorcycle gang in an undercover case. In this particular case, Anchorage didn't contact me personally. The office asked FBI headquarters. The FBI headquarters SWAT program coordinator knew that the Atlanta team was probably the best in the country. He also knew of my attitude about the FBI being a national, not parochial, organization. Although I could have refused, citing heavy workloads and significant cases, I did not. The team went to Anchorage. The experience, as one can imagine, turned into a huge morale builder for the SWAT team and the whole office!

## The Marielitos

I never would have expected that something Fidel Castro, of all people, did—something that had barely registered in my mind seven years earlier—would lead to a defining moment in my career.

In 1980, a downward-spiraling economy and political unrest in Cuba led Castro to sanction uncharacteristically massive emigration of his citizens to the United States. But into this group of ordinary citizens Castro added others: he emptied out the prisons and mental institutions and let those people join the regular folks leaving. In total, over a five-month period 125,000 Cubans left the island in every kind of boat imaginable.

This influx flooded Florida with people. (Because the Cubans left from the port of Mariel these people were called "Marielitos" and the incident has been referred to as the "Mariel boatlift.") Some estimates during the decade calculated that possibly one-third of Miami's population was made up of Marielitos. (And, incidentally, there was little question that they helped to raise the level of crime in Miami.) Though most of the original Mariel immigrants have now integrated into life in Miami, it was not so rosy for the rest of them. Many have been incarcerated since their arrival in the United States.

In fact, all the Marielitos landing on the Florida coast were temporarily detained by the Immigration and Naturalization Service (INS) in camps provided just for that purpose. There were initially so many incarcerated Marielitos that some had to be sent to another temporary camp in Arkansas. Most of them were later released.

This detention allowed the INS to determine who exactly each person was and whether he or she was entitled to enter the United States and be granted political asylum. As you can imagine, with the numbers of people involved, sometimes the process took months before the detainees were released. Keep in mind many of those people imprisoned in Cuba weren't true criminals—they were placed there because of "crimes against Castro" so they actually were political prisoners.

Although throughout the 1980s Castro took back some of the detainees, plenty remained in the United States, and the U.S. government had been trying to negotiate their return for years. By 1987, the nearly three thousand Marielitos who did not qualify for political asylum—because they were mentally incompetent, their true identity and status could not be determined, or they were convicted criminals—were still being held in U.S. custody. Those "detainees," as the remaining Marielitos came to be known, could not be released into the general population and Castro would not permit their return to Cuba. They existed in a purgatory in the American prison system.

The detainees were divided into two main groups. The group consisting of less dangerous detainees, some one thousand of them, was kept in the Oakdale Penitentiary in Louisiana. That facility was not capable of housing maximum-security prisoners. About fifteen hundred hardened criminals and mental cases were kept in the Atlanta Federal Penitentiary, a maximum-security facility built in the late 1800s. But the federal prison system was already overcrowded and the Atlanta facility was an extreme example. It was overflowing with inmates. The remaining detainees were scattered throughout the federal prison system.

Negotiations to return the remaining detainees finally moved forward in November 1987. That's when the trouble really began. Cuba had finally agreed to their return, which was great for the U.S. government but not so great for the Marielitos. In fact, what really created a spark was that even those detainees who had committed minor offenses—drug sales

# The Atlanta Prison Riot

*An aerial view of the U.S. Penitentiary, Atlanta.**

*The author (right) briefs U.S. Attorney General Ed Meese during the Atlanta prison siege.*

*All photos were taken by the FBI and are from the author's collection.

*Detainees riot outside a burning prison building.*

*Detainees, including one holding a weapon, pose with law enforcement officials after surrendering.*

*Homemade bombs collected after the siege ended.*

*Hostages being released.*

*The FBI's negotiation team.*

*The author tours the prison with FBI director William S. Sessions (fifth from left).*

# The Oklahoma City Bombing

*The rear axle of the bomb truck, with the Alfred P. Murrah Federal Building in the background.*

*Part of the frame of the bomb truck on the roof of a building two blocks from the Murrah building, which can be seen in the center of the photo.*

*Artists' conceptions of "Unknown Subject #1" and "Unknown Subject #2."*

*Timothy McVeigh's car in the FBI's evidence processing garage.*

*A briefing for U.S. Attorney General Janet Reno (second from left, at table) in the crime scene command post. Dallas SAC Danny Coulson sits to her left, Oklahoma City SAC Bob Ricks stands one next to him, and the author sits at the table's head.*

*A briefing for FBI director Louis Freeh. Standing on the far right is the administrator of the Drug Enforcement Agency, Tom Constantine. Fourth from the right, also standing, is Larry Potts, deputy director of the FBI.*

and such—would be considered for return to Cuba. But, in reality, none of them wanted to go back. One of them aptly described the situation with this simple statement: "We would rather remain as detainees in the United States than return to Castro's Cuba."

On the Friday before Thanksgiving in 1987, they certainly showed the world just that. Cuban detainees in Oakdale rioted, taking numerous hostages. I called Warden Joseph Petrovsky to find out about the situation in our neck of the woods. While the detainees were very restless and agitated, he said, he was sure that the situation was under control. Nonetheless, I told him that should a riot happen the FBI was ready to assist on a moment's notice. With that on the table, we talked briefly about our upcoming lunch—coincidentally planned for that Monday—and decided to postpone it. Little did I know that we would be eating every meal, together, including Thanksgiving dinner, for the next thirteen days.

I was in my office on Monday morning when, at about 10:00 AM, I received an urgent call from Warden Petrovsky. A riot had just begun in the prison, he tensely told me, and although his staff had fired several shots, the rioting prisoners and detainees had taken an undetermined number of the staff hostage. One or two of the detainees had been wounded by the gunfire, he said, although he was not sure whether any of the staff had been hurt or wounded. (I would later find out that two detainees were wounded and one was killed.) He requested that the FBI respond immediately.

I was not at all surprised by the call. Given the circumstances in Oakdale it appeared that it would be just a matter of time before the detainees in Atlanta would riot. I had already discussed this possibility with my staff the preceding Friday and had put the office on standby for the entire weekend, expecting that something might happen at any time.

But despite the fact that I was expecting it, I knew that this situation would not be easy to control. Not by a long shot. I had a passing familiarity with the prison because the FBI had jurisdiction over any crimes committed there. And even though it was bad before the Cubans moved in, the atmosphere only intensified with their arrival. According to the Bureau of Prisons this was the country's most dangerous facility: guards and staff were twice as likely to be attacked here compared with any other prison. It was in part so dangerous because as the incarcerated detainees felt their chances for freedom slipping away they in turn became more violent.

On those few occasions that I visited the prison after the detainees were there I got an earful and an eyeful. The detainees included some unbelievable degenerates, mental cases, and just plain characters. Remember, Castro had cleaned out the jails and psychiatric institutions. Not only was the noise level in there at the highest volume, it was as though the prisoners never slept. And in some cells they clearly didn't: you'd walk by and you might see them engaging in oral sex.

And then there were certainly some notorious inmates. I'll never forget one murderer incarcerated there, a detainee who went by the name of "El Loco" (the crazy one). He earned that name well while in jail in Cuba. The story goes that the Cuban prison guards became alarmed one day after not hearing any noise coming from his cell. This was odd because there was another prisoner in the same cell. When the guards investigated they found El Loco's cell mate dead, murdered so that El Loco could get his food. And that food possibly included the cell mate, who was said to be only a pile of bones when the guards found him. (Considering that El Loco was thought to be so loco that he was locked up in a cell with a solid steel door and a just a slot for food, it seems weird that he would have been given a cell mate.) So, at the time of the riots we knew that we had at least one cannibal in the house.

Terrific.

Another colorful prisoner housed in Atlanta was Jose Meza Rodriguez, a burly little guy who went by the nickname of "Uno." He landed himself in Cuban jail for cutting off one of his own testicles (hence the nickname) and throwing it at Castro, who was going by in a parade at the time. In the prison system, Uno wanted to keep the mutilation tradition up. He was constantly trying to cut up his body. He had scars all over to prove it, with scar tissue running very deep. This apparently made playing sick very convenient. He liked to scare the new guards by sticking a coat hanger deep inside one of his gouges, so that it appeared as though he had been stabbed. Hilarious. When he wasn't playing pranks he was trying to remove his other testicle. It finally got to be such a problem that Warden Petrovsky had to put him in a rubber room. To give you a handle on what we had to deal with in these riots, imagine that this man at one point led negotiations for the detainees.

## Beginning of the Atlanta Prison Riot

Immediately after getting off the phone with Warden Petrovsky, I notified the entire Atlanta office that a prison riot had indeed begun and it was as bad we could have imagined. To my colleagues' credit, no one was much surprised. We all felt that something was going to happen and that it would be big. We just had no idea how big.

Driving fifteen minutes to the prison from our Atlanta office, I was less concerned with how we would resolve the conflict than how I would deal with the initial hurdle: the potential leadership conflict with Warden Petrovsky.

Who would be in charge? Since the Bureau of Prisons (a part of the Justice Department, just like the FBI) has jurisdiction over the federal prison system and the warden is the person in charge of the prison facility, I was concerned that Petrovsky might think it would be him. Though the FBI had jurisdiction over any criminal offenses committed at a federal prison, we were completely dependent on cooperation from the prison officials to conduct any investigation at the facility. That could be trouble. Yet, in this instance, taking hostages inside the prison is a federal offense, and the warden had specifically asked for the FBI to respond. We might be in luck. But what if he wanted to insist on a joint command?

Emotions run very high in these crises, and decisions made by the commander can have life-or-death implications. In my experience, I've found that in highly volatile situations, like this, it's critical that only one person be in charge. A joint command just does not work, because splitting authority is very confusing to subordinate personnel. Any confusion must be avoided at all costs. Confusion breeds disaster.

With all these thoughts in mind, the gravity of the entire situation became even more apparent as the prison came into view. As I drove closer, I saw a column of thick black smoke rising hundreds of feet in the air above the facility. This only confirmed my estimation that, in no uncertain terms, we were facing a very, very serious situation.

Near the entrance to the prison grounds were a number of Atlanta Fire Department trucks. Their hoses were strung up the large entrance stairway of the administration building and into the entry hall. Smoke was billowing out of the entry hallway but I couldn't see any fire. People were running back and forth, shouting. It was a complete state of mass confusion.

Almost as soon as I entered the administration building I encountered Warden Petrovsky, who nearly threw his arms around me. "Weldon, thank God, you're here," he said. "What do you want me to do?" So much for the concern as to who was going to be in charge. With that simple utterance, he made it clear that the FBI would be directing this situation and that I would be the on-scene commander.

Now, there have been a lot of movies depicting an FBI official getting to the scene of a disaster, loudly proclaiming his arrival, and announcing that he is in charge. In my personal experience, when I arrived at the scene of such a situation I didn't have to announce anything—the law enforcement people there knew me already. Not only that, but in these tense, highly critical situations, I found that most people are eager to give the responsibility to someone else. I never had to tell anyone that I was in charge—it was automatic. In fact, there were some times when I responded to a situation under another law enforcement agency's jurisdiction—just to lend a hand—only to have to convince the senior officials present that I was not the one in charge.

Warden Petrovsky and I immediately went into his office to discuss the situation before our first staff meeting. His staff and mine were there in attendance at the meeting, already working well side by side, and we all got up to speed on what was known.

When I walked into the prison all I basically knew was that the rioters had taken over a large portion of the prison, but I had no specific knowledge about what sections or buildings had been taken over nor did I know which buildings were still under the control of the Bureau of Prisons. I had no idea how many rioters there were or whether there were any prisoners who were not participating in the riot.

What I did know was that hostages had been taken, but I had no idea how many and had no information about whether hostages or Bureau of Prisons staff had been injured or killed. I knew though that at the very beginning of the riot some shots had been fired from the towers. Were any prisoners killed? Injured? At that point, I had no idea. But during my meeting with Warden Petrovsky I wasn't hearing any gunfire. At least that was good news! The last thing we wanted was to have anyone shooting.

Over the next thirteen days Warden Petrovsky and I spent nearly twenty hours a day together. I came to respect him enormously. He was calm and professional in spite of the chaos surrounding us. I can't emphasize how important this attitude is in such a situation. If the leaders become agitated or confused, this immediately is transmitted to subordinates and then the situation deteriorates rapidly. So, in effect, at times as a leader, I became an actor playing a role. No matter what the situation, I knew that I had to appear calm and deliberate, exuding confidence that everything was under control and going according to plan. But such a performance could sometimes be gut wrenching.

## Byzantine Prison

The first thing the SWAT team did was to fall back on old tactics: in a crisis you immediately try to contain a situation. But in this case things were trickier than usual. The prison was so sprawling that there was little way to determine, at least initially, when the situation was contained.

The prison was monstrous, filled with obstacles, nooks, and crannies everywhere. It was the largest prison in the United States, with the entire compound built on three hundred acres of land and the whole twenty-seven acre prison complex surrounded by towering walls. The main prison building was constructed at the turn of the last century, and while it was fortress-like strong, it was antiquated, with seventy-foot granite walls. But instead of rebuilding the facility in later years, the Bureau of Prisons had kept the main building intact and just kept adding to it.

At the time of the riot the massive prison complex was made up of two watchtowers and nine buildings, five of which were cell blocks. There were also several stand-alone buildings, including a hospital, chapel, and dormitory—which housed less dangerous, nonviolent people—known as the American Dorm. The original, main building was the largest and the most imposing structure in the complex, with walls three feet wide at the top. And, yet, despite additions to the prison, this facility was notorious for massive overcrowding. There were often eight prisoners in cells that were ten by twenty feet.

When the riot started I could only rally about one hundred agents out of the Atlanta division, and at the most there were probably twenty or twenty-five SWAT people in the Atlanta SWAT team. Other agents and teams had to be brought in from other FBI offices.

While the Atlanta SWAT team was regarded as perhaps the best SWAT team in the country, we clearly did not have enough people for this situation. However, with the Bureau of Prisons people involved, I was able to bring in more people. And I requested that the other FBI field offices in the region—Savannah, Columbia, Birmingham, Mobile, and Charlotte—send in their SWAT teams as soon as possible. (Because of the ongoing situation at the Louisiana prison, the FBI Hostage Rescue Team was there and not available to us in Atlanta.)

All these teams responded within a few hours, and, in addition, teams from Chicago and New York, dispatched by FBI headquarters, arrived the next day. Altogether there were ultimately about 450 tactical people on the scene: three hundred FBI agents, including SWAT team people; one hundred agents from the Border Patrol Tactical Team, or BORTAC; and fifty U.S. Marshals. In addition, there were an unknown number of Bureau of Prisons (BOP) personnel on hand.

Throughout the riot, the Bureau of Prisons maintained control of the administration building that housed the warden's office as well as Cell Block A. Both buildings were located near the main entry, which allowed for easy movement in and out for our personnel. We, the FBI and the BOP, set up a small command post in the very strategically located warden's office.

The other entrances to the prison were vehicular ones: the West Gate, which was permanently closed, and the East Gate, which had been immediately secured by the prison staff at the onset of the riot. These gates remained secure throughout the situation. With the East Gate closed, the only remaining exit from the compound was on foot, through the central corridor and main gate by the warden's office.

While we knew that we could handle this riot, we had never done anything like this on such a large scale. The number of hostages plus the number of hostage-takers were staggering. There were, all told, twenty-five hundred prisoners in there. At least eleven hundred of them were dangerous and potentially violent. They had taken over one hundred people hostage and these hostages were being threatened constantly with death.

The first building to burn down, as part of the fire that the prisoners started at the beginning of the riot, was the Industries Building, which contained a rather large factory complex. Several storage buildings and warehouses adjacent to the Industries Building were also destroyed. It is not well known, but most prisons have a principal product that they manufacture. This facility made large canvas mail carts. It was in this factory area, or the Industries area, that the riot first broke out.

After the prisoners took over, detainees started to use the factory for a use other than originally intended: to make weapons. They manufactured three-foot-long machetes, the likes of which we'd never seen. (In an interesting side note, after the riot, we talked to the press about what happened. On one of the shows, the *Today Show,* I brought out a machete to show cohost Bryant Gumbel just what we were dealing with. He was just floored: you can bet we were the only guests to bring that kind of prop!)

With this kind of byzantine prison setup, one in which we had no visibility, we just didn't have enough manpower—even when we were fully staffed—to go inside the prison for a proper rescue operation. About all we could do was to try our best to contain the riot while we negotiated with the detainees.

## Barbarians at the Gate

As the uprising began, hostages were handcuffed or bound and split into two different groups and placed in separate buildings inside the compound. One group was held in the chapel and another in the American Dormitory. This kind of intelligence was critical in helping us plan our strategy, but information only came in dribs and drabs from interviews with prisoners and detainees who had surrendered. All during the riot, prisoners and detainees who didn't agree with the rioters turned themselves in. Many of them would come to an access point such as the dining hall or the East Gate during the wee hours and surrender. We debriefed them thoroughly to gather any information we could. How were the hostages being treated? Where were they being held? Who are the leaders? Has anyone been injured or killed?

While we were grappling with the question of which group to rescue first, something else grabbed our attention. Nearly twenty prison employees who had barricaded themselves in Cell Block E were on the line begging to be rescued. This took precedence over anything else. We had to get them out of there right away. A delay in this situation meant death—no question. The thing that we had on our side—for the moment, anyway—was that the prisoners did not yet know these employees were up there. But it was only a matter of time before they would find out.

Besides the obvious problem of the employees being trapped "behind enemy lines," if you will, this bad situation was potentially even more dangerous because Cell Block E was where the worst of the worst offenders were kept, all in solitary lockdown. So, not only would the employees be in danger from the rioting detainees, but also in the mass hysteria if the Cell Block E residents were freed and added into the mix. The adjective "explosive" to describe this situation might be a euphemism. The employees running for their lives when the riot began didn't even think about what they were getting themselves into when they ran to Cell Block E. All they knew was that they had successfully reached an area safe from the rioting—for the moment.

The drama was everywhere. There were huge fires burning all around and the clock was ticking. We also knew that we had to use caution. We would be risking not only our lives and the lives of the barricaded employees, but also the lives of the hostages if the rioters saw us attempting a rescue.

Our operation had to go perfectly. There would be no room for error. To that end, we enlisted assistance from the fire department to develop a plan to get everyone out using ladders over the walls. And these weren't just any walls, mind you. They were forty-foot-high walls—quite a challenge.

But we came up with a plan. We would prop a ladder against the wall vertically and place another one horizontally so that it connected to the fire escape on the exterior of Cell Block E. This maneuver would be risky, no question. What if someone had a fear of heights? After all, it was forty feet in the air and someone might freeze up while crossing. No matter, we had to go ahead. We had no choice. This operation, like any SWAT team operation, would be contingent on speed and this was the quickest method.

We knew that to make this work we needed something to distract the detainees. But that something just kept eluding us. What could we do? We were scratching our heads for what seemed like ages, until someone in my office came up with the perfect idea: get the helicopters, which were already on the scene, to buzz around on the opposite side of the prison.

After we rehearsed the rescue plan extensively on a part of the wall that the detainees couldn't see, and everything was in place, we called the barricaded employees to tell them to get ready. They should be waiting on the third floor near the fire escape to come out the back door.

Now while all this was going on, there was also the matter of twenty-seven employees barricaded in the hospital building next door to Cell Block E. They were yelling and screaming, "Come get us!" and just going crazy for us to rescue them. The noise was almost deafening. Somehow the rioters didn't even notice! They all were in such a frenzy, running back and forth and celebrating their success at taking over the prison. They were in their own worlds. And when they took a breather from hooting and hollering, the helicopters flying overhead distracted everyone.

Despite all the commotion, our plan somehow worked: we took but a few minutes to get everyone out. The employees scrambled across and down the ladders like monkeys. And what about that fear of heights? Forget it. The fear of being captured and killed was more pressing.

By this time the riot was barely seven hours old. With this rescue under our belts, back up at the command post we got down to deciding whether we really could free the people in the hospital. I encouraged a complete dialogue about it and extensive planning sessions, but there was one primary stumbling block: there was no possibility of a covert rescue operation like with Cell Block E. We could not safely rescue every single one of those hostages if we were to retake the prison by force, which was the only way we could get to those employees in the hospital. The only place where we could go over the wall to get the staff barricaded in the hospital was in the rioters' line of sight. To scale the wall and send our folks over wasn't an option. By this point the media were following our every move. Reporters had gathered in increasing numbers and focused attention on us constantly. Pair that with the fact that the prisoners were watching the news coverage on TV, which we knew from prisoner and detainee interviews, and we knew that we couldn't do it.

The Bureau of Prisons people, however, felt differently. If we could save the people in Cell Block E, then why couldn't we save the employees in the hospital? No one wanted to hear "no."

While we were deliberating, darkness fell on the prison. It weighed heavily on everyone's minds that there were about one hundred people already taken hostage—and no one wanted to up that number with the additional people barricaded in the hospital.

The employees were frantically calling us and we could hear the rioters in the background, yelling and pounding on the door—with some kind of ram! Others in the hospital were screaming to our people in the tower nearby, begging to be rescued. The BOP was absolutely convinced that all the people in the hospital would be killed and that the detainees would become crazier with access to narcotics in the hospital pharmacy. And let's not forget that they could become even more of a threat with all the surgical tools in hand.

Based on information I had, I felt that I had no other choice but to refuse to order an emergency rescue. No matter how correct I felt I was, even as I made this announcement, I couldn't help but wonder if I had signed twenty-seven death warrants. My apprehension only intensified minutes later when the prisoners broke through into the hospital. Since we were talking to the employees constantly, we could hear the gut-wrenching invasion through the telephone receiver.

I cannot precisely describe how I felt at that moment, other than just feeling completely alone. While my SWAT team leader, Leon Blakeney, and others assured me that I had done the right thing, the decision was mine and mine alone. On that decision rested the lives of twenty-seven people. I knew if anything happened, to even one person, that I'd have to live with it forever. I would be the person responsible.

By this point three buildings had burned down and fires continued to rage. While firefighters could stop the fire from spreading into the area we controlled, they had no access to stop the inferno from burning the rest of the prison.

We were not winning the battle.

We decided to wait until morning to make our move. Numerous additional personnel were en route and we desperately needed them if we were to initiate any kind of operation to retake the prison and to rescue the hostages. But even based on our additional capability that next morning, it would take too long to reach the hostages. If we attempted a rescue operation that went awry, hostages would be killed. It would take us an hour to break in, considering the prison bars, gates, and obstacles.

Negotiation was the only answer, we all finally agreed. (Some more reluctantly than others, but we all agreed). Even negotiation, however, would take time.

## Self-Appointed Negotiators

Given all the concerns about storming the prison, the negotiation process took on critical significance. Our leader in this area was a highly capable man, Special Agent Diader "Dee" Rosario, a special agent assigned to the Atlanta division, who later served a key role in the Atlanta Olympics bombing case.

A native of Puerto Rico, Dee began his FBI career as a clerical employee in the FBI office in San Juan when I was assigned there. It wasn't long before Dee went on to become a special agent assigned back in Puerto Rico. After several years there he decided to transfer to the U.S. mainland, selecting Atlanta as his office. I was then serving as the SAC of Atlanta and was delighted. Dee was a very talented, capable agent, but at that time I didn't know what an asset he would indeed become. Before coming to Atlanta he had been specially trained as a hostage negotiator. While we had other trained negotiators in Atlanta and the surrounding field divisions, Dee was the only native Spanish-speaking negotiator. In this situation that skill made him invaluable. Dee asked for Special Agent Pedro Toledo to come up from San Juan to assist him so we got him there pronto.

Of course some of the detainees spoke English, but it was their second language. Because Dee was able to communicate effectively in Spanish, he gave them a certain level of comfort and trust. That and the fact that Dee was immediately available—making him also a consistent figure throughout the entire negotiation process—were key factors in our eventual success.

But despite having Dee and Pedro involved, the negotiation process initially was just a circus. Self-appointed detainee negotiators would show up to talk to us. We just assumed they were speaking for the whole group and, very often, oh boy, were we mistaken. We had an open-door policy because we never knew who was empowered to negotiate. Any detainee who wanted to talk to us could come to the door of the dining hall—which the detainees controlled—and speak through the bars. Many talks were actually held that way, but for more formal sessions we had chairs and tables set up in the lobby of the cafeteria.

At any given time we never knew which person really represented the detainees. But we couldn't afford to be picky then because maybe, just maybe, the person on the other side would indeed be empowered to negotiate for the Cubans. We quickly came to realize, however, that the men who came to talk to us represented no one's interests but their own. And, if they did have the whole group of detainees in mind, it didn't matter because they didn't have the authority and respect among other detainees to influence them.

Every day it seemed that there would be new people to negotiate with us. At times we'd be talking to the craziest inmates you'd never hope to meet, let alone negotiate with. Before we had the background on Uno, we actually attempted to negotiate with him when he presented himself at the door. As you can imagine, that wasn't very productive. All told nearly thirty different individuals claimed to represent the inmates' interests.

We were going around in circles until Dee came up with an idea that pretty much saved the whole situation. He had voraciously read all the prison files he could get his hands on, interviewed prisoners who escaped the riot, and grilled the warden and other employees. He was trying to discover who was the most popular among the prisoners. He needed to negotiate with the detainees who were actually able to get something done. Using that method, it wasn't long before he isolated a few prisoners who fit the bill and would talk to us. Finally, after five or six days, we could do some real dealing.

Though we may have found the right people for the job, that didn't mean that things went smoothly from that point. For many, many hours a day we, or our representatives, sat frustrated across the table from the Cubans, trying to figure out a resolution. The negotiating process went around and around. The detainees' representatives would produce a list of demands that we would then try to address. Obviously some or most of things were not items we were empowered to agree to at the negotiation table. So, we had to, practically on an hourly basis—particularly after every session—give a summary of the discussions to Washington for further discussion. At that point talks were held at the Department of Justice level, with Attorney General Ed Meese sitting in, along with the director of the FBI, other policy people from the National Security Council, representatives of the president, and so on.

There was no question that this whole thing was taken very seriously at the highest levels of government. At the Washington meetings requests would be debated for hours on end. Then we were given decisions about what we could offer in terms of a compromise or an agreement to a point that detainees raised. As you can imagine, this was quite a drawn-out process. At the same time, negotiations were going on in Oakdale, Louisiana. This, of course, complicated our negotiations because the government leaders discussed all points in reference to both situations.

Coming out of both prisons, the detainees' number one request was an absolute guarantee that the U.S. government would not deport any of them back to Cuba. We kept telling them that this point was not negotiable. We could not and would not give them that absolute guarantee. This was a point that the folks in Washington were *not* willing to concede—at least not right then.

Next on the detainees' list: a tremendous expansion of their rights in their deportation hearings. A lot of them wanted new hearings altogether, this time with an attorney and witnesses allowed, not just the detainee standing alone before an administrative law judge as before. That would be a challenge, considering that many of them had already had all of their possible hearings—exhausting every legal resource—and the decision had been made to deport them. It was understandable that the detainees wanted to reopen those hearings, but the changes being requested were a radical departure from procedure for these types of cases. The fact they were asking for a changed procedure was a big deal in and of itself. What this meant to us on site was that the situation wasn't even close to being resolved quickly.

But the detainee negotiators did one key thing that proved to us that they were negotiating in good faith. We were particularly concerned about a prisoner the Cubans had freed during the riots. Thomas Silverstein was known as America's most dangerous prisoner because of his habit of murdering inmates, not to mention a guard, and he would certainly kill again if given the chance. We made it very clear to the Cubans that if a single hostage was killed by Silverstein or anyone else, their chances of staying in the United States would die as well. We asked the Cubans to hand Silverstein over as a sign of good faith, but from the outset of our request it wasn't clear that they were planning to follow through.

Or so we thought.

Then, on the fourth day of the riot the Cubans carried a very drugged-up Silverstein to the door. The detainees had trussed him up in typical BOP style: leg irons, handcuffs, and belly chain. That was a very nice early Christmas present. The Cubans had captured Silverstein by handing him a fruit cocktail—one of his favorite foods—but it was laced with some sedatives taken from the pharmacy. He never knew what hit him.

To their credit, the detainees understood that he could have single-handedly ruined their whole goal for the riot.

## Delta Force

With two major incidents going on simultaneously, FBI resources were stretched to the limit. Since the Louisiana riot began before Atlanta's, the FBI Hostage Rescue Team was helping out there and not available to us. Recognizing our shortcomings, FBI headquarters made the decision to request that the U.S. Army's Delta Force, one of the federal government's counterterrorist units, be assigned to the Atlanta riot.

This was, to say the least, highly unusual. There were long-standing rules under *posse comitatus* (Latin for "power or force of the county") that stipulated that military forces were forbidden from participating directly in domestic law enforcement situations. In this instance, however, the attorney general, in consultation with the Defense Department, sought permission from the president for Delta Force to be dispatched to Atlanta and placed under FBI command. With the president's approval, Delta Force arrived the following day. Our instructions were that they were not to be engaged in direct law enforcement activities, but were there for backup. Fine with me.

The presence of the Delta Force at a prison was highly classified and could not be made known to the press or outside agencies. This group is known for its secrecy and any information about it would be strategic intelligence for our enemies. For cover, we equipped the entire contingent with blue FBI jackets and FBI baseball caps.

We primarily used the Delta Force's emergency field hospital, which traveled with the unit. This state-of-the-art hospital, complete with trauma specialists, doctors, nurses, and the ability to treat any type of injury, was set up on the second floor of the administration building. I made sure that all our people knew that if anyone was injured, the best possible medical treatment was immediately available on site. (Normally, we depended on local emergency facilities.)

Our second key use for the Delta Force was its expertise in using explosives to penetrate buildings. Our Atlanta SWAT team, whose knowledge and experience in this area was limited, went to work immediately with Delta on this. Together they rigged the necessary equipment to blow through the prison walls to facilitate emergency entry for a rescue operation—if needed.

Our third use of the Delta Force was its sniper group. The word "sniper" is sort of a misnomer although the personnel are, in fact, trained and equipped as what we traditionally think of as snipers. Their primary function is to be the eyes and ears of the group. With their telescopic sights and their ability to remain undetected, they are able to gather valuable intelligence for the commander. In this instance we used them exactly for that purpose. We needed to know where the hostages were hidden, how they were being guarded, how we could get them in an emergency, and so forth. The snipers furnished this information.

I had several discussions with the Delta Force commander, Brig. Gen. Gary Luck, about the limitations we faced. He and I understood that while snipers were deployed throughout the prison and were equipped with weapons, they were not authorized to open fire. While we knew that we had to keep the Delta Force as a support group, we discussed the possibility that one of the snipers might be in a position to "take out" a detainee who was in the process of harming a hostage. We reached a clear understanding, however, that only I personally could give any green light for the sniper to fire. We had to remember that though the sniper might save the life of that one hostage, the remaining hundred-plus hostages would be in immediate danger of losing their lives without the possibility of our being able to rescue them.

In case the worst happened—the rioters started killing hostages—we constantly rehearsed an immediate assault on the prison. We went out behind the prison to conduct these rehearsals and, with surveyor's tape, we laid out the exact dimensions of the doorways, so we would know what we were dealing with. Each team did a daytime and a nighttime rehearsal, and hardly a day passed where we didn't improve on the plan.

In between rehearsals were briefings where we went over the intelligence that we had gathered. At one of the initial briefings, we learned that there was a network of tunnels under the entire prison connecting the various buildings. We knew as soon as we heard about this, only a few hours into the riots, that we should investigate—immediately. What better way for prisoners to escape?

We sent teams to explore the tunnels and determine how we could secure them. While down there our men caught glimpses of a few prisoners running around in the tunnels, but none even came close to finding an escape route. (And instead of engaging us in an underground battle, the detainees ran away from our men.) What proved really valuable about these tunnels, actually, was information we gained about what parts of the facility the detainees had taken. Our teams in the tunnels reported where they had heard detainees behind some of the tunnel doors, which gave us some indication of where men were. This information helped corroborate and augment what we already knew from prisoners who had given themselves up.

Danny Coulson and Leon spent the whole first night exploring underground while SWAT team members from various field offices guarded different parts of the tunnels. Now this was such a bad assignment that the men involved gave it a fitting name: TURD—Tactical Underground Reconnaissance Detail. The acronym was posted on a sign next to the tunnel entrance. And then there was another choice acronym: SHIT. That stood for Subjects Hiding in Tunnels. The TURDS looked for SHIT.

Danny and Leon conducted scouting sorties constantly, almost every time reclaiming more areas of the prison. While we were sure of many areas that the prisoners had taken over, there was a lot of geography that we weren't sure about and the tunnel system was proving to be our main method of finding answers. The auditorium was one such place, strategically located right above the dining room, which the detainees had taken. The auditorium turned out to be vacant, so we took it over and put U.S. Marshals there to hold down the property. When the detainees found out that we had control of the auditorium, however, they weren't very happy.

The next day (day four of the riot) deputy marshals called us up about a problem in the cafeteria. It was incredibly loud in there, day and night, they said—too loud—and they weren't sure of what to do.

Leon went to check it out and whom did he find? It was none other than our old friend Uno. He and a bunch of other detainees were standing there, at the top of the stairs from the cafeteria to the auditorium, with four hostages. They were holding the highest-ranking one, a lieutenant in the BOP, with a spear under his neck. Uno was trying to make a point that the detainees were going to hurt these guys.

"Get out of the auditorium or I'll kill them," he actually said. Leon, who had dealt with Uno previously and knew how to handle him, smartly calmed him down. He used, what he called, "the good old boy stuff." Leon was from Texas after all and knew a thing or two about the good old boy stuff.

"You don't want to do that. Hell, Uno, I'll kill you. If you kill these people you won't make it down the stairs," said Leon, who was calm, stretching out the situation a little longer. As any good negotiator can tell you, if you can negotiate with someone a greater length of time you can usually wear that person down.

In the meantime, Uno was saying that he had a bomb. He was going to blow Leon up, he said. Leon, to his credit, pretended that he couldn't understand him, pouring on a thick Texas drawl the whole time.

After what seemed like an eternity, Leon admitted that, OK, he knew what they were talking about, but he told them that he didn't believe there was any way that they could have made a bomb. Leon said, "Let me see it. Wait, it's too dark to take a good look."

This sent the Cubans off searching for a flashlight, which took up some more time. Leon almost even got them to pass their "bomb" to him for an "inspection," but at the last minute the other alert Cubans stopped Uno from doing that. Leon was able to defuse the situation anyway, and calmer detainees took over. Ultimately, with lots more talking by Leon, those hostages were returned, unharmed, to the holding area.

One unsettling thing that we had gleaned from prisoners and detainees who turned themselves in was that there were discussions about taking explosives into the tunnels. The detainees were apparently planning to use acetylene torch cylinders to construct bombs. The detainees had the acetylene because of the large amount of construction going on at the prison before the riots broke out. Their plan was for those bombs to be placed under the command post. Luckily, this plan never came close to fruition and after the riot was over we were able to recover the acetylene bombs intact.

## Deadly Misunderstandings

A silver lining during the riots was the absolute dedication and quality of service of the Red Cross and the Salvation Army. Volunteers from both agencies were there in full force, amazing us throughout this whole process. At the very outset of the riot—even in the early, early hours of the first day—they contacted us and helped by erecting feeding stations and a rest station for the benefit of the people working there. Thanks to these volunteers, any one of the law enforcement people, hostage negotiators, or whoever could go into either group's tent and have a meal or cup of coffee or a doughnut at any hour of the day. Or, and just as important, merely sit there for a few minutes to get a break.

In appreciation for their incredible service, at the end of the riot, without any direction and unbeknownst to me, somebody passed the hat. They collected almost $10,000 from all the law enforcement personnel at the riots for donation and requested that the monies be given to the Salvation Army and the Red Cross.

Because they were operating around the clock, so could we. Let's not forget that while we were getting paid, they were volunteers who flew in from all over the country. Some of them were in a delicate situation: a handful of the volunteers were family members of the hostages. But that didn't stop them. They were volunteers and they stood shifts at the tent. The volunteers were with us as long as they were needed.

Those camps were set up out in front of the prison, sitting back about thirty yards from the road, in the grassy front yard. Nearby, we had another tent for families of the hostages. To look at this arrangement you'd think it was a tent city—with everyone camped out right on the grounds—which is exactly what we called it.

Because of the constant news coverage, the hostages knew about the tent city and the relatives outside. The hostage takers were watching a lot of television and just eating up TV coverage of the riot. The whole thing was great for the newscasters—real emotional television. For example, anytime they wanted to interview relatives, they were available. The media took over the stretch of road filled with commercial buildings opposite the prison. They also had tents and some even set up on the roofs of the buildings. It was like media row. There were hundreds of different media representatives out there, including every channel that you've heard of and many that you haven't. These reporters weren't just confined to commercial buildings either. They also rented nearby houses or paid money to owners to rent their front yards, camping out to cover the story.

To put it mildly, it was a three-ring circus. For the most part, the media couldn't see the prisoners, but there was one building inside the wall where they could. The hostage takers could get on top of that building and be visible from the street. So, as you can imagine, they were up there a lot. They climbed up and hung banners for the media to see, because at about a hundred-yard distance, it was too far to communicate verbally.

In general, their ability to communicate with the media was a good thing for us, since it provided information about them. But there was one point when we all wished that we hadn't seen something we did: a Christmas tree.

The hostage takers decided to put up a Christmas tree up on the roof of this building in full view of the media. We took this kind of thing badly. To us it meant, "Oh my God, this thing is going to last until Christmas." It was Thanksgiving and Christmas was still a month away. But, nonetheless, they had a Christmas tree, all decked out with lights on it. To this day, I have no clue where the lights and the tree came from, but sure enough there they were, glittering away. I just kept thinking, "Oh no, another thirty days of this." We weren't sure we could take it. Seeing that Christmas tree really did make our hearts sink. But we were prepared to wait as long as it took.

But the detainees could certainly wait it out, too: prior to the riots the Bureau of Prison had bought tons and tons of food for the facility. Just our luck. As the federal budget cycle was winding down for the year at the end of the summer, the Bureau of Prisons folks had realized that they had quite a bit of money left in the budget, particularly for the Atlanta prison. If they didn't expend the funds allotted to them for the year, the same money wouldn't be allotted for the coming year. So, the Bureau of Prisons had decided that rather than lose those funds they would buy a tremendous store of food. The Atlanta prison would be well stocked. The prison was given tons of staple foods that could last a while without perishing, such as beans, which the Cubans ate a lot of, as well as rice, flour, and canned goods. After the shipment, the prison was set with food that would last the inmates for a year—conservatively.

In a hostage situation this was a terrible thing. They could really hole up in there. Usually, people can only hunker down for as long as they have food and water. In this case, there wasn't a shortage of either. So, their giving up because they were in need of food wasn't going to be a factor. There would be no starving them out in this situation.

Though having the media around generally was helpful for the flow of information, in one case it was nearly deadly. In the early stages of the crisis, misreporting was an all too common occurrence. And when you had rioting prisoners watching the TVs to get information about what we were doing, the whole situation felt like a tinderbox about to burn. One time it almost did.

During day three of the riot, the Chicago SWAT team reported in as a group with thirty or more people dressed in SWAT gear—I would refer to them as ninjas—walking up the front stairs of the administration building. One local TV reporter took a look at the situation and started reporting the wrong story. She fixed cameras on the SWAT team, telling her viewers that it looked as if the FBI was storming the prison to take it back. The detainees watching this went nuts and started making immediate preparations to kill all the hostages.

A group of hostages held in the chapel felt the immediate wrath of the Cubans. They already had them tied up on the floor and blindfolded, but upon hearing the "news" the Cubans poured gasoline on the group. They were standing by to torch them if we initiated an assault. Although it was touch and go for quite a while, fortunately Dee Rosario was able to calm the Cubans down and convince them that the report was not true. He did a lot of that sort of thing.

Dee spent much of this time calming the Cubans down because so many things—whether unintentional, as with the uninformed reporter, or not—caused them to react violently and threaten the lives of the hostages. Any sudden change had an exponential effect on them.

I learned that the hard way. One of the worst reactions we saw was when we switched the language of negotiations from Spanish to English. Things had been going along fine with us negotiating in Spanish, but one of the senior negotiators from Quantico made a persuasive argument that the negotiations should be switched to English. His primary reason was that forcing them to speak English would slow down the process and reduce the volatility of the discussions. I personally gave the order for the switch and it was one of the biggest mistakes I made. Hands down. The Cubans went almost totally out of control. I had no idea that the change would have that effect. Fortunately no lives were lost because of it. Within minutes I ordered the negotiations to be held in Spanish, and Dee, skillfully, was able to calm the situation down over the next few hours. This incident, however, only underscored the group's tremendous volatility.

We honestly had no idea at that point whether the takeover would end with everyone inside still alive.

## The Outsiders

As though there weren't enough moving pieces to deal with during these negotiations, there was another matter to contend with. Many Cuban detainees insisted on bringing in outside negotiators, people whom they trusted.

Their first pick was a religious leader: Auxiliary Bishop Augustin Roman of Miami. Roman was the highest-ranking Cuban-born prelate in South Florida, where there were thousands of Cuban Catholics. Bishop Roman was an important figure to them because of his Cuban background. A good number of the detainees were also devout followers of Santeria, a Cuban religion with African roots and Christian influences. No mainstream religion, it features animal sacrifices and numerous deities.

Their religion didn't matter at all to me. What did make a difference was that the detainee followers looked to Bishop Roman as a trusted person. They wanted him to participate and assure them that the federal government was shooting straight, not playing some kind of game.

My "whatever it takes to contribute to a peaceful resolution" viewpoint was not universally shared. The Bureau of Prisons people were incensed that we agreed to bring in outside negotiators. They felt that outsiders were uncontrollable and could contribute to the violence. And the bishop wasn't the only outside negotiator. There was a group of local attorneys who also wanted to help with the negotiations. These lawyers—local American Civil Liberties Union (ACLU) types—had long been involved in the plight of the Marielitos. Through the years they had been very, very vocal about their opinions. They thought that the U.S. government had mistreated the detainees and aimed their ire squarely at the Bureau of Prisons and U.S. Immigration.

I figured that since the detainees had expressed confidence in these people and in their honesty and integrity, they could possibly help with our negotiation process. That was enough for me to arrange to meet with them. And, to my surprise, the encounter went even better than I could have hoped.

The first thing I did was lay things out very plainly to the lawyers. "You are not a part of these negotiations," I said. "You will not sit at the negotiation table. You will not negotiate on behalf of the government or intervene. You will be there strictly to observe. Your purpose will be to stand behind the government and give the signal to detainees that we are operating in good faith. That's it." To put a finer point on it, I emphatically told them that if they did anything to precipitate or accelerate any violent activities then the full weight of the U.S. government would be brought down on them. I think that did the trick: the attorneys, for their part, convinced me that they understood.

I also continued to argue my case to the BOP people that these lawyers did understand very clearly it was in the best interests of the detainees to see that no harm was done to these hostages. "You may disagree with what the lawyers say," I told the Bureau of Prisons people, "but put that aside for now. There is a common goal. Why can't we come together and resolve this situation? You can all continue to disagree after it's resolved. They can continue to criticize the government, if they so choose. That's their right and prerogative. But if they can help us to resolve this situation then we, by all means, need to accept that help and use their influence." Finally, I got through to them! The Bureau of Prisons people were on board with including outsiders. And, with the mutual goal firmly understood by everyone involved, I felt that outside people could really add to the process.

While all this was happening, the outside negotiators were telling the media that the government had accepted them in good faith. This was good press for us—pretty constant good press—since it was blasted continuously on TV. Taking the rioters' viewing habits into account, we knew that we could influence things by selectively allowing information to be publicized that would help our case. In fact, I'll argue that one of the major factors to help end the crisis was the inclusion of the attorneys and bishop in the process and publicizing that fact. It was widely seen as a testament to the U.S. government's desire to conclude the crisis. Peacefully.

Our goal to resolve things peacefully was so important that we took a risk. By "risk" I'm referring to an internal risk, rather than that these negotiators were a risk to our hostage negotiations. Remember, we were dealing with the bureaucracy of the government. It was a departure from policy to use "outside" negotiators at all, to allow them to participate, even in an indirect way. With any departure from the past, there could have been repercussions. To my knowledge, the Atlanta prison riots marked the first time the FBI had utilized outside negotiators in a large-scale hostage situation. In some hostage situations, where there are only one or two hostage takers, immediate family members are brought in to appeal to the hostage takers to surrender. But doing that here, obviously, would have been chaos, considering that there were over one thousand hostage takers. Even if we swayed one hostage taker by this tactic, the result would have little or no influence over the others.

Using outside negotiators worked so well in Atlanta that years later we used it during negotiations with the Montana Freemen. There we brought in some people who were, shall we say, on the radical edge, with strange and unusual beliefs about government. But what was important to us, both in Montana and Atlanta, was to use outsiders who had credibility with those barricaded inside. People inside believed the radical negotiators would act in their best interest—not the government's.

## Finally Over

It was on Sunday night, November 30, 1997, that we got a huge break. Skillful negotiations, along with help from Bishop Augustin Roman and the other outsiders, were successful in finally bringing the Oakdale riot to a close. After all the drama, the events ended there with a whimper.

But just as we thought our situation was heading in the right direction, and we hoped that the outcome of the Oakdale crisis would help us make progress, things slowed down. Big time. You could say that the process came to a screeching halt.

The detainees in Atlanta learned about the Oakdale resolution but, instead of being relieved, thought their Louisiana brothers had jumped too quickly to sign an agreement that was not in their best interest. They deduced, whether true or not, that the agreement didn't rule out the government's plan to deport them. The Atlanta hostage takers were determined not to make that same mistake.

The Atlanta detainees figured that at this rate they should hold out as long as they could. Since we hadn't done it already, we'd never storm the prison! Although it could be forever until they'd get the deal they wanted, who cared? Staying in prison was looking better than what they feared would be the alternative.

But as far as I was concerned they didn't have forever. The prison siege became the longest in U.S. history by the beginning of December. We'd had enough.

However, some quick thinking on Danny Coulson's part—giving a detainee who was at the negotiating table an eyeful of what appeared to be a whole slew of SWAT team members ready to go—showed them that we meant business. Not long after that the detainees were at the negotiating table with a newfound interest in resolution.

We finally worked out an accord with the six outside negotiators early on Thursday, December 4. Our eight-point agreement promised to review, on a case-by-case basis, each detainee's situation before making a decision to deport.

The government also agreed not to prosecute detainees for damaging government property during the riot itself. Of course, a huge amount of damage—likely totaling into the millions—had occurred. In addition to partial destruction of the buildings, several of them had completely burned down. On an ironic side note, one of the buildings that had been burned had been slated for destruction anyway. It was an old building and its destruction costs were going to be upward of $50,000. In some small respect, this was the one thing to come out of the whole Atlanta mess that saved the government some money.

After the agreement was initialed at the table, the document was brought for a vote in the chapel. The majority of the remaining 1,105 detainees voted in favor. The ones who did were certainly happy. We were, too, when we saw many of the inmates climbing to the roof to hoot and holler. All I kept thinking was, "This will soon be over! Way before Christmas!"

But all was not exactly over. The prisoners wanted Bishop Roman to be present. So that evening he flew up from Miami to pray with them and to be a witness. In the signing ceremony, which itself took negotiations to set up, ten people sat along an oak table with a crucifix in the middle. Roman, who was among the signers, began the ceremony by leading everyone in prayer.

Afterward, the hostages were brought through the doorway of the cafeteria into our custody. We waited on our side and out they came, one by one. That was an emotional experience, no question about it. The hostages emerged looking dazed. They had been living in a state of terror for so long they were emotionally drained. Most looked like prisoners of war. Some, however, walked out bright and chipper, as if it were just ano-ther day at the office. Their reaction was, "Oh, jeez, terrific, I'm out finally." Others emerged mumbling, without saying a word to anybody.

We took every individual off to a site where we processed them, checked them medically, and identified them. This last part was crucial because we had to make sure that we didn't inadvertently get a prisoner detainee posing as a hostage coming out with the group. (We didn't.)

Luckily, the hostages had all been treated well. They had been fed and were in good shape. None had been harmed or beaten or tortured or anything like that. Mentally, it was another story completely. Most were seriously affected by what had gone on.

How could they not be? They had had knives and swords held to their throats. And what about the incident in which the hostages were sitting in a puddle of gas with people ready to torch them? This all had a very serious mental impact on many of the folks. Some years later after the riots were over I had the occasion to speak with Warden Petrovsky, who mentioned, not surprisingly, that many of those hostages never again worked in the prison system.

The hostages had plenty of counseling afterward. They certainly needed it. We did not, however, have on-site counseling, as we did later in Oklahoma City, for everyone affected—including the rescue workers. We didn't have it because the thinking at the time was that since no violence had occurred, there would be no trauma for us. That was unfortunate, because at the Atlanta prison plenty of individuals other than the hostages were pretty shaken up. Only at a later date did on-site counseling become commonplace for everyone.

Often, I can't talk about the riot without getting emotional. During the entire siege, I was totally focused and had no time to become emotional, even though I was under unbelievable stress. Direct responsibility for the lives of the hostages as well as the lives of agents who might have had to go in for a rescue could not be taken lightly. At the time, it was impossible not to think about the Attica, New York, prison riot in 1971. When authorities stormed the prison to resolve the situation, forty-two people died—prisoners as well as hostages. Even today, thinking about what could easily have happened in the Atlanta riots is sobering.

But perhaps those individuals in Attica did not die in vain, because they taught us a valuable lesson. Unless people are being killed or tortured or are in imminent danger, there is no reason to rush to a resolution. Time was not of the essence in a situation like Atlanta's. To act as if it were would definitely have resulted in the loss of many lives. This same lesson was later an important factor with the Montana Freemen, a situation which also resulted in a successful resolution with no casualties.

I am very proud of the fact that the men and women serving with me during that prison riot successfully worked through an extremely dangerous situation with no loss of life. Yet at the same time, it angers me that very little attention has been paid to this considerable success while widespread unfair condemnation has been hurled at the FBI for the events at Ruby Ridge and Waco.

## Atlanta SAC: Challenges

Obviously, the prison riot was a situation unto itself, but the SAC job in Atlanta was quite a change for me. At the time I arrived, there were about 170 agents. The division I was leaving had less than 50. This job covered most of the entire state of Georgia when I started. But by the end of my tenure, my responsibility covered all three districts. Initially, the Atlanta field division covered two judicial districts: the Northern District of Georgia, which was headquartered in Atlanta, and the Middle District, which was in Macon, Georgia. The Southern District, which contained Savannah, was a separate FBI field division, with its own SAC. This was confusing to almost everyone in the state because all of the state and federal agencies were headquartered in Atlanta. The Georgia State Patrol, the Georgia Bureau of Investigation, the DEA, you name it, were in the capital city of Atlanta.

For the most part, these agencies each had a small, subsidiary office in Savannah. This arrangement meant that any major case being worked by the Atlanta office would also be worked by a couple of their agents down in Savannah. As the SAC of the Atlanta office, I found myself in many meetings, representing the FBI and having to talk to people who were working cases in Savannah. Unfortunately, it became obvious our office and I knew nothing about these cases. Once I was already in the meeting, the person would say, "Oh, you're not working that case?" Wasted time. "No, that's our Savannah FBI office," I would have to reply.

This situation was confusing for them and confusing for me. After several years as the Atlanta SAC—it was the FBI after all and I couldn't make those kinds of radical changes without having been there for a while—I made a recommendation to FBIHQ in 1988 that we eliminate the Savannah Field Office and make the Atlanta office cover the entire state of Georgia. That turned into a very major deal because, first of all, the people who lived in Savannah were upset with the prospect that they would no longer have an FBI field office. They felt that they were taxpaying citizens and they deserved an FBI presence as much as Atlanta did, or any other place for that matter. After having had an FBI office in their city for decades, the people of Savannah were not ready to give it up. Their feeling was that any change in that status would diminish

Savannah's importance, not to mention how it could affect the FBI's ability to complete its investigations there.

Congressional representatives from Savannah's district weren't happy either. Constituents were being affected, so they became very interested in what was happening. I can remember going down to Savannah on one occasion to meet with the Citizens Crime Commission. I thought I was going to get tarred and feathered. They were extremely unhappy, asking very pointed questions about why the FBI was doing this or that and saying that the FBI didn't care about locals in Savannah. One elderly lady even went so far as to suggest, "Instead of moving the Savannah office to Atlanta, why don't you move the Atlanta office to Savannah?" That comment did provide some comic relief.

Ultimately, the FBI went forward and eliminated the Savannah Field Office. This happened, in large part, because budgets had been cut in the organization rather stringently. We didn't need both offices and two SACs with duplicate support staffs.

The solution I found for keeping the Savannahians happy was a fair swap. The Savannah office was not eliminated completely, but rather downgraded to a major resident agency. In an effort to save jobs there, the office was designated as a regional computer center and reclassified. Jobs were no longer local and instead supported the entire FBI. In almost every instance grade levels were enhanced because the job descriptions were upgraded, providing an increase in salary and more responsibility for the support staff.

At the outset of this transition, virtually the entire staff of the Savannah FBI office was not very happy either. During the discussion phase of the proposed merger of the two offices, several retired agents met with leaders in the community as well as the local congressman to help fight the merger.

With this situation, it was clear to me that the Savannah office would be extremely hard to manage from Atlanta and that without strong leadership the FBI people in Savannah would never really consider themselves as part of Atlanta.

My solution? Transfer in Harold Jones, an extremely competent supervisor in Atlanta in whom I had complete confidence to be the senior supervisory agent. He accepted the challenge and did a magnificent job, as I had expected.

• • •

The other big challenge in Atlanta was the worst—Barr none.

I'm talking about Bob Barr, at the time the U.S. attorney for the Northern District of Georgia, who eventually went on to serve several terms in Congress. The ultraconservative Barr was perhaps best known as the first member of Congress to call for the impeachment of former president Clinton, but I knew him for other reasons. In my book, Barr was the absolute worst. In his desperate bid for publicity, he made my job extremely difficult by leaking information to the press almost constantly.

It was widely known that Barr had a favorite newspaper reporter with whom he collaborated on articles, *Atlanta Journal-Constitution* reporter Gail Epstein. Whenever we at the FBI were the subjects of one of their joint takedown stories, we'd say that we got hit by the Epstein-Barr syndrome again. All joking aside, I can't tell you how frustrating this was to have confidential information about cases show up on the front page. Not only was it embarrassing, but it often also impeded our work.

At various points other federal law enforcement agencies—the DEA, U.S. Customs, U.S. Marshals, and Secret Service—each came to complain to me about Barr. "You have to do something to get rid of this," they said. "He's killing us!" Isn't it interesting that they all came to the FBI with this problem?

I did what I thought was the right way to proceed. I gathered together material and documents to illustrate how the leaks had caused problems in various cases. In 1988, evidence in hand, I asked Barr to come to my office. When he arrived, I closed the door and we spoke face to face about the matter. Confronting him, I said if he didn't cease and desist all the leaking, I'd have to report it to the Justice Department.

He expressed some concern, but, typical of a politician, he lied. Within a month he was back at the game. I had no choice. His actions finally sent me traveling to Washington, D.C., with articles that contained leaked information. I went to Mike Shaheen, then head of the Justice Department's Office of Professional Responsibility, and made an official complaint.

The result?

Well, I learned a lesson about politics. The simple version: the Justice Department conducted an investigation and didn't do anything. Barr was a political appointee and the Reagan administration was not going to do anything to offend its political base. Its strategy was not to reappoint him when the time came. So, no immediate action was taken. Barr got off easy.

In the meantime, as you can imagine, this made it difficult to work with him for the remainder of his tenure. The U.S. attorney and the SAC traditionally have to work together closely, and from that time forward Mr. Barr wasn't particularly friendly to the FBI.

Even though Barr had done so many questionable things that I didn't think he could shock me anymore, I was wrong. I'll never forget when I saw a quote from him that almost knocked me out of my chair. He was in Congress making a statement about leaks. According to Barr, a sanctimonious son of a bitch if there ever was one, it was unconscionable that law enforcement had leaked information about some case. Politics.

• • •

All in all, Atlanta turned out to be an amazing experience. I enjoyed living there immensely. It was a clean, nice, friendly city, with a terrific quality of life. It even had a Major League Baseball team. I enjoyed being able to catch a few games and tickets were very easy to obtain because during those years the team wasn't doing well.

One thing that I'll always treasure about my five years in Atlanta was that they afforded me the opportunity to get a master's degree. I had wanted to continue my education for many years but had never remained in one place long enough to be able to get a degree. One day while I was visiting Robbie Hamrick, head of the GBI, he informed me about the great academic facilities at Georgia State University, where he was already enrolled. I followed up on his suggestion and enrolled in the next session. The program was structured to last two years and led to a master's degree in criminal justice. It was a long two years. Classes were on Tuesday and Thursday evenings from 6:00 to 9:00 PM continuously all year (including the summer session), except for the Christmas holidays and spring break. I usually spent most of Saturday on campus in the library or the computer lab, preparing papers and doing research.

Sometimes classes directly conflicted with the demands of my job, but all the professors were very understanding. For example, during the Atlanta Federal Penitentiary riot I was not able to attend any classes. In addition, I was scheduled to take a final examination on a course involving the study of penal institutions. I called my professor from the penitentiary to explain why I would have to postpone my examination. He laughed and said, "Don't even worry about the exam. As far as I am concerned you are involved in taking the most serious final exam in the history of penology." When I talked to him after the riots he said that I had passed my exam with an A+ and that is what he had turned in for my grade.

Although I had long-range plans to use the degree for teaching college-level courses, I have not yet taken that step. I may yet do so since I love teaching and lecturing.

● ● ●

When I was approaching five years' service in Atlanta as SAC in the latter part of 1989, I got a call from Deputy Director Floyd Clarke. Director William S. Sessions, he said, had selected me as the assistant director of the Administrative Services Division and that the attorney general had concurred.

I was again totally shocked. This was not something that I was interested in doing. However, as I had learned through many years of service, that didn't matter. I recognized that having served in the Administrative Services Division as the unit chief of the Special Agent Transfer Unit was probably a major factor in my selection. Another contributing factor, I'm sure, was that William Sessions had barely been sworn in as director when the Atlanta Federal Penitentiary riot had occurred and I had had considerable personal contact with him during and after the riot. Plus, the FBI had received very favorable press for the handling of the riot. Once again in my life, pure chance was a major factor in placing me in a position to be noticed and remembered in a favorable way by my superiors.

# 7
# Administrative Services Division and Director Sessions

## Sharing the Black Hat

I didn't realize that when I accepted the position heading up the Administrative Services Division I would end up writing a turnaround story. Administrative Services was responsible for all personnel and budget matters in the FBI. In this respect the FBI is no different than any other organization; it's a constant battle managing an organization's resources.

But managing the FBI's money was a walk in the park compared with managing the FBI's personnel resources. Through the budget process, the FBI receives an allocation of a finite number of special agents; during my tenure (1989–92) that number was approximately twelve thousand. In addition, there were approximately another fourteen thousand clerical and support positions as well as analysts, translators, and a host of other specialized positions. All those positions were assigned to the fifty-six FBI field offices, over four hundred resident agencies throughout the United States, over twenty-five foreign legal attaché offices, and FBI headquarters.

If that were not complex enough, add to it the fact that Congress allocated a certain number of special agents to each program—including white-collar crime, organized crime, terrorism, foreign counterintelligence, narcotics, and reactive crimes. During my time, nineteen programs received allocations. Each program had a program manager assigned to FBI HQ whose responsibility it was to manage the overall program, the cases, and personnel assigned to their program.

After receiving the budget allocation, the program manager had the responsibility of recommending how those resources were to be distributed throughout the organization. Each of the nineteen program managers did the same, all giving their recommendations to the Administrative Services Division. By combining the recommendations for each of the fifty-six field offices and nineteen programs, a total staffing level for each office could be calculated. The result was known as the target staffing level (TSL).

Adding to the complexity of this staffing problem was the Inspection Division. Each field office had to endure, approximately every eighteen months, a complete and thorough review of its operations since the last inspection. Included in the inspection was a review of all active cases in each program, a review of unaddressed work in that program, and an evaluation of the efficacy and efficiency of the program. Finally, the inspector made a recommendation about the staffing in that particular office. Since the FBI was perpetually understaffed in all programs, the inspector almost always recommended a staff level that was more than what had been allocated to that office.

Usually within a few hours after an inspection was completed and the SAC had the inspector's recommendation, that SAC would be knocking at the Administrative Services Division door and demanding that agents be transferred in immediately to bring the office up to the recommended staffing level. The big picture that the individual SACs couldn't (or wouldn't) see was that if you added up all the inspectors' recommended staff levels for all fifty-six offices, the total came to several thousand more agents than we actually had on board. That was one of the reasons that we had a TSL, which factored in the total number of agents that we had to allocate.

The investigative programs were broken down into over three hundred separate case classifications. For example, in the reactive crimes program were kidnappings (classification 7) and bank robberies (classification 91). On top of that, in many classifications there were subclassifications. In the white-collar crime program, for example, there was a subclassification of bank fraud and embezzlement, given a classification of 29. Depending on the value embezzled, the case could be a 29A, 29B, 29C, and so on. As confusing as this is to read about, try to imagine what it was like to implement.

Traditionally, the Administrative Services Division had been considered the bad guy. When we received a request from a field office for more staff, we had to reply in one of two ways, and if we said, "No, we can't do it," that response made that field office very, very angry. Or if we said, "Yes, we'll do it," and then just arbitrarily went through and took some agents from here and a few people from there and others from someplace else, then every place losing personnel would be very upset. We couldn't make everybody happy.

I wanted to change all that. My tactic was to say, "Wait a minute. The Administrative Services Division carries out, facilitates, and administers those things that we are directed to do. We don't make the policy. We don't establish the resources. We don't decide how many white-collar crime agents there should be or where they should be. You in the Criminal Investigation Division—that's your job: you tell us and then we'll carry out your instructions. We will do the transfers and handle the staffing responsibilities."

Instead of trying to find the new agents for the requesting offices, we got them involved in the process. We did this in part so they could understand the complexity of what they were asking, because soon enough they would be on the losing end of another field office's agent request. The first question when they called up with a request to reassign agents to a particular division was whether they were sure that they wouldn't be satisfied with a smaller amount. In some cases they compromised and were happy with, say, half the original number.

The second part of the question was, "Okay, if you agree and you want ten agents to be assigned to this division, where do we take them from? You tell us where those ten agents come from. They don't grow on trees so we have to subtract them from other field offices: take ten from somewhere else so we can add ten over here. You tell us from where to subtract them." The person on the other end of the phone never liked to hear that.

The requesters didn't decide which people to move but did decide from what programs and offices they would originate. They said, for example, "Okay, five white-collar agents have to be moved from Atlanta to Newark." Of course, the requesters weren't very happy about that because now they had to be the bad guy—they had to wear the black hat—by deciding. But the Administrative Services Division moved the specific people: "Okay, here are the five names; here are the five people we're moving." Surprisingly, though, there were no particularly huge conflicts that I can remember.

I only held the job for a little over three years. However, it seemed like ten. There were so many headaches. But we made a lot of progress in those years.

For so long the division's reputation had been quite negative, although it was always considered very powerful because it essentially controlled all the people and all the money. Toward the end of my tenure, by around 1992, we had succeeded in really changing the office from one of service—despite the fact that "service" was our middle name—to one of support. The division that was formerly known as the one that impeded people from getting their jobs done was now the one that enabled them to get their jobs done.

Initiating reforms wasn't easy because many of the practices were entrenched, not only in the division, but also in how the rest of the organization regarded our division. As you can imagine I held an unending series of meetings. It was a very large operation—about one thousand people—and there was a lot of walking around. I went to all the offices, sat down, and talked to the staff about what they were doing and why they were doing it that way. Some people told me that before my visit, they had never even seen or talked to an assistant director.

It's not that the assistant directors in the past didn't want to meet with the staff, but there was so much on their plate that they didn't have the time. When I came in I had to consciously make time to walk around and ensure that everyone knew my door was open. Anybody could come see me at any time. If somebody had a better way to make a mousetrap, I wanted to hear about it.

The staff very much welcomed the change. It was an understaffed division and these people were working their tails off. Previously, without fail, every time they did something there was a storm of criticism. "Why did you take these people away from me? Why did you reallocate this money? Why did you do. . . ?" I sought to change that.

My goal was for people at least to understand why we made the decision that we made and to participate in those decisions to some degree. This helped them to feel they were a part of the process and not a victim of it, which makes a huge difference. When you listen to the troops—the people who are in the trenches, the ones who are actually doing this work—you hear very smart ways to improve the process, making things work a lot more smoothly.

The way I felt about the job was this: it was just a matter of listening to the people, which no one had done. And, as it turned out, it worked.

## Heart Attack

After about two years of heading up the Administrative Services Division, I began to concentrate on fulfilling a goal I'd had for quite some time. My hope had been that I'd be able to return to the field again as an SAC in a place where I ultimately wanted to retire. However, there were many places where I would have gladly settled down. But this goal was still just in the background; it was just a wish that I had.

As it turned out, there were other plans for me. My immediate superior, Jim Greenleaf, the associate deputy director, was leaving. Greenleaf was tapped by former director William Webster, who had left the FBI in 1987 and gone to the Central Intelligence Agency (CIA), to come over to the CIA to help him. When Greenleaf accepted, he created a vacancy in the associate deputy director for administration position. This was a vacancy I gladly filled but, one, unfortunately, that came with many more additional responsibilities.

The FBI is multilayered. Back then there was the director, one deputy serving directly under him, and then under the deputy there were two associate deputy directors. One of the associate deputies handled all the FBI's investigative matters and the other associate handled all administrative matters. And there I was, in the Administrative Services Division, hoping to get out and serve as an SAC in the field. However, Director Sessions made the decision to promote me to associate deputy director, moving me up to the fourth-highest ranking position in the FBI.

Keep in mind that by 1992 I was eligible to retire. It appeared that this would be my last assignment in the FBI; I would be spending the rest of my career in Washington, D.C., rather than returning to a field assignment. I would just stay there in that job until I decided that it was time for me to go. The position was a very interesting one because I had now reporting to me, as the associate deputy director, my old division, the Administrative Services Division, plus the entire Criminal Justice Information System (CJIS) Division as well. While CJIS was an exciting responsibility, that division was undergoing a rather significant conversion to new computer programs, which generated a huge amount of activity. Furthermore, the Information Services Division, or what had been previously called the Records Division, which handled all of the computer applications that the bureau used, also reported to me. Given all this, a substantial amount of my time was required to meet with departmental people and congressional people, not to mention our own internal FBI staff, about these various subjects.

At the time I was promoted, I was still chairing the FBI's Contract Review Board, which reviewed every potential FBI contract valued at more than $200,000. The assistant director of the Administrative Services Division could approve anything less than $200,000, but anything more than that had to go before this board for a full review. In that situation there were presentations made and the board—like any other board—voted whether to award a particular contract to a particular contracting vendor. That kind of activity took up another huge chunk of time.

Then there was my duty involving the FBI Senior Career Board, on which I had served since 1989, when I became assistant director of the Administrative Services Division. This board reviewed candidates and made recommendations to the director, who ultimately made the appointment for all senior executive service positions in the FBI. For each vacant position the board selected three candidates, ranked them in order of preference, and submitted the list to the FBI director for his final approval.

That, too, occupied a fairly significant amount of time because there was a lot of turnover, as there seemed to always be in the FBI. At the senior exective level, 99 percent of those leaving executive positions were retiring, but with the size of the FBI and the number of executive positions that were involved—the FBI had, at that time, about 180 senior executive positions in the organization—there were many vacancies to be filled. If any one of those 180 positions became vacant for any reason, then the Career Board had to become involved. Since we were dealing with high-level careers, a very careful and deliberate consideration was given to each candidate before the board made recommendations.

With all of these existing duties, serving as associate deputy director was a very, very challenging position—more so than I ever could have anticipated. When I moved up into that position—I had started in the Administrative Services Division and continued as the associate deputy director for administration—I really was under a tremendous amount of pressure and strain. The roots of that stress went way, way back to probably the time that I had the position of the transfer unit chief for special agent transfers in the late 1970s. That was a job that I thought at the time was tremendously stressful. However, it was nothing compared with this.

Not long after I settled into my new position I developed an intermittent back pain. I went to a couple of doctors and had a CAT scan and all kinds of tests to determine what was the matter with my back. After all that, finally the specialist said, "You don't have a problem with your back, Mr. Kennedy. Your back is okay. You might, however, consider going to visit a cardiologist."

"A cardiologist?" I thought. What? That was a shocker. "A cardiologist? My pain is back here," I said, pointing to my back. To which he replied, "Well, I know that and you've described everything to me, but in looking at all of your symptoms I think you need to be evaluated by a cardiologist. It's possible that this back pain is actually associated with your heart."

I pretty quickly went to see a cardiologist in Northern Virginia. He gave me a stress test, which indicated that there were possibly problems with my heart. However, he said that I had to have a catheterization in order for him to completely diagnose the problem.

Of course, I agreed to that. As with any FBI investigation I was conducting, I wanted to get to the bottom of this mystery. What was my problem? To that end, I underwent the procedure and the specialist showed me on the screen—one on which I could watch my heart beating, which was an incredible experience—the backside of my heart.

What I saw I'll never forget: one artery was completely blocked. The only reason that I had continued to function without any serious problems was that numerous collateral blood vessels had expanded and grown around that area to feed blood to the affected area of the heart. Over several years as it constricted, I had created my own bypass that kept blood flowing to the backside of my heart.

While this network of vessels kept the blood flowing so that I didn't have a heart attack or have a serious heart problem, things weren't always so stable. When I was under tremendous pressure, or exercised vigorously, the flow of blood to that particular area of the heart was not adequate for the increased demand. I had rather acute angina in the back part of my heart, which created the pain I felt in my back.

My physician didn't seem too concerned. "Your heart is in very good condition otherwise; there don't seem to be any particular serious difficulties at this point. I'm not recommending surgery to bypass the blockage. I'm a very cautious and conservative doctor in that regard and will not recommend that you have any surgery until it's really, really necessary in order for you to continue to function."

Having learned all that, I spent the next year exercising, paying very serious attention to my diet, and taking care of myself, really for the first time in my life. Before I learned of my heart condition, I had never really paid any attention to my situation or to my health because up to then it had always been good. For the first time in my life I was learning that I wasn't going to be immortal. I was going to have to take care of myself.

For over a year I did just that. I purchased a rather expensive treadmill. I had high hopes that having it in my home would be more useful than joining a health club, considering that over the years I had gotten the gym bug from time to time only to be serious for about a month or so and then I wouldn't go again. But it was different this time. Since the machine was in my home I was exercising on the treadmill every single day, religiously. That is until a scary day in December 1992.

I was working out on the treadmill, the same as usual, when I felt the all too familiar pain of angina. Since my condition was such that at any time I vigorously exercised, I experienced angina, I would typically take a nitroglycerin pill immediately before I got on the treadmill (to preempt having any pain) or else I would take the pill after five or ten minutes of exercise when I felt the angina. Once I popped the nitroglycerin pill, however, I was fine throughout my forty-five minute workout.

But on that particular evening things went a little differently. And the timing couldn't have been worse: my wife was out of town visiting her sister in Texas. After five minutes on the treadmill I popped my first nitroglycerin pill, with the expectation that I would keep going strong. Yet, instead of the pain decreasing as it always had in the past, the pain increased. I took another pill and I stayed on the treadmill. Again, the pain did not decrease but increased in intensity. I popped a third nitroglycerin pill. That, in and of itself, indicated a problem. The doctor had told me, "Anytime that you take three nitroglycerin pills without relief you need to go to the hospital immediately."

With the third nitroglycerin pill not only was there no relief—in fact, it was quite the opposite. In addition to the pain, I was sweating like crazy. I went upstairs and jumped in the shower, if you can believe it, really quickly rinsing the sweat off. Then—and I really can't believe I did this—I wasted more precious time debating whether to call an ambulance.

In the meantime, I took two more nitroglycerin pills. Still, there was no relief. My reaction at that point was anger. Not fear, but anger. I thought, "I'm probably having a heart attack and this isn't right. It isn't fair." That's all I kept thinking. "Why should I? I've been exercising, I've been dieting, and here I am having a heart attack."

Then I thought, "Well, should I call an ambulance?"

The reason I even debated, believe it or not, was that we lived in a townhouse complex that was extremely hard to find. We had learned from many lost visitors and cold pizza deliveries that we had to give very explicit directions, repeatedly, or else our house wouldn't be found. Normally—in other words, when I wasn't having a heart attack—I'd walk over to the main street to flag down the visitor who invariably couldn't find our address. So, I could see calling the ambulance and having the paramedics not be able to find the house.

I finally decided to drive myself to the hospital. In retrospect, that was a very foolish thing to do. I could have died on the way or even hurt someone else in a car accident. But I made it. The doctors gave me emergency attention, conducting the battery of necessary blood tests to confirm that in fact, yes, I had had or was having a heart attack. They decided to do a balloon angioplasty, which was similar to the other procedure that I had had. However, in this case rather than just going in and looking around, they inserted a device in the constricted area and inflated a balloon to compress the blockage that had formed inside the artery. The doctor performed the balloon angioplasty in three locations. After the successful procedure, I stayed in the hospital another day or so. However, because of complications of the operation, it was another thirty days of recuperation before I could go back to work.

That's how I spent Christmas 1992—recovering. Kathy came back from Texas as soon as she heard, and although our daughter, Karen, came and stayed for a while I didn't receive a lot of visitors. The doctors told me that I needed rest and did not need to get back to work.

I wasn't completely bored. I received, and I still have, thousands of cards and letters from FBI people all over the world. Every single day the notes came into FBI headquarters and the office periodically sent a courier out to deliver everything to me. Those cards made me a feel a lot better, not only because of the kindness of my colleagues but also because they gave me something to do. I sat at home and prepared responses for a couple of hours every day. That occupied me for a long, long time because I responded personally to each and every one.

Although I may not have been physically ready to go back to work, it didn't take a very long time for me to be mentally ready to jump back into the fray again. If this experience taught me anything, it's this: I don't make a very good patient. I wanted desperately to get back to the office and although I was pretty antsy, I had to sit tight for another few weeks. I wasn't back at my desk until nearly February.

## Fenced In

As I went back to work in February 1993 I was once again thinking that this was my last post—particularly now that I had had the heart attack. On top of that, I was already eligible to retire. But there was something else that didn't sit well with me. At the time the FBI was going through unprecedented difficulties. Allegations had just surfaced against FBI director Sessions.

The charges centered on whether Director Sessions and his wife, Alice, had misused various perks that the FBI had provided. While the couple had access to an automobile and a security detail driver, they were supposed to be used only for work-related travel. The charges stated Director and Mrs. Sessions used them frequently for personal reasons.

What an investigation—an extremely sensitive investigation—into all of those allegations meant was that the FBI would be turned upside down. This was a rather significant and massive investigation of our own director, something, of course, that was almost unprecedented in the FBI. (There had been an investigation many years before into whether the FBI laboratory had constructed some valences for windows in Director Clarence Kelley's personal residence. He was not charged with any wrongdoing as a result of the investigation.)

To make matters even more complicated, the investigation was being conducted by the Inspection Division, or more specifically, the Office of Professional Responsibility, which was under the direction of the Department of Justice. This meant that FBI agents were conducting the actual investigation. They were interviewing people and reviewing records and taking all the necessary steps to conduct a very thorough investigation into these allegations.

While the investigation was ongoing, it was extremely difficult for everyone in the executive ranks of the FBI. Traditionally in the bureau, the director was absolutely above reproach in every way. And yet, here we were with serious allegations made against the director for which he would be later, in effect, dismissed from the FBI. It was disconcerting, as though we'd been told that black was white and white was black.

At the same time, we were still dealing with the occasional allegations of misconduct by other FBI personnel. (It's not that those kinds of things are routine, but they do happen.) One of the more serious allegations that sometimes surfaces against agents is the misuse of a federal automobile, the agent's government car. Proof of misuse results in an automatic thirty days' suspension without pay (what the FBI calls being "on the beach"). As the associate deputy director for administration, I was the person ultimately responsible for these decisions.

Rarely were these automobile violations for anything too egregious. However, the government rules were quite rigid in requiring an automatic thirty-day suspension for any misuse of a government vehicle. But timing is always a curious thing. For the other supposed offenders, getting charged at this particular time was great. For me, it was terrible. Here we were with these serious allegations against the director of the FBI—with no punishment so far—so how could I automatically suspend someone for thirty days for using their car for a non-work-related purpose? It seemed to me that if it applied to an agent then it should certainly apply to the director. I decided that it wasn't prudent to proceed with those kinds of disciplinary matters until the matter with the director was resolved, so I suspended all similar kinds of cases for a time. That period turned out to be shorter than I thought.

The suspension had only been in place a few weeks when it came to the attention of Director Sessions. When he heard about it he became quite upset, ordering that these cases be adjudicated right away. "Nothing should be held up based on the inquiries," he said.

The whole situation became quite controversial within the bureau, though it never became public knowledge outside the bureau, as far as I know. As difficult as my initial decision had been to make, it was nothing compared to my next decision about whether to comply with the director's order. With the FBI rumor mill being what it was, it became well known throughout the FBI that I was personally ordered by Director Sessions to stand down from my position.

In the end I complied with the director's order. Although adhering to the director's wishes forced me to changed my decision, going against what I had thought was the best way to proceed, it did not require me to do anything that was illegal or unethical. Plus, there was nothing I could do about it—except possibly resign.

Even considering the Oklahoma City bombing case and the Atlanta Penitentiary riot, this was one of the tougher situations I went through in the FBI. However, as far as I was concerned, resigning was something that I was not prepared to do. My resignation under these circumstances would make it appear that I had done something wrong. Since I had done nothing wrong, I felt that I had to stay to make that point.

• • •

Mrs. Sessions was unusual compared with any previous director's wife because she was very much involved in the daily work life of Director Sessions. She frequently came into the office and, I think, almost considered herself co-director of the FBI. That may be an overstatement but I think in many ways that this was how she perceived herself. To boot, she absolutely detested Floyd Clarke, the deputy director at the time. She thought that Clarke was conspiring to be the director of the FBI. So, she tried every way that she could to undercut, undermine, and cause problems for Clarke.

Of course, she blamed Clarke—which was totally ridiculous—for the big inquiry launched against her husband. According to Mrs. Sessions, Floyd Clarke led a cabal whose mission was to get her husband out of office. Its "members" included John Hicks, legal counsel for the FBI; me; and others she left unnamed. She surely influenced her husband, because at one point later he, too, even referred to a "cabal" inside the hierarchy of the FBI that had conspired to have him removed from the office.

Within my first three months back at work after the heart attack, as all the allegations about misuse of property began to swirl, the director called me to say that Mrs. Sessions was coming into the office. He wanted Floyd, Hicks, and me to meet with her. Mrs. Sessions wanted to talk about how the fence in the back of her house was in sad state of disrepair and needed to be replaced. Director Sessions told us that it was a security issue.

At the appointed time we went down to the director's conference room to meet with her. The director opened the meeting up by saying that their residence was her domain and that he deferred to Mrs. Sessions in any and all things pertaining to their personal residence. He said that when they moved up from Texas so he could assume the directorship of the FBI, they had purchased this residence, but the property's wooden fence was badly rotted. What's more, their dog, Petey, had gotten out through the fence quite often. But, according to Mrs. Sessions, that wasn't the principal issue. It was a security concern, she said. "We need to have this fence repaired or fixed or replaced."

"This is why you're here—to meet with Alice about how that's going to be done," said the director. With that he got up, went into his office—which was immediately adjacent to the conference room—and closed the door, leaving us there with Mrs. Sessions to discuss the matter.

Since we had been given some advance notice of this meeting, we had done our homework about what exactly constitutes a security fence. It was immediately apparent that what Mrs. Sessions wanted was actually a new wooden *privacy* fence, something six to eight feet in height that completely obscured any view inside their property. However, according to all security experts, a privacy fence doesn't enhance security, it degrades security. The reason is simple: If someone wanted to attack you and you have a privacy fence around your house, they can get behind it unobserved. A true security fence, such as the one that surrounds the White House, is a series of concrete, brick, or stone posts or pillars, with an expanse of iron bars spaced about six inches apart between the pillars so that you can see through. No attackers can hide behind this type of structure. This suggestion, on our part, wasn't acceptable to Mrs. Sessions. It became clear to us that she wanted the fence to be enclosed so the dog couldn't get out. A security fence doesn't keep a dog in since the bars are spaced.

Mrs. Sessions even had pictures of what she wanted. We kept telling her, "No, Mrs. Sessions, we can't authorize that kind of fence to be built because that's a privacy fence. If you want to build a privacy fence then you can do so, but not at government expense. The government should not and could not, and we will not authorize the government expenditures of monies to build this privacy fence for you." How much more direct could we be?

Periodically, the director would come in and brightly say, "Well, have you got everything all fixed up? It's all resolved?" Mrs. Sessions would turn to him, and snarl, "No!" whereupon he would turn around, close the door, and leave us to discuss the fence while he went back to his office. We were there for over two hours, arguing with Mrs. Sessions. We were simply at loggerheads.

At one point I pulled out a newspaper clipping pertaining to Oliver North, the marine lieutenant colonel in the Iran-Contra scandal who testified at length before Congress. Among other scandals involving Ollie North was that the government had built him a fence behind his house. That issue became a matter of some magnitude because it was, in fact, a privacy fence, not a security fence. The upshot of the scandal was that it was inappropriate for the government to spend thousands of dollars to build this privacy fence in his back yard.

I showed the article to her, saying, "Mrs. Sessions, you know how closely observed the FBI is, and the director in particular. If we spend this money it will probably come to light. We can't do this surreptitiously; the public will find out. When they do find out about it . . . let's just say, look what happened to Ollie North."

That tactic didn't work, either. She was not dissuaded at all. She was bound and determined that she was going to have her privacy fence.

Later Mrs. Sessions did an interview with the *Washington Post Magazine* in which she made a reference to this meeting. It was in this article where she first alleged publicly that there had been a cabal within the FBI. No cabal member was named then, however, although in the article she referred to me by name, calling me abusive toward her in that meeting.

That one made me laugh. Really, here we were in the director's conference room with him in the adjacent room and I was abusive to his wife? Not likely.

I was still the assistant director in charge of the Administrative Services Division at the time of the meeting with Mrs. Sessions, so it wasn't until later, after I moved up to the associate deputy director job, that I learned about how she got the fence built. Once she got nowhere with us, the executive staff, she went around us, personally contacting the procurement section chief, who was the person in the bureau managing all purchasing activity for the FBI. For a lack of a better term, she browbeat him into authorizing the construction of a fence. Granted, it was a much more modified fence compared with what she had originally asked for. Rather than being a total privacy fence, with boards set side by side, completely blocking anyone's view, it instead had staggered boards placed in such a way that if you looked sideways could you see through the fence. You couldn't look directly through it—if you did it appeared solid, with one board next to the other board—but, up close to the fence, it would become apparent that the boards were not really next to each other. They were separated by a two-by-four; one board was on one side and the next board was on the other side, alternating the whole length of the fence.

That's not much of a security fence. And, after all that, it's not much of a privacy fence either. It's a hybrid—which is exactly how she convinced the procurement section chief to build it.

Every once in a while, however, one of Mrs. Sessions's demands was valid. But that doesn't mean that then she acted appropriately. She went to great lengths to get the special treatment that she felt she deserved.

Many times when the director was away on business, there would be an embassy reception that Mrs. Sessions wanted to attend. However, since he was out of town she wasn't to be driven around; she wasn't authorized for that, no matter how much she wanted to be. If the director went somewhere then the car and security detail went with him. If she were along for the ride, that was OK. But, without him, she didn't have use of the vehicles and the security detail to travel about as she chose.

Although it's arguable that her life wasn't in any real danger and that she just liked showing up with a security detail, there was another valid side. To be completely fair about this, perhaps she should have had security. How vulnerable is your security system if, in fact, you're protecting the director but leaving his wife to wander around alone at any time of the day or night totally unprotected? It doesn't make any sense. The wife of the president of the United States isn't left alone. She travels with security just like the president. Is it wise to provide all of this personal security for the director and zero for his wife?

No, it isn't. But that's the law, unfortunately. So, it was illegal for us to drive her. Consequently, she was not driven when she was alone, and she constantly complained about this. Now, granted, I never heard of any threats or attempts to harm the director's spouse, and I would be aware of this since the entire time that I was associate deputy director in charge of administration I had responsibility for the director's security detail as well as that for the attorney general. We had twenty-plus people assigned to each.

A lot of tales of Mrs. Sessions's abuse of government perks came out in the investigation. There were no public hearings—just a very thorough investigation reported by the FBI to the Department of Justice (DOJ). The DOJ's ethics office, the Office of Professional Responsibility, produced a 162-page report outlining all of the issues, placing the blame in large part on poor judgment by Director Sessions. In response to their findings, Attorney General William Barr issued him a letter of reprimand. It wasn't long after this that Sessions left office—after President Clinton specifically asked him to do so—in July 1993.

The investigation was a very unhappy time for Sessions. It was also very unfortunate for the FBI that all of these things happened. The shame of it all is that Sessions is a good man. He is not unethical, but he was completely and totally dominated by his wife. She seemed to feel nothing whatsoever was wrong with misusing the entire FBI for her purposes. In her mind, it appeared, the FBI was at her disposal and she could use its personnel or resources to do whatever she wanted.

As for Director Sessions, as far as I know, he's been practicing law since he left the FBI. Although his firm had an office in San Antonio and in Washington, he chose to stay mainly in San Antonio.

Mrs. Sessions eventually got her fence. Although it was modified, she still got it—and it cost the government approximately $10,000.

# 8

# Louie Freeh: Part One

## Flattening the Organization

We couldn't have been more excited when President Clinton named Louis Freeh to become the new director of the FBI in 1993.

Louie was "one of us." He was a young man with a family and had worked the street very successfully as an FBI agent early in his career. We believed that a person who really understood the FBI would do a much better job as the director.

While Louie wasn't the first FBI director to have been previously involved in the organization, he was the first in years. The first, Clarence Kelley, was the director from 1972, after Hoover's death, until 1978, when Webster took office. Kelley had retired from the FBI as a special agent in charge with more than twenty years' service and this helped him become a great director when he was appointed.

Louie initially served in the New York FBI office for a few years, working high-profile organized crime cases. Though he was transferred to FBI headquarters for a fairly brief period of time, he found it stifling. So, he quit the bureau to become a prosecutor in the U.S. Attorney's Office in New York. He served there for a number of years until he was handpicked to work on the case of the bombing death of a federal judge in Birmingham, Alabama.

The Department of Justice selected Louis Freeh to head up the team that would prosecute, once the subject was successfully identified and the case was ready for trial. The FBI jointly ran the investigation, and the bureau picked Larry Potts to head up its part. The close working relationship that developed between the two predictably led to Louie's selection of Potts as his deputy director in early 1995—in spite of Potts receiving a letter of censure in connection with his role during the Ruby Ridge incident. This blemish on Potts's record was eventually seized upon by the media and amplified to the point where he could no longer effectively serve as the deputy director, even though Louie had tremendous confidence in his abilities.

Following the successful handling of the Birmingham bombing case, Louie went back to New York. He was appointed to the federal bench as a U.S. district judge, before being tapped by the president to take over the bureau.

When Louie came back to the FBI it was with a very strong anti-management bias—to put it mildly. This stemmed in large part from his unhappy experience working at headquarters. He made it pretty clear when he first came on board, by his statements and his actions, that he had little confidence in FBI management.

For example, Louie made a point of traveling to all fifty-six of the field offices in the entire FBI almost as soon as he took office, but during these visits he talked almost exclusively to the street agents, spending almost no time with any of the supervisory staff including the SACs. The street agents loved this approach, but the SACs and the field office managers felt that they were completely ignored by the director. They were correct.

Very often an SAC's only contact with Louie during the visit was the airport pickup and drive to the field office. Louie sat down with the agents, spending anywhere from ten minutes to an hour with each squad, while the SAC would sit up in his office. Not only that but every single Friday Louie went down to Quantico and ran five miles with the new agents' class. He was also very religious about attending the graduation of every single new agent's training class. This helped him to reach out and make personal contact directly with individual agents all over the United States. In turn the agents felt as if they could call him—and often did. But when it came time to talking to the SACs, forget it. Louie didn't have time for that.

• • •

Talking to management wasn't the only thing he didn't have time for. Letting us keep our jobs was another.

Louie felt that there were too many managers in the FBI. Practically from the moment he started his job as director he declared that he would make huge changes in the number of staff working at FBI headquarters and flatten the hierarchy of the organization in general.

The field agents couldn't have been happier. For years they had been complaining to sympathetic congressmen and Department of Justice officials that there were too many agents at FBI headquarters. When Louie arrived, there were something like nine hundred agents assigned to headquarters and those nine hundred agents represented approximately 8 percent of the FBI's total eleven thousand agents. Those who knew no better deemed the FBI a top-heavy organization in need of streamlining. Considering that Louie was a field agent through and through, it's not surprising that one of Louie's early declarations was that he intended to flatten FBI management. Even though there was little that any of us could do to stop it, I knew at the time that this would ultimately be harmful to the FBI.

Those of us who were involved in the administration of the bureau—where I had served from 1989 to that point in 1993 when Louie took charge—tried to argue the case that fewer than half of those nine hundred agents had anything to do with the day-to-day management of the FBI. They were involved, for example, in such things as the Criminal Justice Information Services Division, once known as the Identification Division. Of those agents, many were maintaining a central fingerprint repository for criminal justice throughout the United States. Others were serving state and local law enforcement obligations, and dozens of others were assigned to FBIHQ but were seconded to the CIA, DOJ, Congress, and other federal agencies. In addition there were about one hundred scientific experts and expert witnesses in various fields assigned to the FBI laboratory. The majority of cases they worked were state and local, since state and local investigators all over the United States could submit evidence to the FBI laboratory for scientific examination free of charge. The result was the submission of evidence for hundreds of thousands of cases—rape, murder, you name it. So these agents really shouldn't have been counted as part of the FBI management structure.

Over one hundred agents were permanently assigned to the Training Division and were involved in new agent training, National Academy sessions, and a host of other training situations for other federal, state, and local law enforcement officers, as well as for significant commitment to international training seminars. When you subtracted all these—and other—agents, you're left with less than half of the nine hundred total. The actual percentage of agents involved in headquarters management was 4 percent.

That's a pretty low number, but since I wasn't the director, it wasn't my decision to make. Louie thought 4 percent was still too high. He set rules to make sure that people who had been at headquarters for more than three or four years were transferred out to the field. I believe this to be the most serious mistake he made as director. His view was that any person who had served at FBIHQ for more than four years was a drone and needed to be returned to the field. While surely this was true in some cases, it certainly wasn't accurate to the extent that Louie and many of the field agents believed.

I can recall one instance when an agent who had been assigned to the FBI laboratory for almost twenty years was to be transferred to the field to work applicant cases. I intervened and stopped the transfer because during his time in the lab the agent had developed into the world's foremost authority on a specific type of physical evidence. He had written papers on the subject and was frequently asked to advise criminal laboratories throughout the world regarding this type of evidence. What a waste this would have been for the FBI, and the forensic science community as a whole, to send this guy to work as a street agent for the last few years of his service.

But he was only one person. Countless agents who worked for years to gain a tremendous expertise in, say, organized crime or counterintelligence were shifted into other areas. People who, over the course of their careers, had built up an impressive body of knowledge were being thrown out of their positions.

Authorities in Chinese intelligence agencies and operations that the Chinese were having in the United States would be rotated back into the field after five years under Louie's plan. This resulted in the destruction of the expertise and experience that the Chinese espionage group had built up. And then of course you had some very green supervisors running this program for the entire FBI. Many of them didn't know what they were doing. This wound up crippling FBI headquarters.

One could argue that Louie's personnel transfer policy was the reason why we had the Wen Ho Lee situation at the Los Alamos National Laboratory. The FBI made some very serious mistakes in that case. This was absolutely because of the lack of experience and expertise left at FBI headquarters by the late 1990s. Nuclear scientist Lee was accused of spying in 1999 but was acquitted months later of serious espionage charges. Dr. Lee was not completely acquitted of everything, however. He had downloaded some classified information onto unclassified computers in his home and these were violations, offenses to which he pled guilty.

Had more experienced Chinese experts been involved, the case could have been handled more smoothly. Instead, the whole thing made the front pages and gave the FBI a great, big, black eye. Another one.

Of course, more than just Chinese experts were shuffled around. Naturally, this leads to questions about 9/11. Any connection? That's stretching it in my opinion. While I don't think we can link any specific terrorist case to the downsizing, a brain drain clearly occurred.

Unfortunately, decimation of headquarters over the first two or three years of Louie's directorship was devastating to the FBI. Louie, it seems, eventually realized this too. In the later years of his tenure, he added more and more staff to FBIHQ. Ironically, at the time of his departure there were many more agents working there than when he started.

## You Flatten Me

When Louie said that he would be flattening the organization I didn't realize that would include me.

Ten days into his tenure as director he walked into my office and closed the door. After a minute or two of conversation, he said, "Well, Weldon, I've decided that I'm going to reorganize FBI headquarters. It's top heavy and so I've decided to eliminate two executive positions—both the ADD [associate deputy director] for investigations and the ADD for administration."

I was totally taken aback. This was a bolt from the blue, but I understood because I had seen how other directors acted when they arrived. When Webster and Sessions each came into the FBI as the director, they put people with whom they felt comfortable in positions of leadership. I expected Louie to do the same and shift those of us in the executive positions elsewhere. I was not one of his top people; in fact, I had never met the man before he was appointed. So, while this shift was expected, I never guessed that it would happen so early in the game.

In my case, I had the option to retire if I so chose, but I wasn't quite ready. One of the main reasons for my hesitation was, frankly, financial. Only a very short time before this, Congress had finally given the senior executive staff a rather substantial raise. Congress had been holding back for years, either responding to requests with no raise or by capping the salaries of senior executive staffers. Since I had been given a substantial raise, it was very important from a retirement standpoint for me to stay on active service for a bit longer. Staying longer would make a big difference in my retirement annuity because the system took what was called a high three-year salary average to use as the base for the formula that calculated one's annuity.

Not to mention that I wasn't really ready to retire. I loved the FBI and everything that I did in it. Louie sensed this as well, and he was aware of my service and what I had done in the organization.

"I certainly don't want to force you out of the FBI so I'm asking you what you would like to do. I'm eliminating your job. It doesn't have to be tomorrow but within a reasonable period of time I want to do away with this position. So, I'll give you three or four months, if you need it, to determine and select what job you would like to have elsewhere in the FBI," said Louie.

That was it—a very short meeting.

What to do? I knew I had a lot of thinking ahead of me. Jim Ahearn, the special agent in charge of the Phoenix division, was nearing retirement—or, as we would soon see, firing—so that position would soon be open. That was appealing because my family, particularly my wife, really loved Phoenix. We had been out to Phoenix for years on our vacations and had fallen in love with Arizona.

A week later I went back to Louie with my idea for a transfer: I wanted to be the special agent in charge of the Phoenix office when Jim Ahearn retired. "That's fine. That's what we'll do then," said Louie.

I was so excited I could hardly stand it. From the outside it probably looked odd that I was thrilled over what amounted to a demotion. Here I was, the fourth-highest ranking person in the FBI, going back to a field office to be in charge of just one field division. However, because of the way the FBI structures salary—I was grade executive level 6 (ES6)—I would not have a change in pay or grade.

Actually, the transfer amounted to a raise. My base pay and benefits remained the same and on top of that I would have exclusive use of a government vehicle. Plus any person in the FBI will tell you that the best job in the organization is being a special agent in charge of a field division. Large, small, or medium sized—it doesn't really make a whole lot of difference. You have your own staff, you are the boss, and you are in charge of what goes on in your area. Of course, you answer to headquarters and you answer to the director but not on a day-in, day-out basis. You obviously have a lot of rules and regulations that you have to comply with—and you have to make sure of compliance—but you are essentially running your own fiefdom. And, as long as everything is running well, there is very minimal oversight from FBI headquarters.

Phoenix also has a lower cost of living than Washington. I had been concerned that I was going to have to retire in Washington, D.C., or if I chose to go somewhere else I would have to pay for the move. Now I had decided where I wanted to retire and the FBI was going to move me there. Not only that, but my first love was fieldwork. So, getting an opportunity to go back in the field—when I had anticipated retiring at headquarters—was a thrill!

There was no downside to this equation at all. It was all plus, plus, plus as far as I was concerned. My family was excited about it, I was excited about it, and so we planned to go as soon as Ahearn retired. News of him putting in paperwork to do so didn't come that much later—he was set to leave in January—and Louie was good to his word about my transfer.

However, the transfer wasn't so smooth for my predecessor.

## No Comment

The story reached the desk of the attorney general quickly in December 1993. And, once there, the news didn't dawdle en route to Louie's desk, either.

I can only assume that these two got on the phone to each other immediately, but I do know what happened next for a fact. Louie put a call in to Phoenix SAC Jim Ahearn.

"I'm reading this article that appeared in a local newspaper. It quotes you as saying that Janet Reno went to Washington and forgot she's the nation's prosecutor: 'She's become a social worker.' Is this an accurate quote, Jim? Is that what you said or is this some problem with the reporter?" asked Louie.

Jim said, '"No sir, that's accurate. That's what I said."

Even the *Arizona Republic* reporter who interviewed him knew the quote would be controversial. He asked Jim if he was sure he wanted it to be printed. Absolutely, said Jim, who figured he was just a few days away from retirement and could say what he liked without repercussion. In fact, in the same article, he said that he was leaving the FBI in part because of the bureaucracy. But what really ticked him off was Reno's stance on promoting early childhood care to combat crime. Ahearn thought she was more of a child welfare person than an attorney general. One thing in particular that didn't sit well in the bureau was Reno's strong support for what the FBI called the "Delinquent Dads statute," which stipulated that the FBI would have to investigate deadbeat fathers who didn't pay child support. This would double the FBI's total normal caseload but Congress had not appropriated any funds for enforcement of this new statute.

Though the statute held up, FBI agents made it a very low priority. Some time after the statute was enacted, Attorney General Reno checked in on the number of prosecutions there had been. When she found out how few there were, she was incensed. Her subsequent memos demanding an increase in the number of cases being investigated only further irritated the agents. The feeling was that the Delinquent Dad cases did not rise to a level that justified an agency like the FBI doing the investigation, nor did they merit prosecution by the attorney general's office as major criminal violations.

Louie didn't care for those opinions or for outspokenness.

"Well, I don't agree with this quote and I think it's very damaging. You are immediately removed as the special agent in charge of the Phoenix Field Office. The ASAC is now the acting SAC. Transfer me over to his office."

Ahearn could hardly believe it. He wasn't the only one.

Larry McCormick, the ASAC got the surprise of this life. His phone rang and on the other end he was greeted with "This is Louie Freeh." At that point he'd never met Louie and getting a phone call from the director of the FBI was akin to getting a phone call from God. "I've just been on the line with Ahearn," said Louie. "And I have removed him as the special agent in charge of the Phoenix Field Division. I want you to go over to his office now and get his gun, badge, and credentials. Then you are to escort him from the building."

Nothing like this had ever happened in the FBI, even going back to the Hoover days. McCormick did what Louie asked, of course, but everyone in the office was in shock. Ahearn was suspended, placed on administrative leave until he retired. His departure didn't take long since there wasn't much for Ahearn to pack. His preparation for retirement had largely taken care of that: he was only six days away from retiring at the time of his suspension.

This happened very early in Louie's administration. Ahearn wasn't the only one to learn the hard way about how Louie felt about agents speaking to the press. In late 1993, Jim Fox, assistant director in charge of the New York Field Office, was getting ready to retire when he, too, gave a regrettable interview to a local newspaper reporter. He made some comments about one of the cooperating witnesses in the World Trade Center bombing case. Specifically, he said a particular informant, Emid Ali Salem, who had become very vocal in the media disparaging the FBI, in fact hadn't given the bureau any information that would have been useful in preventing the bombing. Nonetheless, what Fox disregarded—and violated—was a federal court's gag order on making any comments about the case. As a result he, too, received a phone call from Louie, not unlike the one Ahearn received.

The fact that Fox was defending the way the FBI handled the World Trade Center bombing was no matter. Nor did it matter that Fox was a thirty-year veteran, only three weeks from retirement, or that he had played a visible role in the aftermath of the World Trade Center bombing. He was suspended until his retirement and forced to leave the FBI building immediately, under escort.

To put it mildly, these two incidents had a chilling effect on SACs' willingness to talk to the press. If you did an interview with the press and Louie Freeh or the attorney general or someone else of that rank decided they didn't like what you said, well, you were history. Immediately, SACs almost across the board discontinued any kind of contact or association with the media. I really think that such a lack of information is a recipe for disaster, since the public is entitled to know some things about what the government—particularly the FBI—is doing. When the press can't legitimately get information from an FBI spokesperson, be it an SAC or some other spokesperson, then they go elsewhere. Now this other source, the subject of the case, the subject of the inquiry, his or her attorney, or some other person with an axe to grind may or may not be providing accurate information. That person may just be providing his or her own personal version of the facts.

This lack of information frustrates reporters who are trying to do their job, which is to get information to the public. No wonder reporters are angry when they are constantly running into blank walls and can't even get the time of day from legitimate spokespersons from the FBI. As a result, when somebody speaks up and says something good about the FBI it doesn't get printed.

In the *Washington Post*, for example, during Louis Freeh's tenure, whenever a big FBI case unfolded and a lot of arrests were made, an interesting thing happened: throughout the entire article there would be no mention of the FBI. Instead, the article just mentioned that "federal agents" did this or that, but nothing about the FBI. Unless you knew, independently from the newspaper, that the FBI worked the case, you wouldn't know which agency did the investigation since federal agents could work for any number of groups such as the DEA, Bureau of Alcohol, Tobacco, Firearms, and Explosives (ATF), or Secret Service.

You can imagine how this affected agents who worked very hard on a case to bring it to a prosecution. The way the *Washington Post* was reporting, when a good case was brought to a successful conclusion the general public would have no idea that the FBI was responsible. Yet, when someone like, say, Frederick Whitehurst, a member of the FBI laboratory, wanted to make some negative comments about the FBI, guess where they ended up? The front page and on all the news media. Everywhere you looked for a period in the mid-'90s Frederick Whitehurst was saying that the FBI laboratory was lousy.

This kind of press treatment persisted throughout the entire time that Louie was director. It's just my personal opinion, of course, but I could make a pretty good case that the attitude on the part of the press went something like this: "There are haughty, arrogant, uncooperative people in the FBI, and any chance I get to whittle them down a notch or two, I'm going to do just that."

The lesson? Sometimes no information to the press can only translate into misinformation to the public.

It was not just the FBI's refusal to provide the press with information that contributed to a negative perception of the bureau; misinformation provided by others helped, too. In the wake of 9/11, New York mayor Rudy Giuliani often talked to the media and even went before Congress to speak about a lack of cooperation by the FBI with local law enforcement.

The facts in the matter, however, tell a different story. For about twenty years the FBI has had a Joint Terrorism Task Force in New York City. This Joint Terrorism Task Force is even housed in the FBI offices and there are over one hundred New York City Police Department detectives working permanently as a part of this task force. I never understood how Giuliani or anybody else for that matter could say that this is not a cooperative effort or that there's any kind of withholding of information from local law enforcement. They are part and parcel of a task force that is charged with investigating all major terrorism cases in the New York City area. These one hundred officers work in the FBI space every single day and have access to all but the most sensitive information. Some information is maintained on a "need to know" basis, and like most FBI agents, all members of the task force do not have unrestricted access to this information. This task force was responsible for the investigation of the 1993 bombing of the World Trade Center as well as the 9/11 attacks.

New York isn't the only location. There are numerous terrorism task forces around the United States and in virtually every major city. A task force includes some FBI agents, other federal agents, and some local and/or state officers, and a complete and total exchange of information takes place. When I was the SAC in Phoenix, for example, I had six or seven different kinds of task forces working in the office. One was dedicated to narcotics, another to fugitives, another to white-collar crime, another to public corruption, and so on.

If there is no interagency cooperation, then that is news to me and everyone else with whom I worked across the entire spectrum of law enforcement agencies on the federal, state, and local level.

The cumulative effect of the negative press coverage, with little or no counterbalance, is devastating to the FBI. It negatively affects morale and consequently hampers effectiveness and productivity. It also negatively impacts the FBI's relationships with other agencies. More important, it lowers the public's confidence in the FBI, which results in less cooperation between citizens and agents. Since the public's cooperation is, in my opinion, a cornerstone of the FBI's success, any lessening of that cooperation will hamper the FBI's ability to do its job in protecting the public.

# 9

# SAC in Phoenix and the Oklahoma City Bombing

## Phoenix Rising

On a personal level, this was set to be the move of a lifetime. Kathy and I had decided to build our dream house right outside of Phoenix, in the suburb of Scottsdale, which is a beautiful place. It was to be our retirement home, which we had been dreaming about for years. We just needed to move to Arizona to make it happen, and, thanks to Louie, there we were! My wife was passionate about building the house, working with a local architect, and helping to design all the details of the house. My son-in-law at the time was a jack-of-all-trades. He knew quite a bit about building to begin with, but he obtained his contractor's license for this project. We went into a partnership with him to build the house and just had a ball with the whole thing. Not only was it a great opportunity to get to know him better, but also it's always nice when you get to work with family.

In the meantime, we moved into an apartment and put our stuff in storage. However, as fate would have it, even once it was built I wouldn't get to spend all that much time in my dream house.

This assignment as the SAC in Phoenix was one of the most interesting of my career. Although the Phoenix SAC ran only a medium-sized field division, the job covered a huge jurisdiction—the entire state of Arizona. When I first started I thought that the reason that the job would be so exciting would be because of all the work solving crimes on the many Indian reservations in the state. Little did I know about the big crime I would soon be tackling and that it would have nothing to do with Native Americans.

The FBI office in Arizona has more investigations of Native American cases than any other FBI office. Arizona has the third-largest Indian population, behind California and Oklahoma, of any state in the nation. The federal jurisdiction is very broad. Many of the Indian reservations have their own police departments and jurisdiction from the Tribal Authority to conduct investigations and, in fact, prosecute individuals for criminal violations. But with significant cases, such as murder or rape, the FBI has jurisdiction.

One of the things that we were able to accomplish, however, was to start a dialogue about establishing a joint FBI-Navajo Task Force. Although there had always been cooperation, we thought that a task force would be an appropriate vehicle to draw our efforts much closer together and make a much more effective law enforcement approach. The FBI traditionally has been very successful with these kinds of joint task forces. For example, the Safe Streets Task Forces are operating in most major cities. In these task forces, federal agents team up with local law enforcement investigators, as well as federal and state prosecutors, to reduce local street gang and drug-related violence. In this instance we formed the first Safe Trails Task Force, consisting of twelve Navajo tribal policemen and four special agents of the FBI. We had a wonderful kick-off ceremony that was attended by U.S. Attorney Janet Napolitano, Navajo tribal leaders, several members of my staff, and me, as well as by the new members of the task force.

● ● ●

When I arrived in Arizona in February 1994, I was no stranger to FBI cooperation with outside parties. And, ironically, the place where I was most experienced in this matter was actually in Phoenix.

A few years prior, when I had been at headquarters as the assistant director of Administrative Services, my predecessor in the SAC job, Jim Ahearn, had come to me for help. He had witnessed the success that the Phoenix Police Department had had with the Citizens Police Academy, a long-standing program in various cities that teaches interested citizens about how the police department works as well as its policies and procedures. It's all conducted through a series of classes taught by police officers. Some of the topics typically covered are: training, communications, canine, patrol, SWAT, and recruiting. "Understanding Through Education" is its slogan; the program's main goal is to alleviate misunderstandings between the public and law enforcement. Jim thought that the FBI could benefit, too, through just such a program and I agreed.

Funding is not such an easy thing to come by in the FBI, or any government agency for that matter. We put our heads together and figured out some ways to scrape together a few hundred dollars from headquarters to get the program going. And the staff of the Phoenix office of the FBI was so eager for the program that members put in money out of their own pockets too. Some of the people in the office voluntarily prepared food at their own expense to bring in to the classes.

The first FBI Citizens Academy was born in Phoenix. Every Wednesday night for six weeks, twenty citizens, a real cross-section of the community, came to the FBI offices to learn about what we do. They were carefully selected, representing various geographic areas, demographics, and professions. There were members of the media, CEOs, and citizens from various minority and special interest groups. (All had to pass a background check, of course.)

Everyone really enjoyed the different classes. One night was white-collar crime night, for example, with the supervisor of the white-collar crime squad leading a session that talked about cases that were being worked on by the office. Another night was devoted to narcotics and another to organized crime. Then there was also the Saturday session with the demonstration of a SWAT exercise and firearms lesson. Participants at the range learned to fire all the weapons that the FBI uses: the shotgun, various handguns, the MP5 machine gun, and so forth. Afterward, there was a cookout for the students and their families.

After I became SAC in Phoenix, I continued the FBI Citizens Academy. With every session, we made slight improvements and adjustments. Since the participants particularly liked the sessions in which they solved a problem, as well as got out of the classroom, we put together a session that was a simulation of a bank robbery. An academy graduate lent to us the use of a former bank building, now empty, that he owned. Students played customers and tellers and two guys from the Hostage Rescue Team came in with shotguns firing blanks, as they were "robbing" the bank. Following the robbery we had an "investigation." The students were interviewed about the appearance of the robbers, what they said, and so on. Forensics people came in to recover the empty shell casings and dust for fingerprints in the escape car. This was like an audience participation episode of *CSI* or *Law & Order*.

I was so thrilled with the success of the first program that I flew down from Washington for the graduation. What really impressed me were the reactions from the participants, in particular, that of the head of the local branch of the National Association for the Advancement of Colored People (NAACP). "When I was first invited to this academy," he said, "I was very suspicious, but I accepted out of curiosity about what the FBI was going to do, whether they were going to try to make me an informant or do something to me. But I want to tell you that this has been the most educational experience I've ever had and I want to encourage you to have these all over the country. I really feel like I know—and can trust—the FBI now." Well, he got his wish. We started to encourage SACs across the country to start these kinds of programs in their cities, and despite the hard work and cost, often out of the pockets of the SAC and office staffers, a lot of them did it anyway. Today, there are academies at forty-nine of the fifty-six FBI offices, almost half of which were started after 9/11.

Not only did these programs benefit the citizens but they were beneficial to us at the FBI as well. For example, after I became SAC in Phoenix I had a nice network of people knowledgeable about the FBI who stood ready to assist in any way that they could. The NAACP leader, for example, was instrumental to us in preventing what could have been a tinderbox of a situation. A black man who was a double amputee died as he was resisting arrest by the Phoenix Police Department. Almost immediately,

I was on the phone with this NAACP leader and he and I spoke nearly every day during the investigation. (The FBI conducted the investigation into this incident as a potential violation of civil rights, over which the FBI has jurisdiction.) He, meanwhile, was calming down the community, assuring citizens this was a very vigorous and complete investigation and that they should cease any demonstrations or protests. We were very candid with him, keeping him apprised of what was going on, and he was very appreciative because we weren't hiding the ball or trying to pull any fast ones. I can't imagine the potential misunderstandings and crises that could have erupted had this leader not participated in the academy.

● ● ●

After my bad experiences with Bob Barr, the U.S. attorney for the Northern District of Georgia, I was determined to forge a better relationship with the U.S. attorney for Arizona. The importance of this relationship cannot be overemphasized. The FBI investigates cases and then presents them to the U.S. attorney for prosecution. If there is poor coordination between the investigator and the prosecutor, the results are very damaging and could even result in the bad guy going free—not a very good outcome from those responsible for protecting the public.

I got lucky. Janet Napolitano, the current governor of Arizona, had recently been sworn in as U.S. attorney for Arizona before my arrival. We immediately established a good rapport. We began a routine of meeting privately for breakfast every other week, schedules permitting. We frankly discussed priorities, cases, and problems, which we worked through to our mutual benefit.

She very wisely launched an outreach program to local and state law enforcement agencies. She and I, along with other federal agency heads, such as the SACs of the Secret Service, ATF, DEA, and others, would travel together to cities in Arizona for meetings with local law enforcement and local prosecutors. The open dialogues improved cooperation among all the agencies.

Little did I know how soon I would be applying some of the lessons I'd learned from working with Janet.

## Proceed to Oklahoma City Immediately

Although my selection to be the on-scene commander at the Oklahoma City bombing (OKBOMB) site sounded like a terrific vote of confidence (which it was), the situation was a little more complicated than that. For many, many years—in fact, for most of the FBI's history—when there was a major incident or major case of any kind, the special agent in charge of the office where the incident occurred was automatically the on-scene commander. Whatever investigative activity there was or whatever FBI activity was involved, that person was automatically designated on-scene commander, by default, if for no other reason. That was just the way the FBI organization was. Since the days of Hoover that's how assignments were made—with rare exception.

After Louie came on board—and after Waco—there had been a rather exhaustive review of command and control procedures used by the FBI in major crisis events. The result? Louie made the decision about who the on-scene commander should be. He didn't want it done by default because he was concerned that a major incident could occur with a brand-new and relatively inexperienced special agent in charge in the area. The agent might be good in other respects but maybe not particularly good or proficient at being a major crisis manager—a role that requires a different set of skills.

Louie and the FBI agonized over this issue because there was a lot of disagreement within the FBI about whether on-scene commanders should be selected this way. I can recall a conference in Quantico where this was a major topic of discussion. There, almost all the SACs were unanimous in feeling that if something occurred in an SAC's territory then that SAC should be the person in charge of the event and the investigation. Anything otherwise would be an insult. We'd be questioning his or her credibility and ability to manage a major case.

After all, the reasoning went, "Didn't the FBI have enough confidence to name the person to a major post, namely that of being a special agent in charge?" Consequently, that person should be qualified to handle any crisis that might occur. If the SAC couldn't handle a major crisis, then that person should be removed.

Louie, however, stood before the entire group and said, "Look, I'm the director—I'm the person ultimately responsible for the conduct of the FBI in a major case and I want to feel comfortable that we have applied the best that we could under the circumstances. I want to feel comfortable with whom I name to be the on-scene commander so I reserve that right and will do that." He just laid down the law.

There was a little grousing but that's the decision that was made. End of story. Keep in mind that this was when he was the new director and everyone was excited that one of our own was going to run the organization. Louie, as we all would learn, had a strong bias against the leadership of the FBI and seemed to rally against its established bureaucracy. Though his decision was controversial, especially among the SACs, street agents were behind him.

Then Louie went one step further by deciding that there should be some special training in crisis management for a select number of SACs so that the FBI would be better able to respond. Obviously, he didn't feel confident that all fifty-six field offices were commanded by people who had enough background and experience in this particular area to be able to handle anything that might happen in their respective territories.

Louie started a training series for a special group of about a dozen SACs, which he selected personally, as well as for another dozen Department of Justice attorneys who would be involved in crisis management situations. Since I had been the on-scene commander during the largest single FBI hostage operation ever conducted, I was asked to attend and lecture about it.

I don't really know, because I never heard directly from Louie, exactly how he came to his decision about making me on-scene commander at Oklahoma City. When the bomb went off, I can only guess he was thinking, "Who do I have and who is the most experienced as far as managing crises?" Although he was not the director at the time of the Atlanta Penitentiary riot—that occurred in 1987, long before he was appointed—someone on his staff must have told him about me.

Bob Ricks was the SAC of the Oklahoma City Field Office and would have automatically been the agent in charge of the case and the on-scene commander under the old rules. Bob was an accomplished, experienced agent who was respected by the citizens. I had had some contact with him, though not a lot of direct professional association.

One thing I did know was that Bob was somewhat controversial because of Waco. During the crisis he assisted the on-scene commander, Jeff Jamar, who was the SAC of the San Antonio Field Office. As part of his duties, Bob handled the press during a significant part of the case and had a number of press conferences. So, it was not surprising that after he returned to his office in Oklahoma City he was called upon on numerous occasions to speak publicly about Waco and the role that he played. However, after legal proceedings began and there was a trial in progress in Texas, the federal trial judge issued a gag order and instructed anyone connected with the case must maintain silence, giving no interviews.

Bob didn't exactly abide by this. After making a speech at a civic group meeting—as SACs frequently do—a reporter asked him a question about Waco, to which Bob responded and was quoted in a local newspaper. Now, I don't recall the quote but everyone at the bureau learned quickly that Louie was incensed about it. This was not surprising, as Louie did not take kindly to comments to the press of any kind. Although I don't know this for sure, my strong belief is that this was why Bob wasn't appointed to oversee the Oklahoma City investigation.

Though my experience of being on-scene commander turned out to be a blessing, it was certainly in disguise when I first heard the news. Not only was this going to be the first major test of our new crisis management plan but also here I was, a special agent in charge myself, flying from Phoenix, Arizona, about to land in Oklahoma City and take over a major case in another SAC's territory. As you can imagine, the situation created some big diplomacy issues, not only with regard to Bob Ricks himself, but also with the entire perception of the FBI and its leadership. As the SAC there, Ricks had a tremendous amount of contact with federal, local, and state law enforcement in the Oklahoma City area and was knowledgeable about the abilities and personalities involved.

I, on the other hand, did not and was not. I didn't know any of the staff, didn't know anything about the capabilities of the local law enforcement, and didn't know on whom I could rely for what. Not only that, but there was the issue of the SAC's internal standing within his own office. The office would normally be looking to Bob Ricks for leadership and suddenly here's this other person whom they don't know, coming in to be in charge and run the operation. At the FBI there is a great deal of focus on the leadership in each particular office. All people assigned there, from the newest clerk out of high school on up, want to see a strong SAC who not only earns their respect but who also has respect from other members of law enforcement. It helps them in their work. If a major case happens in their jurisdiction and the local SAC isn't in charge, a huge morale problem can develop. Why isn't he or she running the show? The fact that the local SAC is not in charge raises questions in their minds about his or her ability.

Very early on I decided that the first thing I had to do when I landed was make sure that there was a complete understanding between Bob and me. The working relationship had to be as professional as possible and we couldn't let personality or hurt feelings get in the way. It was important that he be left with dignity and the ability to run his own office as well as maintain his standing as the senior federal law enforcement official in Oklahoma.

But it didn't appear I was going to be landing in Oklahoma anytime soon. As the weather whirled outside, all these thoughts did the same thing in my mind as I traveled the seemingly never-ending trip there. I had to connect through Dallas, but because of heavy storms I was stuck waiting there until the wee hours. It wasn't until I finally looked up—or rather looked down—from my thoughts that I realized I was still wearing the same suit I had on since early the day before. Although I was more than ready to get to Oklahoma, in retrospect, this waiting period was a good time for me to collect my thoughts and get a plan together.

Needless to say, it's a good thing I'm not one who talks to himself, considering most of the passengers sitting around me were members of the media. The waiting area was filled with news crews, complete with cameras and equipment, the whole thing. They were desperate for information about the bombing, talking about the case and what they knew about it but mostly what they didn't. It must have been some kind of miracle that they didn't notice me and realize the part that I was about to play. In the meantime, I just sat there like a mouse.

And why not grab a little peace right now? The circus for me would be in more than full swing in just a few hours.

## Blank Check

After all the travel, delays, storms, and everything else, it was very early on the morning of April 20, 1995, by the time I finally arrived in Oklahoma City. The area adjacent to the Alfred P. Murrah Federal Building smelled like smoke and looked like a war zone, with glass and debris everywhere. In the short time I walked around the area the glass badly cut up my dress shoes.

I immediately went over to the command center, where I was given a briefing by Danny Coulson, the SAC from Dallas, Texas, and Bob Ricks. Coulson had gotten the call early on, too, and he had driven from Dallas immediately. A large contingent of FBI personnel, including special agents and technical and support staff, drove the few hours in their vehicles from there.

I knew that my first obligation was to make sure that there was a complete understanding between Bob and me as to what was going to happen—who was going to be in charge of what.

"I didn't choose to come here, Bob," I said. That was the first point I made. "This is not my choice. I was named to do this by Louie. You're here and obviously it's not your choice either, but the bottom line is that we have to live with it. This is a major catastrophe and we have to appear totally united. Not only that, but we have to do a fantastic job. Otherwise, you, the FBI, and I are going to be subject to a tremendous amount of criticism, and rightfully so, if we don't put this on a priority level and conduct ourselves completely professionally. That said, what I would like you to do is since you have the knowledge of local and state law enforcement, as well as contact with the governor [Governor Frank Keating, who happened to be a former FBI agent], is to be the primary liaison between the FBI and local and state law enforcement. That will be your function. There, obviously, are a lot of things that I don't know and maybe will never know about the capabilities, strengths, and weaknesses of not only individual components of law enforcement here, but also of the individual people who are in command of various components of local and state law enforcement. Therefore, I'm going to depend on you to be the liaison and advise me about what should be done with regard to these individuals. Not only that, but I'm going to be here for a month or two, then I'm going home. You'll still be here. You'll still be the special agent in charge, so it's going to be extremely important, with you as the liaison, that we strengthen that relationship rather than let that relationship deteriorate."

That made sense to Bob and this became our understanding. Bob took charge as the liaison with law enforcement and Danny Coulson headed up things at the crime scene itself, the actual coordination of the FBI, and other activities involving the investigation at the bomb site. I handled press matters, presided at all meetings about the case, and coordinated with FBI headquarters.

There were people on duty through the night, with more arriving. To help out with the management of the investigation, another SAC, Neil Gallagher, came in from New Orleans, and Mike Wilson, the Houston division SAC, showed up too. Even though I was the on-scene commander, I couldn't stay there twenty-four hours a day. There needed to be some ranking FBI decision makers on scene around the clock so that in the event of a major situation, an appropriate decision could be made without a major delay to wake me up and get me up to speed on the situation.

That morning we spent our time organizing who was going to do what. Neil Gallagher and Mike Wilson were on the night shift. Ricks and myself would be on during the day, along with Coulson. The five of us would work whatever hours we had to—that was understood without even talking about it—which would amount to twelve to eighteen hours a day.

During the first night the FBI had set up a temporary command post in an abandoned building several blocks from the actual bomb site but close enough that all the windows had been blown out. The whole area, however, was cordoned off. There was a garage-type bay on the lower floor and an upstairs with a series of closed-off rooms that we used as conference rooms, then a work area with partitions, and another open area.

Initially, the people on site had set up the upstairs as a food area, where we had about twenty phone lines installed. When I realized that, I immediately had the food area removed to the first floor. I had visions of people wandering in, picking up a sandwich, and settling in. After all, this was an investigation area. This upstairs area had a unique purpose: key executives could come to this area to talk about the investigation and have briefings on the status. We couldn't have other people wandering in and out.

As we settled into our command post we were spending a lot of time just getting the physical plant set up. It helped enormously that we were on Bell Telephone's property since we had to have all kinds of extra phone lines, electric lines, office equipment, radio and communications equipment, computers, and who knows what all else brought in. To put it simply, the challenge here was to establish a completely operating, full-blown, major case, FBI operational center in what had been a virtually abandoned warehouse facility with all of the windows blown out.

One good stroke of luck we had was that there were no real budget restrictions. In a major case like this there's no such thing as a budget. For example, there was a conference call that a few of us were on with Louie in which I mentioned that we might need to do analysis that was going to cost $100,000.

Some of the other folks on the line said, "One hundred thousand dollars? Oh, well." Forget it.

Louie's response was different: "I don't care how much it costs, do it. Go with it, don't worry about money."

Louie's attitude permeated the whole case. From my experience with the Atlanta Federal Penitentiary, I can attest that when you're in a crisis mode like this one, and given all the pressures and importance placed on this case, the last thing you need is to be worried about was a few dollars here or there. Luckily, Louie made sure that money was not a consideration here.

We had, in effect, a blank check. You need to go rent furniture, go rent furniture. You need to buy all kinds of equipment—duplicating equipment, computer equipment, whatever you need—go get it. Just get it. That was quite a change from normal FBI operations.

## In Media Res

That very first morning, the top priority was to get me completely briefed on the case. We knew that there was going to be, and already was to a certain extent, a huge amount of media focus. A young fellow by the name of Mike Kortan had been sent out from headquarters to help get me prepared.

Kortan was a media guy who was going to be my right hand as far as media matters were concerned. A former street agent, Kortan was fairly new to the public relations side of things at the time of this crisis. But we had to work through things together, considering that the plan was to do two media briefings daily: one in the morning around 10:00 AM and another in the afternoon around 4:00 PM. This would be trial by fire for the both us!

I would be conducting all the press conferences in conjunction with the chief of police of Oklahoma City, Sam Gonzales (who became a good friend). That meant that the first thing I had to do on that first morning in Oklahoma City was to prepare myself for a major news conference shortly. There was a lot of back-and-forth about what would be included, what kind of statements we would make, what would be the content, and what kind of questions we would answer. Who would ever have guessed that one of the most difficult things that an FBI SAC has to do is to learn how to deal with the media?

Something that I learned was that in a situation of this magnitude you must keep the American people informed about what's going on. (This, no doubt, could be the subject for an entire separate book.) In a major case like this, and particularly if public safety is involved, the public is entitled to know what is being done to protect it.

Yet, as strongly as I feel that the public is entitled to know what's going on, I do realize that there are some items that just cannot be disclosed, because doing so is illegal. According to Rule 6e of the Federal Rules of Criminal Procedure any information obtained from a grand jury inquiry is secret. You cannot publicly disclose what was obtained through a grand jury investigation except during the trial itself. That kind of information is very, very tightly controlled and you cannot make comments. Period. If you violate that secrecy then you're subject to criminal prosecution.

So, here you are, standing in front of the press, and you have all this information because it's germane to the investigation itself. But when a question is asked you have to separate in your mind what you may tell the media legally versus what you can't tell because it would be illegal to disclose.

However, I had learned in the case in Atlanta that if you don't tell the press anything, then it starts making things up. Combine that frame of reference with the knowledge that Louie had summarily terminated two special agents in charge because of statements made to the press, and the whole situation becomes much less like giving a speech and more like playing Russian roulette. Adding to the uncertainty of this equation is that you can't control what people write. You may have something attributed to you in the form of a quote that you didn't actually say.

So, I spent a considerable amount of that time getting completely briefed on the case—where we were at that time, what we knew, and what we didn't know then—and preparing myself mentally to go into the media lion's den.

When the moment arrived I slowly walked through the back door of the city auditorium, where the conference was being held. The police and Mike Kortan escorted me. The chief was already there and the two of us met at the back door and went in together. As we were going onto the stage I saw just how packed the auditorium was. It was overwhelming. I had never seen so many cameras and so many media people in my life, from every publication you can imagine, national and international. An accurate description by many, including my friend Randy Collier, who was a stringer for *Newsweek* at the time, was "media frenzy."

I had a prepared statement, not my personal statement, but one that had been worked back and forth among media people at FBI headquarters and Kortan. It had been massaged enough by those two groups to be considered "press proof." I read the prepared statement regarding the investigation's progress and then we opened up for questions.

I decided early on that because these press conferences were such mayhem, I would actually take the time given to answer each question to really think about what I was being asked. I would pause, think about it, and then I would restate the question.

This tactic did several things for me. It gave me time to think and it made the question clear to whoever was listening. Having seen a lot of press conferences, I knew that sometimes the viewer or listener can't hear the question clearly, because it was likely coming from somewhere without a bank of mikes. When the speaker responded, those listening in the audience (or tuned in to audio or video) didn't have a reference. I would usually start my response with: "The question is . . ."

By doing that, I was able to slow the whole thing down. Instead of all of these people yelling and screaming and putting mikes in my face, I was able to curtail the feeding frenzy. Things were slowed to a very measured pace. As for those press people who were shouting and waving their microphones in my face, I just wouldn't pay attention to them. In fact, I told more than one of them to sit down. Though I never raised my voice, they seemed to learn very quickly to play by my rules and act professionally or be ignored.

I think that I was able to work well with members of the press because I showed respect for them. I treated them the way I would treat any colleague and not talk down to them as I have seen so many others do during press conferences. This treatment, in turn, I believe, led to mutual respect. I tried to get to every single reporter I could and answer their questions the best I could without hurting the case, the FBI, or any other law enforcement agency. But maybe, more important than anything else in my ability to deal with the media was that the media perceived me, so I was told, as a very honest person and didn't question the veracity of anything I said. Once you prove yourself untrustworthy to the media, you go down a slippery slope.

## Crime Scene

There really was only one controversial incident that occurred while working the bombing case. In fact, many who participated in or were involved somehow with this case said that it was just an absolute model of cooperation between federal, state, and local agencies. You did not see any dissension or disagreement. It was just amazing: people at every level worked together, with an interest only in cooperating so that the bombers could be brought to justice.

The organization in charge of rescuing and recovering people—both living and dead—was the Oklahoma City Fire Department. Period. And Fire Chief Gary Marrs was in charge. We at the FBI, meanwhile, were assisting from the investigative side. We would step in and secure the evidence.

With that operational structure, we rocked along for a day with no problems. But that turned out to be a short twenty-four hours. The Oklahoma chief of police, Sam Gonzales, came in with something on his mind. "Weldon, please meet with Gary Marrs. He has a problem," he said.

Gary said, "FEMA [the Federal Emergency Management Agency] is insisting that we use listening devices and other electronic probing devices to see, hear, and detect people still in the rubble. The problem is that this is slowing everything down.

"We need to be careful because the movement of heavy blocks could kill people in the rubble, but our posture is that if we wait too long, then a survivor might die if we are unable to reach them in time. I need to you to intervene."

This, however, wasn't my bailiwick. The fire department was in charge of rescue operations. Arrangements were made for us to have a joint meeting with FEMA and the fire department at their command post, which was located in a part of the Alfred P. Murrah Federal Building that was still standing, to try to resolve this issue.

Emotions were running very high. There were strong feelings on both sides and shouting and pounding on the table. FEMA thought that the fire department was endangering people's lives by moving fast with heavy equipment. The fire department was equally disturbed and upset because they knew people in rubble are often badly injured and, therefore, need help quickly. To improve chances of survival the heavy stuff had to be moved out of the way as fast as possible.

Both groups wanted to find and save any survivors, but they had two radically different approaches. And they laid all this in my lap. Although I was able to communicate to the FEMA people that I felt that they needed to move faster, I was not in a position to overrule FEMA. They were working at the direction of the president of the United States.

That meant that it was time for Louie to intervene. So, I called and told him what was happening. He, in turn, called Janet Reno, who called President Clinton. This was quite a phone chain. I don't know what the conversations and discussions were like, past mine with Louie, but pretty quickly someone on the president's staff called the director of FEMA, James Lee Witt, who was on site. He was instructed to stand aside and let the fire department do what they needed to do.

FEMA, of course, obeyed—what choice did the people have?—but suffice it to say, they weren't happy about it. Up until that time FEMA had been purchasing equipment and supplies, sometimes by the truckload for all the people working at the site, including FBI personnel. Suddenly, however, FEMA said that going forward the FBI would have to pay for any equipment it used but that FEMA would still be able to furnish equipment for the state and local agency personnel at no charge. It never ceases to surprise me that you can find petty politics pretty much everywhere you look.

That was the only conflict in the entire Oklahoma City investigation that rose up to my level. And in this conflict, both sides were doing what they needed to do without any ulterior motives. Each side *was* doing only what it thought necessary to save whoever was in the rubble. In FEMA's case you can't really blame its people for wanting to deal with the rescue in a traditional way. After all, they were used to handling natural disasters, earthquakes, and the like. At the time, Oklahoma City was FEMA's largest mobilization of urban search and rescue teams.

But throw another factor into it: unlike with earthquakes and other natural disasters, this was a crime scene, and a major criminal investigation was taking place.

## Twisted Metal

Within hours of the explosion one of the most significant pieces of evidence in the investigation was found. The twisted rear axle assembly of a truck. It was about 650 feet away from the bomb site and had crashed into a car parked in front of an apartment house. Now, of course, it was lying in plain view out on the street, but it wasn't found immediately because the crime scene was a twenty-square-block area. There was evidence everywhere, including on top of buildings two and three blocks away. It was difficult in the early stages to determine what was and what was not significant.

However, we knew immediately that the axle was important to us. From that axle assembly we were able to determine the truck's serial number, or vehicle identification number (VIN), which enabled us to determine the manufacturer of the truck, Ford. The early discovery of this key piece of evidence was critical in speeding up the investigation.

Once we determined the maker of the truck it was very simple to go to Ford and ask who bought it. The Ford people were quick to tell us that the 1993 twenty-foot Ford truck had been sold to Ryder and it was a rental. Ryder? That immediately piqued our interest because Ryder was the same brand that had been used in the World Trade Center bombing in 1993 in New York City. Did this mean that the perpetrators were Middle Eastern? This was a thought that certainly ran through our heads. As we all now know, the bombers weren't Middle Eastern and the Ryder truck usage was merely coincidental, but at the time we figured that a connection could be a possibility.

We dispatched agents to Ryder headquarters in Miami, Florida, to investigate further. Though the truck had a Florida license plate, Ryder searched its computerized records to see if it could be traced to another part of the country. Bingo! The truck in question was from Elliott's Auto Body, a rental agency in Junction City, Kansas, where a "Robert Kling" had rented it on April 17 a little after 4:00 PM. On the surface this information may not sound like a big deal, but believe me, it was. Junction City is due north of Oklahoma City—244 miles and about a four-hour drive away by interstate highway. The proximity of the rental agency to the bombing site was very significant.

It didn't take us long to get our agents to Elliott's Auto Body. In fact, nothing in those first days seemed to take very long. That we were able to find the axle and connect it to Elliott's all within one day was extremely helpful to the success of the investigation. Once at Elliott's we interviewed the folks there, in addition to checking their records, to find out what happened to this truck. Right off the bat they were able to show us the paperwork about the rental. This "Robert Kling" supposedly lived in Idaho, but we quickly ascertained that this was a phony address. No driver's license existed in Idaho for Robert Kling. But in the course of our investigation, we wound up checking driver's license records in all fifty states. There wasn't a Robert Kling who came anywhere close to who we were looking for.

There we were, temporarily at a dead end. We knew what the truck was, we knew where it had been rented, but that was it. So we started interviews, very intensive interviews I should add, of the three people present at the truck rental center at the time of the Ryder rental to determine everything they knew. We flew in an artist to do an artist's conception drawing from recollections of the folks at the rental agency. It took a number of hours for the artist to produce likenesses of the two people who came to rent the truck. The result of the artist's work was an image of what we called Unknown Subjects (Unsubs) in the FBI lexicon. In this case, there were two images, and with Unsub #1, or John Doe #1, the image was very close, as it would turn out, to that of the actual bomber, Timothy McVeigh. Unsub #1, the primary person, was the one who actually went to the rental counter and rented the truck. Eldon Elliott, the owner, later testified that he remembered Timothy McVeigh's face because McVeigh, unlike most clients, had waived damage insurance on the vehicle.

(But a witness at the rental agency also remembered something else—McVeigh was accompanied by another man. As *Simple Truths*, the seminal book on the Oklahoma City bombing, describes it, the search for Unsub #2 would receive more public and media attention than anything else in the case.)

We now had the faces of the renters. Yes, the name could be a phony one, but having the face was a big deal. It was a surprise to some that the bombers looked like white male Americans, not Middle Easterners or of foreign descent. And from talking to the people at the truck rental counter, the main suspect, Unsub #1, sounded like somebody's next-door neighbor in Middle America. That was a surprise to many of us because with the World Trade Center bombing in recent memory, and with all the perpetrators in that crime being from the Middle East, many of us, including me, thought that these bombers could be from there as well.

At the time our details were not solid, obviously, but we thought the Unsub #1 was of medium build, 5' 10" or 5' 11", 180 to 185 pounds, with a light-brown crew cut, and possibly right-handed. We believed the second man, Unsub #2, also had a medium build, around 5' 9" or 5' 10", and about 175 to 180 pounds, with brown hair and a tattoo on his left arm. He was possibly a smoker. He was darker, but he didn't look Middle Eastern, either. This Unsub resembled a number of different suspects, including a solider from Ft. Riley, Kansas, who was at the rental office the next day.

We had two images to take to the American people and tell them as quickly as we could: "This is what we've learned so far and we need your help. We need you to help us identify who these people may be." The name Robert Kling might have been a phony one, but it gave us a bridge to connect with the next clue. To that end I went on national TV on

Thursday afternoon, the day after the bombing, to do just that and released composite sketches of two men—labeled "John Doe #1" and "John Doe #2."

The world now was on notice that we had descriptions of people associated with the bombing. Not only that, but we were soliciting their assistance, to call 1-800-905-1514, with any leads. The phone number led to a bank of phones in Washington, D.C., manned by FBI agents and FBI operators. We knew that we would immediately start receiving phone calls and we were correct. We had tens of thousands of phone calls coming in. It certainly didn't hurt that right after my press conference Attorney General Janet Reno announced a $2 million reward for information leading to the bombers' arrest and conviction.

The vast majority of the calls turned out to be dead-end leads. With this kind of request for help you can imagine all the kinds of things that can happen. You have people who legitimately think they recognize a drawing as someone whom they knew or were associated with in the past. Unfortunately, you have some people who come forward with an ulterior motive. They call in about a former neighbor or former boyfriend or ex-husband, or whoever, just to cause problems for that individual. Keep in mind that we had to take every one of those leads and pursue it to the final degree. We had to find that person, interview him or her, and determine if the person had an alibi or was somehow connected or associated with this case. Also, remember that at this time we didn't know for certain whether the suspects were American or foreigners. And if they were American, they could have been aided by foreigners.

Even after we had released the sketches, there were a lot of theories and rumors about who might have been involved. There was talk of a possible third man, an Oklahoma resident named Abraham Ahmad, who had left Oklahoma on the day of the explosion. On his way to Amman, Jordan, he was stopped on a connecting leg of his trip in London for "acting nervous."

His luggage went on to Rome, where Italian officials said it contained wires and tools that, while they could be used in electronic repair, were also consistent with those used for explosives. Knowing that speculation of this kind was extremely premature, however, I was careful to insist to the press he was just a "possible witness" and not a suspect. After FBI interrogation, he was cleared.

At the same time, there was a spotlight on three Middle Eastern–looking men who had been arrested in Oklahoma and Texas. Though I didn't confirm at the time that we had arrested anyone in connection with the bombing, the three men were picked up Wednesday night. They were held on immigration charges after stopping an Oklahoma state trooper to ask directions on Wednesday, the same day as the bombing. The officer thought something about them was suspicious, so he wrote down their car's license plate number. That plate, however, turned out to be registered to a blue Chevrolet Cavalier rental car and not the vehicle they were driving—a huge red flag. The Cavalier was from National Car Rental at Dallas/Fort Worth International Airport and was rented by one of the men, a Queens, New York, cabdriver, who was originally from Pakistan. The rental car was later found with one of the men, parked right outside an Oklahoma City motel.

Needless to say, the men were heavily interrogated. Their Dallas apartment was searched and their property tested for explosives residue. In the end, though, they were found not to have anything to do with the case.

It's not surprising that there would have been suspicion about Middle Easterners. The bombing took place only two years after the World Trade Center bombing, in which a Ryder rental truck had also been used. Additionally, there were initial indications that the bomb was composed of ammonium nitrate and fuel oil, called ANFO, which can be made with a mixture of fertilizers and kerosene. A homemade ANFO bomb was also used in the 1993 World Trade Center explosion. In the early 1990s ANFO, unfortunately, was quite popular. From 1990 to the end of 1994, there were eighteen ANFO bombings or attempted bombings in America, two of which were at Internal Revenue Service (IRS) facilities in Phoenix and Los Angeles. The one in LA involved a car bomb.

And then there was the question of motive. Among other ideas, we pursued the concept that the attack targeted the U.S. Drug Enforcement Administration in Oklahoma, whose state headquarters had been on the seventh and ninth floors of the Alfred P. Murrah Federal Building. And, indeed, in the attack several DEA employees were among the missing.

However, going by the sketches, we began to suspect even more strongly that the suspects could have had some connection to survivalist or extremist religious cults. We noted that the Oklahoma bombing took place exactly two years to the day after the Waco incident. In addition, the Oklahoma City incident happened on the same day that a member of another right-wing extremist group, the Order, was executed in Arkansas for the murder of a pawnshop owner whom he thought was Jewish.

We settled in at that point for what might have turned out to be a very long haul. After disseminating the drawings—the biggest thing we had to go on at that point—the next step was to go door-to-door, house-to-house, business-to-business in Junction City, Kansas, with these drawings. Did anybody in the town, besides the people at the rental agency, recognize these people? If so, would they have any information that we could use? We would soon find out.

## Don't Tread on Me

Once we focused on the town of Junction City, Kansas, it didn't take long before we found someone who would help our investigation. The manager of the Dreamland Motel on the edge of town, Lea McGown, recognized the man federal agents had only known as Robert Kling.

"That's Tim McVeigh," she said as soon as she saw the Kling drawing. Not only that, but he had parked a large yellow Ryder truck in the motel lot, which she remembered was the same color as the old Mercury Marquis he arrived in. She also gave the agents the address that he registered under at the motel.

This could be big. Of course, the name Robert Kling was phony, but this could be the lead we were hoping for.

We started the machinery. We ran the name and address through all the databases to see if anything came up. Sure enough, within a few hours it did. There was a match.

An ATF agent working in the Oklahoma City headquarters had run the name through the National Crime Information Center computer. A hit! The Oklahoma Highway Patrol had made an inquiry on that name on April 19—the day of the bombing. A few phone calls later and we realized that we might have just found our man.

An Oklahoma State trooper named Charlie Hanger had made the inquiry into McVeigh as part of a routine traffic stop on the interstate north of Oklahoma City in a town called Perry. Trooper Hanger was about seventy-five miles from the bombing site when, about an hour and a half after the explosion, he saw an old beat-up car driving without a license plate. He pulled over the garish 1977 Mercury Grand Marquis; the driver was pleasant enough when he got out to meet him. The driver, Timothy McVeigh, explained he'd just bought the car and that's why he didn't have the plate. When Hanger asked if he had insurance or registration, he said that because the car was newly purchased—although he didn't have any kind of receipt—all the documentation was being sent to his new address.

As he gave Trooper Hanger his driver's license, the officer saw that he did happen to be carrying something: a gun. The traffic violator was sporting a Glock semiautomatic pistol on a shoulder holster. He also had with him an ammo clip and a knife.

Time for jail, Mr. McVeigh. He was escorted into Hanger's patrol car, after being ordered to leave his locked car by the side of the road. So, there it was—a nearly undisturbed crime scene. It was sort of like one of the Egyptian tombs. We caught quite a lucky break.

En route to the jail, Hanger had his dispatcher do a check on McVeigh's Michigan driver's license and the gun. The dispatcher came back to Hanger with some intriguing info: McVeigh's New York concealed weapon permit was not legal in Oklahoma. That was it—McVeigh was done. He was soon booked on four misdemeanor charges: unlawfully carrying a concealed weapon, transporting a loaded firearm in a motor vehicle, failing to display a current license plate, and failing to maintain proof of insurance.

• • •

The ATF agent got some good news when he called the Noble County Jail to see if the inquiry on McVeigh had led to an actual booking. It had. Our suspect was already in jail the whole time! Amazing. But, at the time of that phone call, he was about to be taken to a bond hearing.

Who would have ever guessed that something as routine as a traffic arrest would turn out to be so significant? Not only did we have a real name but we also had a real person—in jail already. A more thorough search later of McVeigh's car was extremely beneficial. In the car we found traces of PETN, an explosive. That was, to put it mildly, a big turning point in the investigation. It was overwhelming, absolutely overwhelming. Though it took a lot of the pressure off, our discovery generated new pressure of its own. While we had a person in custody, we had a drawing of another person. The idea of something unknown was gnawing at us. This John Doe #2 was someone the rental agent said was with McVeigh at the time he rented the truck. What we also didn't know was whether there were other conspirators who might be involved. We had only one person. Were there one, two, three, or ten others?

And our one person wasn't talking. He wasn't cooperating at all. So the pressure was very intense, because it was very possible that we had part of a conspiracy that was ongoing. Who was to say that we couldn't have another bombing at any moment?

The defense attorneys for McVeigh, not to mention various conspiracy theorists as well as authors seeking a sensational story, among others, frequently allege that once the FBI found McVeigh, we focused exclusively on him. They charge that we subsequently failed to identify other conspirators.

Nothing could be further from the truth. These baseless allegations really make me angry.

The real story is that after we had McVeigh in custody, it was imperative that we identify *any* and all others possibly involved. If other conspirators remained on the loose and committed another bombing with significant loss of life, wouldn't the FBI in general—and I in particular—be responsible for that failure? You bet we would. That knowledge was a powerful driver affecting everyone working on the case. We left no stone unturned and pursued every lead to the bitter end.

In December 2006, the House of Representatives Oversight and Investigations Subcommittee of the House International Relations Committee released a chairman's report entitled "The Oklahoma City Bombing: Was There a Foreign Connection?"

According to the report, the subcommittee focused primarily on two theories that "seemed to be based on factual evidence that, if verified, would indicate a foreign participation in the bombing."

In the details of the report there was speculation about whether the bombers had Middle Eastern connections. The report then comments that since al Qaeda terrorist Ramsi Yousef and Terry Nichols were in the Philippines at the same time, there was "opportunity" for interaction between Nichols and Yousef. Later in the report, the authors reach the conclusion that while there may have been opportunity for a linkup, "the proof, however, has not been established." In my opinion this is an understatement. Since there is no evidence that it happened, how does one prove that there never was such a meeting?

Let me give an example of another piece of "evidence." The report mentions that an employee at a tire store saw McVeigh and a "dark" passenger at his place of employment at 8:45 AM on the morning of the bombing and asked for directions to 5th and Harvey Streets (the location of the Murrah building). When I first heard this report in the command post my reaction was, "I cannot believe that the bomber did not know how to get to his target only fifteen minutes before the bomb was detonated." I dismissed the report as fictional—as were numerous other reports of sightings. As a part of the investigation, however, the FBI located and interviewed every single person who had a rented a Ryder truck during the pertinent time period. An elderly couple who was moving cross-country gave information that on the morning of April 19 they had gotten up very early and driven for a couple of hours before reaching Oklahoma City. There, they pulled off the interstate and located a place to have breakfast. After breakfast they returned to the truck to continue their journey. However, they got lost in downtown Oklahoma City and could not locate the entrance to the interstate. They stopped to ask for directions shortly before 9:00AM at—can you believe it?—a tire store! This is just one of the many dozens of reports which were thoroughly investigated and disproved. In fact, during the trial a defense attorney commented that at least half of Oklahoma City must have seen McVeigh on the morning of the bombing or else he had a large number of twin brothers.

The report also fails to mention that McVeigh and Nichols were using a telephone card for approximately eighteen months before the bombing and that this was their primary method of communication. Every call of the thousands they made during this period was traced and the recipient interviewed.

It was by this method that the call to Elohim City, where McVeigh was attempting to locate Andreas Strassmeir, a known right-wing extremist from Germany, was unearthed. Other calls identified persons who had been contacted to purchase racing fuel and other bomb components. If there indeed were other conspirators, and I am convinced that there were not, the telephone records would have identified them even if other investigation failed to do so.

The committee report also highlighted the fact that in early 1995 information was received that in the first search of Terry Nichols's house the FBI missed a stash of explosives. The information included specific information from a jailhouse informant in prison with Nichols on how to find the explosives, which were, according to the information received, still underneath the floorboards of his house. A second search was successful in locating the explosive materials where the lead stated they could be located. The report stipulated that this episode was enough to "precipitate an investigation to determine what else may have been missed or mis-analyzed in the original bombing probe."

As embarrassing as this was for the FBI, I submit that it is understandable and was not a "startling" development as characterized in the committee report. Let me explain. When a federal judge issues a search warrant, the body of the warrant identifies not only the places to be searched but what items are being sought in connection with the crime. The Nicholses' house and its garage were virtual treasure troves of information pertinent to the Oklahoma City bombing. For example, receipts were located for the purchase of four thousand pounds of ammonium nitrate fertilizer, a key ingredient of the ANFO-type bomb proven to have been used in the Oklahoma City case.

What a search warrant does *not* do is give the searching authorities license to tear up the property, knock down walls, rip up floorboards, or do any other damage to the structure or its contents. The only exception would be if credible information was received (which was the case in the second search) that evidentiary material was concealed in the walls, under the floorboards, or in a location otherwise inaccessible to a normal, legal search. In any case, the finding of additional explosive materials in Terry Nichols's residence has absolutely no bearing on the original question posed by the committee, "Was There a Foreign Connection?" or even if there were any other unidentified conspirators.

In my review of the committee report I could find only one new fact: in an interview Nichols admitted to the committee investigators that he was responsible for the robbery of Roger Moore in Arkansas. While the FBI long suspected he had been involved in this crime, it had no positive identification or physical evidence as proof. Timothy McVeigh was closely associated with Moore and had even been his houseguest. Even Moore suspected that McVeigh was somehow involved, although it was clear that he did not personally participate in the actual robbery. Nichols's admission provides further proof of the conspiracy between Nichols and McVeigh and eliminates speculation as to whether additional conspirators were involved in this phase of the overall operation.

Prior to this report, in 2004 there was a resurgence of conspiracy theorists (some of whom are mentioned in the committee report) whose ill-founded ruminations and speculations based on rumor, innuendo, and false information gained some publicity. As a result, the FBI prudently undertook a massive and comprehensive review of the OKBOMB case. A team of experienced FBI agents examined the entire investigation, including thousands of documents, with the purpose of determining if there were leads that were not covered or any avenues of investigation that were not fully explored. Their finding? All participants and conspirators in the OKBOMB case were identified in the original investigation. There was no credible information uncovered indicating otherwise nor was any avenue of investigation neglected.

Therefore, I completely disagree with the committee's ambiguous finding: "Whether or not there was a foreign connection to the bombing is inconclusive." The report went on to say, "This investigation determined that many pieces of so-called evidence backing various theories of a foreign involvement were not based in fact." I can only regret that the committee did not accurately state its findings and admit "*all* pieces of so-called evidence backing various theories of a foreign involvement were not based in fact."

The last sentence of the report reads: "The overall assessment is inconclusive on the varied theories." In my lexicon that is a "cop-out." The body of the report itself demonstrates that while there are unanswered questions (which is true of every investigation ever conducted or reported on by human beings), it is quite conclusive that the committee found not a shred of evidence contrary to the FBI investigation.

Cases of the magnitude of OKBOMB, the assassination of President Kennedy, 9/11, and others invariably draw the interest of conspiracy theorists; some are legitimate but most are seeking publicity or notoriety. I will never forget watching an episode of the television show *Nightline* that aired shortly after the bombing. The show was broadcast from a small church located in rural Michigan near Terry Nichols's family farm. The packed audience was questioned regarding their attitude about the bombing and the possible involvement of members of the Nichols family. Ted Koppel commented that he had heard rumors to the effect that the government might be involved in the bombing itself. He asked for a show of hands of those people who believed that to be the case. Almost half the audience raised their hands! With that as a starting point I guess that I shouldn't be surprised that some of the crazy conspiracy theories gain credence or even precipitate a congressional inquiry.

Eclipsed only by the 9/11 investigation, the OKBOMB case remains one of the most comprehensive investigations ever conducted and, I believe, an outstanding example of the FBI operating at its best.

I can imagine the scenario if other conspirators had successfully carried out a bombing after Oklahoma City. First, there would be a media frenzy bashing the FBI for failure to "connect the dots," "shake the trees," and "freely exchange information" with other agencies. Many relatives of victims and survivors would appear on all the talk shows, demanding that blame be affixed for the failure to protect their loved ones. Next, dozens of armchair experts would be brought forth to go into detail about how the investigation should have been run and how inept and clumsy the FBI investigators were. Then, books would be written with all manner of off-the-wall conspiracy theories and accusations of illegal activity. Finally, congressional hearings would be demanded. Hungry politicians would loudly proclaim that the FBI was broken and desperately in need of a complete overhaul. In the hearings, the politicians who were members of the same political party as the sitting president would be very sympathetic to the FBI and its leadership, but the opposing party would relentlessly bash the FBI and demand that heads roll.

A strange scenario? We had ample precedent. Just look at the Ruby Ridge hearings, the Waco hearings, and, more recently, the 9/11 hearings. I have no doubt that the same scenario would have played out had other conspirators in Oklahoma City been successful in another bombing.

The really sad thing to me is that the FBI is not broken now, nor has it ever been. It is the finest law enforcement agency in the world and has been phenomenally successful at protecting the U.S. public from crime and terrorism.

Is it perfect? Of course not. Are mistakes sometimes made by the human beings who work for the FBI? Of course. The American people had better pray that the politicians calling for a change in the culture of the FBI are *not* successful. In my thirty-three-plus years in the FBI, I was consistently exposed to men and women who made enormous sacrifices and even put their lives on the line to protect the American people. The FBI that I that know and love will do a magnificent job and improve performance if given the tools (the Patriot Act), the funding (new computers and technology), and additional staff (special agents, analysts, and support staff) to do so.

Once we had McVeigh in custody, we began the backtracking, piecing together his life. Since we had the real name of the suspect it was time to put his story together. A tremendous amount of investigative activity flows from the discovery of a suspect and his actual name. We track back into this person's history to determine who he is, where he lived, where he went to school, where he worked, and the identities of all of his associates.

An early finding in McVeigh's case was that he was not too long out of the army. As we went through his acquaintances and family, among other people significant to his past whom we contacted, we very quickly found the name of Terry Nichols, an army buddy. We were able to determine that Terry Nichols lived in Herington, Kansas, although his family had a farm in Michigan. Herington was but a few miles from Junction City, Kansas, where the truck was rented. This was another significant development.

It looked as if this other person was potentially involved in the bombing, so we put Nichols under surveillance. Why? Several reasons: we named him as an associate and a friend of Timothy McVeigh's. That's not an allegation of any kind of criminal misconduct, of course, but even more important was the fact that if there were other unknown conspirators involved in the episode, it was very important that we had the name of a potential conspirator who's out, loose, and moving around. Let's put him under surveillance, and let's see whom he contacts and see if we can identify other people who might be involved with Nichols.

Herington, Kansas, however, was a little, tiny town. It didn't take very long before Nichols became aware that he was under surveillance. A big tip-off: he heard his name mentioned on the radio. The announcer didn't say that Nichols was under surveillance, but rather that he had been named as somebody who might be associated with the bombing. I'm not sure exactly what the radio program said, but the bottom line was that Nichols heard his name on the radio. Upon hearing it he immediately drove to the police station and turned himself in only a few hours after the surveillance began. He was with his wife and son, trying to act as though he were innocent.

It wasn't the first time he tried this act. He had spent a good deal of time and thought on his alibi. Very elaborately, on the morning of the bombing, he tried to give every appearance that he was in Herington, Kansas, when the bomb went off. He paid a utility bill in person that day and he bought some gas. He did several things that morning before and after 9:02 AM, when the bomb exploded. Keep in mind that this is about a four-hour drive north of Oklahoma City.

We didn't know all the things that he did on the morning of the bombing until later. Even so, when we first took Nichols into custody and began interviewing him, he initially appeared to be cooperative. Now this meant something to the case, because we had two people in custody and the second one was telling us a little bit—at least—about what his association was with Timothy McVeigh. We may not have known then what his involvement in the bombing was, but he did make it very clear that he was involved somehow with McVeigh. He admitted to us that, yes, he knew McVeigh and was a friend of his. In fact, he spent nine hours telling us a lot of useful information. Some tidbits: he had given McVeigh a ride from Oklahoma City three days prior to the bombing. Oh, and McVeigh had warned him something big was about to occur.

So, at this point we're really rolling. In the meantime, while we were questioning Nichols, agents found a second associate of McVeigh's, Michael Fortier. We'd come up with his name from reviewing McVeigh's army associates. All three of these men had served together in the same army unit.

They had a real common connection, so going forward we would be paying a lot of attention to army buddy Fortier, particularly after we learned of his right-wing extremist sympathies. That meant that a rather big part of the investigation centered on Kingman, Arizona, where Fortier lived. We placed Fortier under surveillance and ultimately took him into custody. Fortier's trailer had a "Don't Tread on Me" flag. (It's not difficult to see why he and McVeigh were friends.) This third man became quite cooperative as the case went on, and, eventually, he testified on behalf of the government.

By the time we found Fortier, we were only seventy-two hours past the deadly explosion. We could barely run fast enough to keep up with how quickly everything was developing. One fact developed leads to another fact, which developed leads to another, which developed leads to another. The pace was just like wildfire.

Interestingly enough, even though I was sitting there with a rather large contingent in Oklahoma City at the so-called office of origin—and we're controlling the case—significant parts of the investigation were not taking place there. In fact, the real active part of the investigation was going on elsewhere. Oklahoma City, essentially, was a search and rescue operation along with a bomb crime scene search, where we tried to collect whatever evidence might be found at the bomb site. The really productive witnesses and interviews that produced information and intelligence, well, all that was actually going on elsewhere: Junction City, Kansas; Kingman, Arizona; Decker, Michigan; and Herington, Kansas, just to name a few.

## Daily Grind

The first week was just a constant expansion of the case and the development of new information and fresh leads. Then the case eased into the long haul. Once we had all three suspects identified and in custody, then it was just a matter of sorting out all the leads that developed. We needed to construct and keep up to date a time line, day by day, minute by minute, if necessary.

For example, one huge part of the investigation had to do with phone records and tracking down where these people had traveled, when they had been there, and how long they had stayed. Piece by piece, the picture came together, eventually, but a lot of our work was just extremely tedious.

To give a flavor of the kind of detail work that went on (and on): the FBI obtained all of the motel registrations for the previous year in a six-state area. This included the actual registration cards and documents with which guests signed in. Cards also contained the guest's name, address, and vehicle tag or other identifying information. We had several tractor-trailer-loads of those kinds of documents. So, we took over a huge gymnasium at Ft. Riley, Kansas, and set up about a hundred desks. A white-gloved agent at each desk would look at registration cards to compare them against a whole number of "knowns."

We knew, for example, that on the registration card signed by McVeigh at the Dreamland Motel, he wrote the address 3616 N. Van Dyke Road, Decker, Michigan. So, the agents looked for that address or anything reading Decker, Michigan, on every registration card. We were looking for the name of Timothy McVeigh as well as Robert Kling. We were also looking for the names Michael Fortier or Terry Nichols, as well as corresponding addresses in Herington, Kansas, or Kingman, Arizona. Basically, we were looking for any registration that looked like it might be connected to this group of people.

The agents went through tens of thousands of motel records. From that pool they found a number of instances where one of the three men registered using the Decker, Michigan, address but attached to a name that we hadn't heard of before. We'd also find other phony addresses on registrations with names or aliases that we knew were associated with McVeigh or Nichols. The lists were constantly updated, adding names and addresses.

When we found a registration at a motel for a given date that fit one of the aliases or addresses, it would trigger a flurry of activity in the area of that motel. We would pull the phone records for the particular room. We went to pay phones in a multiblock area surrounding the motel and subpoenaed the records from the phone company of all calls during the time the person was registered at the hotel. Pouring through those records was mind-numbing work. However, in these kinds of cases mind-numbing work is what often produces positive results. We were then able to identify any number of instances where we found a town or city or place where the suspects had been—information that we had not known previously.

In some cases we found that the reason the three traveled was because there was a gun show in town. As we pieced the evidence together, we were able to determine that one of the ways McVeigh made money was through his work as a firearms expert. He bought, sold, and traded at gun shows. He and Nichols traveled all over the United States to do this.

We were looking for any and all leads. In many cases, you don't actually know what you're looking for. We did know what we needed to find out: where they were every single day and with whom they might have been in contact. We needed to reconstruct every move and made every effort to accomplish that.

As we kept investigating we didn't find any more people of interest. That's why even today when people ask, "Wasn't there something about that Unknown Subject #2? Weren't there other conspirators out there who were never identified?" To this I always reply, "Absolutely not."

The Unsub #2 turned out to be someone's memory playing tricks on him. One of the witnesses at Elliott's Auto Body Shop "remembered" that McVeigh walked in with another man. But after a thorough investigation it turned out that the person in question actually came in a day later, accompanying someone else who was also picking up a Ryder truck. Both men were totally innocent.

Goodbye, Unsub #2. You have no idea how often witnesses' memories play tricks on them.

There's no possible way there were other conspirators, because through our investigation I believe that we knew every telephone call that McVeigh, Nichols, and Fortier made for about an eighteen-month period. Though these people were using prepaid telephone cards, we were able to get records for all of the calls. While today it seems that you can buy prepaid phone cards at just about every drugstore and deli around, it wasn't that way then. This was 1995 and phone cards were mostly ordered through the mail. You actually had to write for one and this was something Terry Nichols did often. Another thing he did plenty of was hold onto everything—he never threw out his checks or any records. We found a mother lode of evidence when we searched his house in Kansas.

McVeigh and Nichols had ordered telephone cards through an organization in California that they thought they could trust to keep information confidential. They bought the cards under a phony name and felt free to use them on their travels all over the place. Once we got the records, the information was plenty rich, showing such things as calls placed to buy some of the materials needed for the bombing. But again that meant hours and hours of combing through more records.

Since no one in our group had a crystal ball, it was all hard, hard work. Agents put in tens of thousands of hours of drudgery to find that one lead, that one registration card at the motel that we hadn't known about previously, which led to a phone number that we didn't know about. And eventually, in this case, we were able to reconstruct every move, contact, and telephone call any of the three made for approximately eighteen months prior to April 19, 1995.

I can say with total confidence that we identified all three conspirators in this case and arrested them. McVeigh's sister, Nichols's wife, and Fortier's wife had limited knowledge, but none of them was materially involved. No other person, other than these three, was involved in this bombing—despite what the conspiracy theorists might say.

## Leaks

The only really frustrating part of the case was that a tremendous amount of information was leaked to the press. The leaks shouldn't have been surprising, however, considering the number of people involved.

On hand in both the rescue and investigative parts of the operation, there were, all told, some two hundred FBI agents and forensic specialists; about seventy-five agents from the Bureau of Alcohol, Tobacco, and Firearms; at least forty-five U.S. Marshals; and thirty criminal investigators for the Internal Revenue Service. The IRS lost several employees in the explosion. On top of that, there were also representatives from the Drug Enforcement Administration, Department of Justice, and the U.S. District Attorney's Office.

At the very first meeting that I had at the command post on the morning of April 20, I felt like I was staring at all of them. As I walked into the meeting and started looking around, to my surprise, it was standing room only. There were probably fifty, maybe seventy-five, people in this room. Of course, I didn't know any of them really, except for the FBI people. Beyond them there were the state, local, and other federal agency people. I did not know who all of these people were, which caused me a great deal of concern.

"There have been some developments that we have to attend to," I told the room. "I'll get back to you later." With that, the crowd dispersed. I immediately called a smaller group of FBI personnel together, including Bob Ricks, Danny Coulson, Neil Gallagher, and Mike Wilson—all SACs. "Look," I said, "I've got to cut this back. We can't have seventy-five people in here, first of all. Second, we have to know who every one of these people is. We can't just allow any Tom, Dick, or Harry wandering by to come into these planning sessions."

The problem was that we couldn't just kick people out. While the FBI was in charge, the Oklahoma City bombing was a major joint investigation involving numerous federal, state, and local agencies. These other groups were full partners that had to be included. We went through and identified those whom we believed should be involved in the meeting. Individuals were selected from every agency represented at the bombing investigation. No agency was left out. We made sure of that. What we also made sure of was that they couldn't bring two, three, or four people along with them into the meeting. There was to be no entourage, just one or two people. We asked each agency to restrict participants to those with a "need to know" and they did exactly that.

Once cut back to a smaller size, the group was more manageable, but even so there were twenty or so people. We were very candid in those meetings—which took place every morning—discussing problems with the investigation and the direction it was taking and listening to any and all suggestions that anyone wanted to bring forward as to what should be done. We hammered through the questions and issues and came up with a plan for how we were going to proceed each day.

After those meetings we would hook up by conference call with the other command posts that were handling different parts of the investigation: Junction City, Kansas; Kingman, Arizona; Decker, Michigan; and others. And, of course, there was the FBI command post in Washington, D.C., not to mention the other agency people in that command post, too. In a given conference call we might have as many as two hundred people participating from all over the United States and representing an alphabet soup of federal, state, and local agencies.

Unfortunately, that many agencies involved with that many people often meant that a lot of information leaked. I had learned through experience that in any major case there are bound to be leaks, and Oklahoma City was no exception. There's not much one can do about it. We could only warn people and plead with them to hold the information close, not to disseminate it. But after all was said and done, when a case is this intense, there are going to be people who will leak information. Purposefully.

Leakers think, "Hey, I'm on the inside and I really, really know what's going on! Boy, I attended a meeting! Let me tell you what they were talking about." That's really juicy stuff: inside information from someone who participated in the discussion. Even though the journalist doesn't quote the source, the leaker stills feels important, I suppose, though of course I can't say for sure what their motivations are. There are some instances when leakers have had a long-time association with a particular newsperson or feel comfortable discussing things with that newsperson, and believe that they won't be betrayed or double-crossed.

In these conference calls Louie, Janet Reno, the director of the U.S. Marshals, the DEA administrator, the head of the Secret Service, and the heads of the relevant agencies had people from their staffs who would be in attendance and be free to participate. It was also assumed that they would report back to their bosses about what happened. I certainly knew a lot about reporting back to headquarters. I was having several conference calls a day with Washington, giving a briefing of what was taking place. On the other end of the line were: the director; the assistant director in charge of counterterrorism, Robert Bryant; his deputy assistant director, John O'Neill, who perished on 9/11 in the World Trade Center; the deputy director at the time, Larry Potts; and the general counsel, Howard Shapiro. And these were just the principals. There were a lot of other people on the line, too. However, it was not assumed that the contents of our briefings would be on CNN or the networks an hour later, as was sometimes the case.

The leaking became a constant nuisance, as you can imagine, but it came to a head when I made trip to Kingman, Arizona, where a major part of the investigation was being conducted, only to come across something very disturbing.

A Phoenix FBI agent approached me and asked, "Boss, have you seen this?"

No, I certainly had not. In my hands, though, I was now looking at the source of many of these tremendous leaks. Without my knowledge, ATF reps in Oklahoma City were sending a summary document to their headquarters about each of our meetings. And without the reps' knowledge, ATF headquarters was disseminating the document daily to all ATF offices across the United States. Who knows what they were doing with it besides giving it to the media! I exploded.

I had an immediate conference with the ATF agents to stop this practice. The two high-ranking ATF agents who were working directly in the command post with me were good people and were embarrassed and upset by what had happened. They were only keeping their headquarters briefed, which was entirely appropriate for them to be doing. But it was entirely inappropriate for ATF headquarters to disseminate this information throughout the entire agency. Though this isn't the standard kind of thing you think of when you think "leak," it was still very hurtful.

No doubt there is a lesson here for those who say that *all* information should be completely shared. In my experience, every time we fully disclosed information to everyone, there were significant leaks that hurt the investigation.

However, in an investigation the size of the Oklahoma bombing, there was bound to be more than one leak. As it turned out, a male ATF street agent, sent to Oklahoma City to work the case, was allegedly having a romantic relationship with a female reporter covering the bombing. Wouldn't you know it that on a regular and consistent basis she kept getting all of the details of our investigation correct in her reporting?

This leak was never proven, but it wasn't too long before the ATF agent was sent back to his home office—after which, not surprisingly, her reporting immediately seemed to get a little less accurate.

## Over but Not Over

A month into the investigation it became clear that some decisions had to be made about how the case was going to play out over the long haul. By that point it was obvious that this was going to be a very long-lasting investigation. There would have to be a significant group of people assigned up to and through the actual trials.

Then there was the question of who was going to be permanently in charge of the investigation. I made it clear from the onset that the person would not be me. I was soon going to reach the age of fifty-seven, the FBI's mandatory retirement age. My plan was go to back to Phoenix to finish out my time and retire in September 1995. Discussions began about who would take this case from me and then run it through the final trial date. A number of names were cast about and the decision ultimately was made to select Danny Defenbaugh, who was assigned as an inspector in the FBI's Inspection Division in Washington.

Danny was incredibly knowledgeable about bombing cases, having spent a number of years in the FBI laboratory. That was crucial in his selection since Oklahoma City was the largest bombing case the FBI had ever worked. With his background and experience he was a natural, because essentially this was going to be a case largely built from forensic evidence since there were no eyewitnesses. Another qualified person, Jack McCoy, who was serving as an ASAC at the time, was picked to serve as Danny's deputy.

"Forensics" is a word thrown around a lot but not necessarily widely understood. Simply put, forensics is the study of scientific evidence in a criminal investigation. For example, take clothing. There were significant findings when we analyzed the clothing that McVeigh was arrested in. The lab uncovered explosive material and residue. McVeigh also had a knife that the lab found to have explosive material on it as well.

In June, after Defenbaugh arrived and settled into his new position, I was on the next plane back to Phoenix. This trip was a lot less stressful than the inbound flight. The flight back was probably the first time during the whole investigation that I actually got to catch my breath and reflect. What a way to end my career! I had the good fortune to be asked to head up a significant investigation, with importance to the lives and families of so many good people. I felt that everyone working the case had done a terrific job. I was very proud of how the FBI performed and how we were perceived.

Back in Arizona I was busy preparing for my retirement in September. I got back from Oklahoma City in time to see the completion of our dream retirement home in Scottsdale after a year of construction. I was thrilled and couldn't wait to ease into retirement there.

Right about the same time a huge amount of publicity and controversy developed over Louie's appointment of Larry Potts to be the deputy director. This appointment had been made much earlier in the year, but it wasn't until June that the press took hold of it. As mentioned earlier, Larry Potts was a central figure in the 1992 Ruby Ridge investigation. During my FBI career I had had some involvement with practically every major case. Ruby Ridge, thank goodness, wasn't one of them.

Larry wasn't so lucky. The Ruby Ridge siege began with an ATF inquiry into the activities of a white separatist named Randy Weaver, who was living in Ruby Ridge, Idaho, in a very remote mountain cabin. The ATF had been investigating Weaver for various firearms violations for some time. On any given day a number of U.S. Marshals would be in the area on foot, surveilling the house where Randy Weaver lived with his wife, Vicki, and their children. The marshals were there to apprehend him after he had failed to appear in court on a weapons charge; an arrest warrant had been issued. On August 21, 1992, a gunfight erupted. One of the marshals and Weaver's teenage son were killed.

After this the FBI was brought in because it has jurisdiction when there is a killing of a federal officer. In the meantime, Randy Weaver holed up in the cabin with his wife, his remaining child, and an associate, Kevin Harris. They weren't surrendering. The FBI surrounded the area. On August 22, 1992, an FBI sniper shot Harris when he was outside. The shot passed through Harris and hit and killed Randy Weaver's wife. Unseen by the sniper, she was standing on the other side of the door from Harris and holding her baby in her arms. The child survived, as did Harris.

The siege continued for days afterward. Randy finally surrendered and was taken into custody. By the end, his wife was dead, his son was dead, and a U. S. Marshal was dead. A controversy erupted over who had authorized the sniper's shot and under what circumstances it was fired. There was more than one congressional inquiry, not to mention a Department of Justice inquiry. There was also an FBI inquiry, which some called a whitewash. The inquiries seemed to never end. In fact, they probably are still going on in some form.

Larry Potts was a central figure in all of this because of his position. During the siege he was the assistant director of the Criminal Investigation Division of the FBI. A key issue hinged on whether Larry had authorized a change to the protocols, or "rules of engagement," that the FBI uses in possible armed confrontations. Larry, to this day, denies he authorized any change, yet others maintain otherwise.

Normal rules of engagement specify shooting to protect oneself or others only if those individuals are in imminent danger. Now, in this case, the controversy surrounded documentation in which the SWAT on-scene commander had written that any person, armed and outside the cabin, could be fired upon. The commander's instructions didn't say anything about whether or not that person had to be aiming at or shooting at anybody. To say if they were outside the cabin and armed then they could be shot was a departure from policy. In this case, as the shooter testified, he shot to save somebody's life. He said that he thought that Harris was going to shoot at the government helicopter flying overhead, and so he shot first.

There was great embarrassment and a huge amount of publicity focusing on who authorized what, when they authorized it, who knew what, and when they knew it. It didn't help matters that Larry had been promoted in the time since the siege. Ultimately, it became very apparent that Larry Potts could not continue to serve as the deputy director. He was simply too controversial.

Larry volunteered to step down and at about the same time was put on suspension by the Department of Justice for the remainder of the investigation. Louie Freeh found himself looking around for a replacement. Soon, he found me.

So, I'm back in Arizona—very much enjoying being there—and it's early in August 1995 when everything reached a critical point with Larry. When we heard about Larry stepping down, Kathy immediately asked me what I would do if Louie asked me to serve as the deputy. I had a good laugh over that one. After all, Louie couldn't wait to get rid of me when he first took office! He wanted his own team and I wasn't known to him at that time. Yes, I had done a good job in Oklahoma City—or at least I thought so—but that and being appointed as deputy director are two very different matters.

It was with some surprise that a couple of days later I got a call from Floyd Clarke, who had been the deputy when Louie first took office. They had become very close, but Floyd had retired about six months after Louie became director. If anything, they had become closer after Floyd retired and I knew that Louie frequently sought Floyd's advice.

Floyd quickly got to the point. Louie had asked him to call me and to sound me out about serving as deputy director. They both knew that I was only weeks away from mandatory retirement. That could be waived since Louie felt that I was badly needed in the wake of the criticism about the appointment of Larry Potts.

Why would Louie want me? Larry was relatively young and inexperienced and was an FOL (friend of Louie's). I was none of the above. My experience, coupled with the national exposure brought by the Oklahoma City case, made me an ideal candidate to offset those criticisms. I told Floyd that I would think about it and call Louie the next day.

That night I hardly slept. On the one hand, I was flattered and honored that Louie would even consider me. On the other hand, it would be a financial setback and I would have to leave Kathy in the new house in Arizona and rent a place in Washington.

In the end it was an easy decision. I had spent over thirty years of my life serving an organization I loved and now was being asked to serve as the highest-ranking career FBI special agent. (The president appoints the director.) How could I say no? Kathy, who had predicted that I would get the call, knew what my answer would be before I did.

I called Louie. It wasn't a long conversation. I accepted the appointment, which then had to go to Attorney General Janet Reno for final approval. I agreed to report within two weeks.

So much for enjoying our dream house—not to mention my retirement!

# 10
# Louie Freeh: Part Two

## Deputy

This may not be much of a surprise but no one got rich by working for the FBI. In fact most of us, including me, incurred debts of tens of thousands of dollars throughout our careers.

I was all too aware of this when I was asked to be the deputy director.

One of the first things that came to my mind was the cost of taking on such a job. Considering that it would involve a move to Washington, I was worried about expenses, such as renting an apartment and paying for a phone and utilities. I had asked Louie that I be placed on temporary duty status instead of accepting the job as a permanent transfer. That meant that not only would trips home be paid for, but also I would have the aforementioned living expenses covered, as well as a per diem. Considering that Kathy was going to stay back at our home in Arizona, I was in no financial position to be maintaining two residences, and since I was only planning on staying as deputy director for one year, it didn't make sense to sell our house. What I didn't know then was that I would be staying on the job for a total of eighteen months.

However, Louie and the attorney general discussed it and decided that picking up such expenses was out of the question. The deputy director position, they said, was a permanent transfer, not a temporary one. As a permanent transferee, I wasn't eligible for any compensation on top of my salary other than moving expenses, said Louie. Since I was not planning on selling my Scottsdale house and moving Kathy to Washington, D.C., that meant that the government basically only had to pay for my one-way ticket from Phoenix to Washington. Considering that Louie and Janet Reno were two of the most straight-arrow people that I had ever met, I shouldn't have been at all surprised that they weren't willing to bend the rules for me, even slightly.

I imagine that their rigidity was partially attributable to what happened with Director Sessions, but even more so it came from their own sense of propriety. For example, when the attorney general flew down to her home in Florida to visit her family, she would insist on buying her own ticket in coach and refused to let the airlines upgrade her to first class under any circumstances. Louie would act the same way when he traveled. In every instance they refused to accept any kind of financial consideration.

The transfer ended up costing me approximately $2,000 a month out of pocket for housing, food, and other various expenses. Since Washington, D.C., was my permanent duty station, any time I went back to Phoenix I had to pay for it. For the period that I served as the deputy director, it conservatively cost me about $35,000. This was extra cost, not including the normal household costs back in Phoenix. That amount was a big chunk of my salary since I earned the same salary as I had when serving as SAC—grade ES6—which came out to about $120,000 a year.

All these moves took their toll on my savings, and I was not a very wealthy man to begin with. I had transferred so many times—and every time it cost me money. In some cases I also lost money on the sale of property. For example, when I left Washington, D.C., I sold the townhouse that we owned in Arlington, Virginia, when I was serving as an associate deputy director for Sessions for $35,000 less than I paid for it. Had I known what was going to happen, I could have just held on to it and moved back in! Instead, I ended up renting an apartment nearby, actually very close to where I had lived as a trainee some thirty years earlier.

Notwithstanding the personal financial sacrifice, it was a distinct honor to be asked to serve and I happily did so. Louie and I had a very good understanding and it was a great experience.

• • •

At the beginning of September 1995 I was the deputy director, the second-ranking position in the organization and the highest nonpolitical-appointment position. I had gone as far as anyone could hope to go within the ranks of the FBI. In the time I had been away from D.C., about a year and eight months, Louie had instituted a lot of changes. Now there was only one deputy director and no associate deputy directors, which was one of the jobs that I had held. All the assistant directors reported to the deputy. Furthermore, technically all of the SACs also reported through the deputy to the director. So, to put it another way, one person, the deputy, was handling the job that was formerly handled by three people.

Given all this, the deputy director position became a twenty-four-hour-a-day job. This took a toll, because not only was the position very mentally demanding, but it seemed to never stop.

As the number two to Louie, in particular, I really had my hands full. The one saving grace was that I couldn't travel with him. There was a prohibition against us traveling together—for obvious reasons. But then again when he was away that meant that I had to do not only my job but also step in and handle many of his responsibilities. As it turns out, it wasn't such a bad thing that we didn't travel together. Those who traveled with Louie hated it. It was grueling because Louie didn't want to spend the night away from Washington, D.C. However, he wanted to visit every FBI field office in the country. He would get in the FBI airplane at 5:30 AM and fly to wherever it was, even if it was the West Coast, and return that same night. Depending on the time zone, it could be a *very* long day.

In most instances, Louie went on a five-mile run right after he landed at the field office. (Only his security detail was compelled to do that portion of the trip, however.) Once he finished and got cleaned up, he went to the field office, where he had meetings lined up with supervisors and the agents on the staff. Then he had a working lunch to which he invited the local chief of police and the U.S. attorney and other law enforcement or criminal justice dignitaries. After lunch he would continue meetings with squads in the office until around 3:00 PM, when he would head back to the airport to fly to Washington, D.C. It was a killer.

When he made international trips, it was at the same pace. Obviously he couldn't go to Europe just overnight, but I think during one trip he was in five countries in three days. It was just like a death march. People who traveled with him had no free time whatsoever. They went from early, early in the morning until the wee hours of the night. As you can imagine, I was very pleased to be the one holding down the fort in Washington, D.C., while Louie was away.

Louie was very much a hands-on, roll-up-the-sleeves, and get-right-in-the-middle-of-it kind of a person. This was particularly true if the situation were case related. He just loved working on cases. That was his orientation. He'd been a street agent; he'd worked cases as an agent. When he was a prosecutor he tried cases. When he was a judge he heard cases.

The most difficult challenge that I faced was that I wanted to be a true deputy in every respect, but I found that pretty difficult to do because Louie was very interested and very deeply involved in operational matters personally. It was highly unusual to have the director involved in the small details of cases. There were two high-profile cases during the time I was there where I saw the effects of when Louie got in the middle of things—the Montana Freemen case and the investigation of Richard Jewell after the bombing at the Atlanta Olympics. One was met with resounding success, while the other would end up tainting Louie's legacy for years to come.

## Lessons: Some Learned, Others Not

For eighty-one days in the spring of 1996, the FBI faced a standoff, one of the longest law enforcement sieges in the history of the United States, with antigovernment extremists who called themselves the Montana Freemen. They were holed up on a remote farm in rural Montana, defying any and all authority. Was this going to be Waco II?

We certainly hoped not. In Waco, eighty people died, many of whom were children. Everyone at the bureau, including Louie, who was not director at the time of Waco, had learned a lot from that debacle, as well as from Ruby Ridge. From the outset it was very apparent that we were not going to initiate any sort of action to forcibly try to take over the farm. We were prepared to wait it out, however long that took. However, during this case, an FBI director was personally involved.

Composed mainly of down-on-their-luck farmers and crooks, these right-wing "patriots," the Montana Freemen, were bound together by a common belief that the federal government had no authority over them. They felt that they should have jurisdiction over themselves, and that they could print their own money and issue their own arrest warrants. They were located on nearly one thousand acres of land, a property they renamed "Justus Township." It was originally the farm of the Clark family, members of the Montana Freemen, who had lost it to foreclosure for nonpayment of the mortgage and taxes.

Though their viewpoints were an outgrowth of the more radical Posse Comitatus group of the 1970s and 1980s, the Montana Freemen seemed to focus on being con artists rather than strictly being survivalists. They made millions by putting together crooked money orders, often by using cooked-up liens filed against the property of government officials and then writing money orders or checks with their "property" as collateral! These people even taught classes on fraud to people around the country during weekend "seminars." Ostensibly, their goal was to spread their ideology and methodology in order to undermine the U.S. banking system. The Freemen were a thorn in the local law enforcement's side, to say the least. They issued "warrants" for the arrest of some public officials whom they wanted to try in their own "common law court." They even had a million-dollar bounty on the head of the local prosecutor.

Though the FBI had long been aware of this group, we were cautious about coming in and using force to clean up the situation—because of the Waco and Ruby Ridge incidents. Though we were slowly making inroads, the actions of one of our undercover agents inadvertently took the case in a whole new direction.

We were successful in getting an undercover person into the group. The agent posed as an electronics salesman, attended one of their seminars, and offered to cash millions of dollars worth of fake checks for them. In turn, they told him about some of their less savory plans. The

Freemen needed some large cars so that they could kidnap two of their enemies, a local sheriff and the aforementioned prosecutor; try them for treason; and then hang them.

Beyond telling us about their intentions, the agent brought back all kinds of intelligence to us about how many people were present at the farm, what their attitude was, what their strengths were, what their weaknesses were, and so forth.

Since the agent had expertise in two-way FM radio systems, the Freemen were asking him questions about how they could improve their radio communications. There were many blind spots on the farm where there were communication gaps. So, as they were consulting with our agent about how to improve that situation, he was reporting their weaknesses back to us.

We had ascertained there were actually two leaders of the group, and we figured if those two were apprehended, then essentially the group would fall apart. With that intelligence we had formulated a plan in which our agent would get these two leaders to one of the high spots on the property, where he would propose building an antenna so that whole property would receive much better radio coverage. But before this took place, we would set up an arrest team secretly in that area. When the leaders were brought away from the main group, our team would strike. That was the plan.

Yes, but it was to be the subject of hours of debate and argument and discussion as to how exactly this was going to be done. There were other proposals that we considered, including having our source bring in another FBI person or two in an undercover role. That was discussed at some great length but ultimately rejected as being too risky. Finally, we settled on the original plan of arresting these two individuals. Though dangerous, as these two leaders were armed at all times, it still seemed to be the best route. The arrest would take place away from the women and children and therefore not endanger innocent bystanders.

We went over the plan ad infinitum. We studied our aerial photographs and all kinds of information to plan where our people would be placed and how they were going to infiltrate. We went back and forth on details for weeks until we finally decided to go ahead with it.

The agent did his job and got the two away from the rest of the group. As he was pointing out where he would put up the antenna, our team stormed in and apprehended the two without incident. No shots were fired. Nobody was injured. We then ordered the other ten or so men for whom we had arrest warrants to surrender. They were wanted on a variety of federal charges, including threatening a U.S. court judge and $1.8 million in check fraud.

Unfortunately, we weren't going to be lucky. As far as the people in the compound were concerned, even though their two leaders had been taken into custody, their group didn't break down. If anything, they were more strongly resolved that they weren't going to give in. On that day, March 25, 2006, twenty-one Freemen barricaded themselves in buildings on the farm. So started the standoff that would outlast the fifty-one days at Waco and the nine-day occupation of Wounded Knee in 1973. And we had lost our undercover man, since as far as they knew we had arrested him too.

During the Waco siege U.S. Army vehicles were used and agents wore camouflage gear. This generated a lot of criticism and confusion about whether the military was being used. For this siege we approached things very gingerly. Instead of wearing camouflage, the agents stationed outside the property wore civilian clothes; instead of armored vehicles, they drove civilian cars. There were no military, black-painted helicopters. Agents didn't completely surround the property, either. Every movement on our part was completely planned out. We made pleas on television to get the Freemen to surrender. Most unusually, we contacted other militia groups in an effort to improve public relations and trust with these types of people. The FBI couldn't afford to have any mistakes—or any casualties—on either side.

To that end, Louie became directly and totally involved. The special agent in charge, Tom Kubic, and the case agent from Salt Lake City (Montana is in their territory) traveled to Washington on at least two occasions for planning and briefing sessions with Louie and a number of FBI HQ personnel. These were very exhaustive, very detailed meetings on exactly how we were going to proceed. I can't say that it was unheard of, but it was very unusual, even in a pretty significant case like this one, to have the director involved in such a detailed way, making decisions on the progress of the case and how it was going to be handled.

Of particular concern to him was the relationship between the FBI negotiators and the Hostage Rescue Team (HRT). During the Waco operation there had been some obvious friction between the HRT folks and the negotiators. Louie was determined, and rightly so, that there would not be a repeat of Waco.

His involvement in the Montana situation overall was positive but very burdensome on the Salt Lake City SAC and on Robin Montgomery, who was the SAC of the newly formed Crisis Incident Response Group (CIRG), which included the HRT personnel as well as the hostage negotiation team. These two groups had been combined following Waco to make sure that there was no tension between them and that any disagreements between the two would be understood and addressed.

Louie even had me personally travel to Montana to conduct an on-site review of the case and to determine if everything was being managed properly. He wanted me to get a firsthand look at the situation: meet with people on the scene, look at the command post setup, determine whether we were adequately staffed, and so on. I spent a couple of days there and, needless to say, conditions were pretty rough. At that point in mid-April, about three weeks into the siege, one agent had been killed when he lost control of his vehicle while driving one of the unpaved roads in the middle of rural Montana.

To ensure a peaceful resolution, dozens of outside experts were brought in, as well as people with beliefs similar to those of the Freemen. We operated on the same theory that I had operated on in Atlanta: no matter how radical or weird the person might seem in terms of their beliefs, if we thought that there was even a possibility that an individual could establish some rapport with the Freemen and talk some sense into them, then we would give that individual access. We let outside negotiators have conversations with the Freemen to convince them that the best course of action for them would be to lay down their arms and surrender peaceably so that no one got hurt. And so we went through a series of individuals whom we tried to use in that fashion, but even the radicals returned, tearing their hair out in frustration, saying that these people were crazy. "I can't talk any sense into them. I give up!" You have no idea how many people said this. This went on day after day and week after week.

The motley crew of extremist negotiators included a Green Beret Vietnam War veteran who had become a radical, a retired police officer who recruited police officers to become extremists, and Charles Duke, a Republican state senator in Colorado who had been supportive of militias. We even considered an offer to negotiate from Randy Weaver, the central figure in the Ruby Ridge case, but we turned him down.

The only person, extremist or otherwise, who really seemed to have much luck in getting through to them was a lawyer, Kirk Lyons, from the CAUSE Foundation, a legal action group that defends right-wing extremists. (CAUSE, by the way, stands for the areas in which the organization thinks that Aryan whites are being attacked: Canada, Australia, the United States, and Europe.) Lyons's client list includes its fair share of radicals and neo-Nazis, as well as some Branch Davidians. At the time of the Freemen case, Lyons was suing the government on behalf of some of the Waco survivors to the tune of $330 million.

Lyons had offered his services early on. Initially we said no, but since nothing was working, including cutting power to the farm—although arguably, that helped bring about the end—we reconsidered. As mediator after mediator, outside the FBI and inside the FBI, failed to resolve the Montana standoff, the FBI was ready to give Lyons his chance. So, he wrote a letter to the Freemen, after which we flew him and some of his colleagues to Montana to talk to them.

After speaking with the holed-up Freemen, he told us that the Freemen would never surrender until they had the "blessing" of the real leader of the group, LeRoy Schweitzer, whose arrest had triggered the standoff. Schweitzer, meanwhile, was in jail in Helena, Montana, waiting to be tried for fraud and conspiracy, among other charges.

To get that "blessing," Lyons had the outlandish notion that we should let the Freemen's interim leader and a former owner of the farm, Edwin Clark, temporarily leave the compound and fly him and Lyons to see Schweitzer. What? He wanted us to take a man that we had warrants to arrest, fly him in an FBI plane for a jailhouse meeting, then bring him back into the standoff, and release him!

This was unheard of. But to Louie's credit he took this necessary risk in order to resolve the crisis peacefully. And it worked. Schweitzer gave us his okay and Lyons helped put together an agreement. The following day, Clark ushered all of the remaining Freemen out of the compound safely. Our only concession was agreeing to let a Montana state legislator, Karl Ohs, safeguard some Freemen documents that these radicals maintained would prove government wrongdoing. No gunfire, no injuries, and no deaths, with the exception of the agent killed in the automobile accident.

We had learned our lessons and applied them well—especially Louie, whose willingness to authorize unorthodox measures had an overall positive effect on the case.

• • •

Just a few weeks later, however, the investigation into the bombing at the Atlanta Olympics became another story entirely. Although Louie was not on site when the bombing investigation started, he certainly got directly involved in the situation. But this time the results were disastrous.

The case began around 1:00 AM on Saturday, July 27, 1996, when a bomb hidden in a green knapsack exploded in Atlanta's Centennial Olympic Park, which was filled with crowds at the time. One woman was killed and 111 others were injured.

Richard Jewell, a private security guard working in the park who had discovered the bomb minutes before it exploded, was initially considered a hero because he alerted police and got people out of the way. The media loved him, and he gave interviews everywhere.

Diader "Dee" Rosario, with whom I had such a successful experience working with during the Atlanta prison riots, was one of the two case agents. Dee took a look at Jewell's profile and decided that he was one of a number of people whom the FBI needed to interview. Jewell was the only one who saw the knapsack initially. It's not uncommon that people like firemen and policemen will commit a crime so they can be the first to directly respond to it. Jewell was a cop wannabe who came out looking like a savior.

Dee and his fellow case agent Don Johnson questioned Jewell in an unorthodox way. They went to his apartment and asked him to come to the local FBI headquarters under a setup—asking Jewell to help them make a training tape. Jewell said yes, drove himself there, and agreed to be interviewed for the "training exercise tape."

Beforehand there was a big discussion between Louie and the agents in Atlanta about whether or not to read Jewell his Miranda rights. The decision was no—he should just come into the interview room and get started.

Initially, things were proceeding as planned. That is until Johnson was called out of the interview room. He was told that Louie had phoned and changed his mind. In the interest of caution, said Louie, someone should read Jewell his rights, *even though* the interview had already started.

So, Johnson went back and asked Jewell to read and sign a waiver of rights. Then they would start the interview again.

Richard Jewell read the form. And he said, "No, I'm not signing this and at this point, heck, it's better if I terminate the interview." So he left. The interview itself was cursory—it had barely even gotten started before Jewell left—so the case agents interpreted his leaving as the reaction of a potentially guilty person.

A few days later word leaked out that Jewell was a suspect when the *Atlanta Journal-Constitution* came out with the headline: "FBI Suspects Hero Guard May Have Planted Bomb." The media went crazy, camping out on Jewell's doorstep and playing up his suspected role big time. Every paper splashed his name and identity on page one. He was all over TV as the prime suspect in the Atlanta bombing. In reality, there are FBI interviews any time there is a big case with a number of potential suspects. That's par for the course. And in many of the interviews the suspects are found not to be connected at all to the case. The Oklahoma City investigation was a prime example of that: we interviewed dozens of potential suspects but fortunately without press coverage.

It ultimately turned out that Jewell, too, was not connected in any form, not even involved from afar. He was cleared of being a suspect. No matter. The handling of the situation had a terrible impact on the FBI because Jewell didn't hesitate to go public.

He filed suits against a lot of people, including the newspaper reporters as well as the FBI. It seemed pretty clear that he had a case. Being named a primary suspect was very damaging to Jewell's reputation and ability to make a living. In the short-term, the media swarmed all over him; he literally couldn't go anywhere or do anything. When finally the media frenzy cooled down he was still known, nationally and internationally, as Richard Jewell, one of the suspects in the Atlanta bombing case. He settled his suit against the FBI for an undisclosed amount of money.

I was not involved in this case, except peripherally when I made a trip to Atlanta for a press conference. (Remember, Louie hated press conferences.) There we displayed a reconstruction of the knapsack and asked for information from anyone who had seen it or the person carrying it before it exploded. We also asked people who were in the park that night to allow us to review their photographs and videos in an attempt to recover an image of the person who brought the knapsack into the park.

Louie was a great case agent, but trying to micromanage a case, especially one of this magnitude, from afar simply doesn't work—as this case so glaringly proves. As usual, hindsight is 20/20, but it is apparent that if the agents had been allowed to do their job, Jewell's interview would have been different. Louie's interruption of Jewell's interview really threw everything into turmoil and that, together with the leak of Jewell's name, gave the bureau a big black eye.

The one thing that I was relieved about was that the case luckily didn't affect Dee's career. He continued his assignment in Atlanta until his retirement.

● ● ●

Epilogue: On May 31, 2003, Eric Rudolph, a thirty-six-year-old army veteran and white supremacist, was arrested. He pled guilty to the Olympics bombing as well as to three others. He is currently serving a life sentence.

## International House

One of the brilliant things that Louie did was recognize that crime, as we evolved and went forward into the computer age, was truly international. The days of Hoover running down "Pretty Boy" Floyd as he committed bank robberies from one state to another were long gone. Instead, we began to have situations in which, for example, a Russian in Georgia (the former Russian state) used a laptop computer to access bank files in New

York City, transferred $10 million out of the bank, and deposited it into various accounts in South America.

Without international cooperation, how do you investigate such a crime? How do you bring those people to justice? Track them down? Identify them? That's a tough, tough thing to do. Unless you have very strong international relationships and presence, you're not going to be able to do it. So early on in Louie's administration we began a five-year plan to double the number of agents posted internationally and double the number of legal attaché offices. As part of that plan we tried to strengthen the liaison between the FBI and law enforcement officials in countries to which these new attaché people were posted.

This was all part of Louie's vision that we really had to strengthen the presence of the FBI significantly on an international level if we were going to be successful in combating crime and terrorism, because crime wasn't just taking place in the United States—it had evolved and criminals operated across borders in the international arena. If we didn't have the apparatus in place to appropriately investigate those kinds of cases then we would be sadly deficient.

One of the most significant areas of criminal activity was Moscow itself. We initially assigned two agents to Moscow, but later had to expand because the program was so successful—there was an abundance of criminal casework. Besides Russians committing crimes in the United States, there were citizens from the United States who committed criminal acts, fraud, or other crimes in Russia and would then flee back to America. It was a two-way street. In some cases we would conduct investigations in the United States to assist the Russian police. We were working hand in hand. In fact, Bill Kinane, with whom I also work at Guardsmark, was our first legal attaché in Moscow. A fluent Russian speaker, he opened the office in 1995 and served there for five years.

It was an interesting time. The daily operation under Louie Freeh's directorship involved a steady stream of international visitors to the FBI. Louie and I would receive them together if both of us were there, but if he were not there then I would receive them alone. Typically, we would discuss international cooperation and how the FBI could be of assistance to them. Many of the visitors were from foreign delegations that were lobbying the FBI to establish a presence in their country. There were more requests than we could accommodate. We had a limited budget so there were only a select number of offices that we could open. Countries would vie with one another to get an FBI office.

One way that Louie devised for the FBI to become more involved internationally was through the opening of the International Law Enforcement Academy (ILEA) in Budapest, Hungary, which he persuaded the State Department to fund. The FBI did all the work in putting the academy into operation and provided the instructors.

After the collapse of the iron curtain, there were a large number of Communist countries that, for the first time, were not going to be operating as police states. They were going to be operating in a constitutional and legal framework, with some respect for the law. Most of those countries and their law enforcement personnel didn't immediately understand that. They didn't comprehend, for example, that they couldn't detain and physically torture people to get a confession out of them. They would ask, "What? You mean I can't put the thumbscrews on anymore?" They really didn't know what to do. So, the purpose of ILEA was to try to teach former Eastern Bloc police agencies a new framework for how the police function in a free society. This was not an easy task.

I visited ILEA after I had left the bureau and was struck by how it was like a mini United Nations. There's a large tiered classroom with translation booths in the back; the students put on their earphones and select the language translation they'd like to hear. In any one class they may have four, five, or six languages because the students are not all from the same country. They are from all over the former Eastern Bloc.

Today ILEA has thousands of graduates. It was modeled in many ways after the National Academy that the FBI has run for over fifty years at Quantico. The FBI academy is regarded as the West Point of law enforcement. It's a very highly sought after professional development course. In many departments it's used as part of their promotional scheme—if you've not graduated from the National Academy, then you are not eligible for promotion to the highest ranks of the department. Every year law enforcement officers from around the country are selected to attend.

Hoover created the National Academy because he wanted to accomplish several things, with the number one objective being to raise the professionalism of law enforcement. During the 1920s and 1930s, law enforcement was not a very highly regarded profession and it certainly wasn't very professional. Hoover's idea was that the FBI needed to raise the bar in law enforcement throughout the country.

While the students are learning to be better law enforcement professionals, we are simultaneously educating them about the FBI. If we have a National Academy graduate who's the chief of police of a given city in the United States, he or she for the most part (and I never saw any exception to this) has a great deal of loyalty and affinity to, and belief in, the FBI. He or she works more closely with the FBI and the FBI has a lot more confidence in this individual because the FBI has investigated the student's background before any appointment to the academy is approved. Before that person even goes into the academy, the FBI is satisfied that he or she is a professional, honest individual who can be trusted. The same care is taken in selecting students for ILEA. The network of graduates enhances law enforcement in all the former Eastern Bloc countries and is of great value to the FBI and law enforcement in general.

## All in the Family

Louie consistently made it perfectly clear to everyone—and in that list I am including President Clinton, who appointed him, and Attorney General Janet Reno—that his first priority was his family. I was in Louie's office once when Janet Reno called him about an important meeting that she was scheduling for 5:30 that afternoon. "Can't make it," he responded. "I have to go to my son's soccer game. I'll send Weldon in my place." That made it crystal clear to me that his statements about his family having top priority were not rhetoric but fact.

In spite of Louie's physical appearance as steely-eyed, square-jawed, and tough, possessing a demeanor that one expects from the director of the FBI (although he is a small guy), he was a contradiction. When I was serving as the deputy, in 1995, Louie and Marilyn had their fifth child, Liam Patrick Freeh, and Louie took paternity leave. He had done this at previous jobs, so he must have reasoned, why not as head of the FBI? Paternity leave was something new to FBI leaders, however. Hoover did not have a family. However, if he had, I can't imagine that he would have signed up for paternity leave. Louie, however, was a new kind of leader.

Initially, the general public was only aware of some of his gung-ho enthusiasm for fatherhood, but not much. That's in large part because he did not like dealing with the press at all. This is kind of ironic because he generally did it well, I thought. He couldn't avoid it entirely, of course. He participated in numerous interviews. Under the right amount of duress he sometimes agreed to a media meeting or an article. However, if he could find a way, such as if the topic was a specific case, he would have somebody else do it. Because of this I ended up doing more media interviews than I would have ever guessed.

His affinity for his children was common knowledge among the agents, who loved it. While the agents had been given permission to take family leave before Louie came in, I can only imagine that they certainly felt more comfortable doing so after he did it. In government circles such as Congress, it seemed that his family devotion was welcomed, too. There, as far as I know, the attitude toward it was along the lines of "This is kind of refreshing. Here he is, the epitome of the G-man, but he's got very strong family ties and he maintains a strong family interest."

When Louie was out on paternity leave I talked to him daily during that time, but he came into the office only on a few occasions. Important documents for his signature were regularly sent to his home. But I must say that my holding down the fort when he was away really did remind me of when I was temporarily thrust into the top leadership spot in Boston after the SAC retired. If anything happened I would be the person in charge of the entire FBI. That was a heady assignment. Luckily, no major crisis happened during the several weeks he was on leave.

Even after Louie returned to a regular work schedule, it was more or less on a part-time basis. He frequently would abbreviate his hours to accommodate family needs such as visits to doctors. The baby was born in the later part of September and Louie did not return to a full schedule until January.

His sons, numbering six by the time he left the FBI, were a big handful. I have no problem saying that because he certainly told stories about them. He would tell the story, for example, of the ceremony at the Rose Garden when Clinton publicly nominated him to the director position. All the high-ranking bureau officials were in attendance, including me, because at the time I was the fourth-ranking person in the bureau.

Marilyn was there with their then four boys, who were running around like crazy. At one point when one of the older boys was standing near a fountain, one of his younger brothers ran up behind him and pushed him in. The kid was dripping wet at the ceremony. Louie had to go over and pick him up. But Clinton got a laugh out of it. Boy, were these kids full of life. They were not intimidated by anybody or any office.

Louie's wife, Marilyn, must have been worn to a frazzle just keeping up with her sons. She's a super lady, but they would have been a handful for anyone. Louie would occasionally give her some relief by taking them for a few hours so she could go shopping or just have some free time. There would be occasions when I walked into Louie's office and he would be feeding a baby on the couch. The American public never saw that. Other times all of his boys would be there, especially when the kids were off from school in the summertime or during school vacations.

When they were in the office, the kids had the run of the place. One of the interesting things about Louie's office was that it had an inner office, a personal office, in addition to a conference room on the other side where he would receive visiting dignitaries or have meetings with visitors outside of the FBI. However, his inner office was something different. There was one whole wall that held school paintings and the little arts and crafts that the boys had made. The things you'd normally see hanging on somebody's refrigerator covered an entire wall in the FBI director's office.

Louie wasn't particularly concerned about his personal public image but he was very concerned about any negative impact his image or standing would have on the FBI. In this case his devotion to his family actually helped to improve his public image. We had more than one conversation during difficult times when he would ask if I thought that his being the director was hurting the bureau. I believe he was totally serious on those occasions when he said that he would resign as director rather than discredit the FBI.

Louie Freeh was sworn in during September 1993 and stayed in office until the summer of 2001—two years shy of the ten-year tenure of an FBI director—when he left early to make some money. That was his stated reason, which I firmly believe. By that time he had six boys. The oldest one was approaching his teens and in the next few years Louie was going to have boys starting to go to college. As it was, he had them in private Catholic schools that were costing him an arm and a leg.

Raising these boys on his salary was difficult. He had no money, no investments, no family money, nothing. His wife didn't work outside the home. So, he lived payday to payday, like every other agent.

That's why he took his next position, as senior vice chairman and general counsel at Maryland Bank National Association, an issuer of credit cards. They paid him a lot of money so he was able to do well financially. It had been a sacrifice in the first place for him to leave the federal bench to join the FBI. While federal judges don't become wealthy people, their compensation is higher than that of the FBI director. Though their compensation is only a fraction of what a very competent attorney would make, it is nevertheless a lifetime appointment.

As a judge, Louie could have supported his family comfortably, but he chose instead to accept the offer of director, giving up that lifetime appointment for a ten-year appointment maximum, where he made statutorily less than $150,000 and ran a $3 billion enterprise with 28,800 employees worldwide. The president had it nearly just as bad. At that time the president's salary was only $200,000.

It is ridiculous that we expect government people to sacrifice as they have to do, because a person who is really capable of running that kind of operation in the private industry would command three, four, or five times as much salary. Besides paying them peanuts, many of our high-ranking government executives, particularly the FBI director, are subjected to unbelievable scrutiny. They are under a high-power microscope from the time their names surface as potential appointees. Critics and opponents constantly look for weak points and mistakes to publicly criticize them and, in some cases, even fabricate stories in order to discredit them or their agency.

Being the director of the FBI requires a high degree of intelligence, skill, and dedication. In addition, one's luck, whether good or bad, also plays a role. In this regard Louie had very good luck: he left office a scant three months before the 9/11 attacks.

# 11

# Preparation for Retirement

## Future Endeavors

When I went to work as the deputy director, I agreed with Louie up front that I would do the job for a year. That was it. Well, you can be sure that those twelve months went by like a blur. Toward the end of them, however, I began thinking about when it would be time for me to leave. Around month ten, I started talking to Louie about it on an occasional basis—it was not the easiest topic to broach with him. I guess I should find that flattering.

Finally, in the fall of 1996, we talked about it more seriously. I asked him if he had a successor for me in mind. He did. (Whew.) It was William J. Esposito, who at that time was already an assistant director serving in division 6, the Criminal Investigation Division. He had been the SAC in San Diego and had done a good job there, before Louie brought him into headquarters. With that transition in place, I decided to leave in the spring.

"Take your time," he said. This was good to hear. I wanted to look around a little bit and see what might be open. I was looking forward to retirement but badly needed to augment my pension for a few years prior to completely retiring. Little did I know then the wrong move I almost made.

• • •

The Salt Lake City Olympic Committee at the time was looking for a head of security for the upcoming games in the winter of 2002. A friend gave me the lead and suggested I contact Tom Welch, who was cohead of the Salt Lake City Organizing Committee. After a brief phone conversation, Welch made arrangements for me go to Salt Lake City for interviews around holiday time. The meetings went well and they extended me a very, very attractive job offer.

I wanted some time to think about it. Guardsmark, a world leader in providing contract security services, had already expressed interest in me and it was a place I knew that I wanted to consider strongly. My old friend from my FBI training class, Don Pettus, had retired from the FBI several years before and he was already working at Guardsmark and doing quite well. He encouraged me to talk to Ira Lipman, Guardsmark's founder, chairman, and president, to see if there might be any opportunities for me there.

Besides Guardsmark, though, there was another completely different alternative. When I was SAC of Atlanta, I had gone back to school, getting my master's degree in criminal justice at Georgia State University. I had always loved teaching and enjoyed the relationship with the students. Teaching had been my vague long-range plan, and I considered that I might want to teach full-time one day, but I didn't really get serious about it until it came time for me to retire.

I talked to Georgia State and a couple of other schools about the idea. However, after some searching, both of the regular and soul variety, I realized eventually that it wasn't what I wanted to do. First of all, I really felt like I needed to earn some serious income and academia was not the place to do this.

I decided I really needed to find a job in which I could improve my financial situation. So, my options boiled down to only two: Salt Lake Olympic Committee or Guardsmark.

I didn't actually go to Guardsmark, whose headquarters were in Memphis, for a full set of interviews until late January 1997. And, boy, was that a grueling day; I hadn't had a real job interview for thirty-five years. The Salt Lake interviews, on the other hand, were kind of laid back, very casual. We met in the office, we had lunch, and we had dinner. It was a very loose and fuzzy kind of deal.

Nonetheless, I had some serious reservations about the structure of the Salt Lake City operation. I knew a bit about how the Olympics worked since I had some exposure to the planning process from my time in Atlanta before I left there in 1989. I contacted some of the people I had worked with for those 1996 games and asked for input, such as how they would approach the director of security position.

The first pointer they gave me: nail down the budget for security. In spite of the fact that these are sports games, this is a business. The investors intend to make a profit. They have spent a lot of money and time and effort bringing the Olympics to Salt Lake City, so losing money is not part of the agenda. One of the areas that they will possibly find that they can skimp on, my contacts warned me, may be security, unless there's some real specific scare. (Keep in mind that 9/11 wasn't even fathomable at that time.) "You're going to find that they'll charge you with the responsibility of having a very high level of security," they told me, "but they won't give you the budget to do it with."

That, of course, wasn't the only problem I would have encountered working for the Salt Lake Olympic Committee. No matter what I asked my interviewers, I couldn't get a straight, direct answer from them. Who would I directly report to? There was a lot of mishmash about that and the bottom line was that they didn't really know. They hadn't bothered to think it through. What would the security budget be? It got really mushy about how much was going to be allocated and who would make the decisions. My interviewers were very, very unclear on this point.

Given all this, I became quite uneasy. That's the only way I could describe my reaction. My sixth sense must have kicked in. These Olympic people were very friendly and extremely anxious for me to come on board. However, it turns out that during the whole interview process they were well on their way to being indicted on criminal charges.

The very same people who interviewed me were among the boldfaced names that later appeared in the headlines next to the word "scandal." They were being indicted because of alleged misconduct in bribing the Olympic Committee to select Salt Lake City as the site for the 2002 Winter Games. Even though they were later acquitted, it was still not a situation that I would have wanted to be associated with.

I shudder to think about how that scandal would not only have tarred my reputation but also reflected poorly on the FBI at a time when it definitely did not need any negative press. Sixth sense, guardian angel, whatever you want to call it, you can only imagine my relief at not taking that job the day the news broke about the scandal, which was after I was comfortably settled in as the vice chairman of Guardsmark.

The reason the Olympic people were so anxious to have me probably had more to do with my position as deputy director of the FBI than anything else. They probably had some ideas that by bringing me into the scenario, I would perhaps lend some credibility to what they were doing and how they were doing it. They might have thought I might provide some shield in the event the thing turned ugly, which it did.

Since I was on a personal job quest, I did not discuss my planned visit with the Salt Lake Olympic Committee with anyone, certainly not with the local FBI office, who never knew that I was there. Even though I had no concrete information on which to base my decision, I called Mr. Welch to decline the offer.

Guardsmark, a company recognized for its sterling ethics program, couldn't have been a more different organization. I flew back down to Memphis again one morning not too long after I realized that Salt Lake was not for me. My day started early, with me boarding the plane at 6:00 AM and then spending the entire day going through interviews. My final interview was with the head of the company, Ira Lipman. Although we hit it off and our meeting resulted in an offer, I didn't immediately accept it.

Despite the Olympics situation, I was still in the exploratory phase of my job search and not ready to accept any offer. Although, of course, the Guardsmark offer was night and day compared with the Salt Lake proposition, I had a lot of things on my mind, and I decided to wait until my actual retirement from the FBI to make a commitment.

And so when that day had come and gone and I was on my way back from Washington to Scottsdale, I stopped off in Memphis to spend another day at Guardsmark. After all, if this was going to be the next stage in my career, I'd better make sure that my decision was the right one.

On this trip I had my wife with me. And boy, were we treated like royalty. Ira Lipman is a very gracious and considerate host. He put us up in the Peabody Hotel, the famous landmark known for the ducks that march through its lobby, and had an enormous bouquet of flowers waiting for Kathy. When Ira Lipman made his offer again, I finally accepted. I would be starting on April 1, 1997.

It wasn't a tough decision. Besides the exciting challenge of the work, the offer was very good from a financial standpoint. If I worked at least two or three years—which at that point was my intention—I would do well financially.

The catch, of course, was that it involved yet another move. Here I'd built my retirement home in Scottsdale, Arizona, and now I was going to move to Memphis. However, that city was attractive because of the accessibility it offered to see my children and grandchildren. Our son Milton lived in Oklahoma City with his family and our other son, Darrell, lived in Atlanta with his wife. Memphis was equidistant between the two.

From a family standpoint this was great. It put us closer to our boys than Kathy and I had been in some time and meant that we were going to be able to visit them often. Anytime we had a three-day weekend we'd be able to scoot down to Atlanta or over to Oklahoma City and spend time with the kids. Our daughter, Karen, was living in Anchorage—where she still is today. She was up there working as a pilot for Alaska Airlines and was therefore able to fly on FedEx, because of an agreement between the two companies. Since Memphis was the FedEx hub, there was a direct flight that was only seven hours.

Everything was rosy and the move from Scottsdale worked out great, for a few months at least. And then, ironically, Milton was offered a job with the U.S. Border Patrol in Casa Grande, Arizona, just south of Phoenix. He had worked for the Border Patrol earlier in his career, and despite his exciting work for U.S. Immigration he had become disenchanted and missed his former job.

Not too long after that Darrell, who had been working for years and going to night school, finally got his bachelor's degree in environmental development. I was so proud of him. Immediately after his graduation he started looking for a job. You'll never guess where he found one—Phoenix. He had landed a job with a major home builder.

Within a few months, both of my sons moved to where I had just left. Milton and his wife, Beth, already had three children: Cody, Ciara, and Savannah. Then Darrell and his wife, Angie, had a little boy, Collin, and later a little girl, Zadie. So, now we're up to five grandchildren who all live in the southwestern United States. And we grandparents were living in Memphis!

Timing can be a funny thing. However, I knew we'd end up back in Arizona eventually. In the meantime I would be facing some exciting new challenges that I never could have imagined in the FBI.

## Last Hurrah

One of the most memorable moments in my life was the retirement party that the FBI threw for me. Nearly seven hundred people attended the formal going-away dinner in the ballroom of Arlington's Crystal City Marriott hotel. My entire family was there, including my sister and brother and their families. Only my mother wasn't able to be there, because her health wasn't good.

There were so many presentations to be made by local and foreign law enforcement agencies that we had to hold them in a separate room before the formal dinner. I was thrilled to be honored by such great organizations as the Royal Canadian Mounted Police (RCMP) and Britain's MI5 and MI6 services. In addition, there was representation from Sweden, Spain, Germany, Italy, Japan, Mexico, and others.

As a result of all this, my home office is chock-full of plaques and commemorations. I have so many that most of them are packed in boxes and stored. Hanging above the fireplace in my office is a carved wooden FBI seal, three feet in diameter, presented to me by the Federal Bureau of Prisons. On bookshelves are several small statues, including one from the RCMP, one from the FBI Special Agents Association, one from the Major City Chiefs of Police Association, and one from the FBI National Academy Associates.

The whole thing had the feel of a patriotic event. By my request, the master of ceremonies was Bill Gavin, an old FBI friend. Our friendship would continue to grow as he later worked with me at Guardsmark. With his affable personality and quick wit, he was the perfect choice.

Together Bill and I decided to limit the number of speakers so that people would be engaged. After all, we did have the pre-event in the separate room. Bill also put together a slide show, without my knowledge, that was very touching and funny. He was also the narrator. I found more than a few surprises in this retrospective of my career. The audience got quite a kick out of the picture of me as an infant dressed only in my birthday suit, with the exception of a sailor hat.

I was particularly touched by some of the people who showed up to say good-bye. Louie said something I'll never forget: "He is one of those rare people in government who has made a difference. All of us in the FBI will miss his clear thinking, keen judgment, and boundless energy." Janet Reno came up to the podium and said, "In the most difficult of times, and facing the most strenuous challenges, he has always performed with only one goal in mind—the well-being and safety of the American people." While she was up there, she also gave me a big bear hug. It became a little family joke after that. My wife would refer to my "girlfriend"—the attorney general!

I was also thrilled with the nice letters I received both from people who were there and those who couldn't make it. There were many from people I worked with during the Atlanta prison riots. One person, John R. Kingston, supervisory special agent in the Economic Crimes Unit at FBIHQ, took the time to thank me for my patience in handling the uprising. Even years later I think it was so thoughtful he wrote that to me.

Other letters came from people I had worked with at various points in my career. Some of these included letters from Charles "Bud" Meeks, executive director of the National Sheriffs' Association; J. P. R. Murray, commissioner of the RCMP; Tom Constantine, head of the DEA; and George Tenet, then acting director of the CIA, who thanked me for breaking down barriers and improving collaboration between the FBI and the CIA. I even received a letter from President Clinton congratulating me on my career.

Some letters that I particularly relish came from some of the FBI agents and support employees. One person, David J. Baldovin, a special agent in Memphis, told me that I was "an agent's agent, understanding what is really happening on the street while ascending to high positions within the bureau." In my opinion, that was the highest compliment I could get, since I have always had such a great deal of admiration and respect for all special agents of the FBI.

# 12

# Outlook on the Future of the FBI

The FBI is the principal investigative arm of the U.S. Department of Justice and an institution with the mission "to uphold the law through the investigation of violations of federal criminal law; to protect the United States from foreign intelligence and terrorist activities; to provide leadership and law enforcement assistance to federal, state, local, and international agencies; and to perform these responsibilities in a manner that is responsive to the needs of the public and is faithful to the Constitution of the United States." I am concerned that under the current—and I believe, temporary—pressures being brought on the FBI by the focus on terrorism, the very fabric of the FBI will be altered so significantly that its ability to fulfill its mission will be compromised.

Nearly six years have now passed since the attacks of 9/11 and the resulting decision to make terrorism the number one priority for the FBI. Significant resources have been shifted (over two thousand special agents) away from other investigative programs into terrorism. While the shift is appropriate considering the threats faced by the United States at this time, the failure to backfill the resources taken away from other programs will have long-term, serious, adverse consequences for the FBI and the American public.

Since the beginning of the FBI's history, stemming back from the Theodore Roosevelt administration, the focus of the FBI has been ever evolving. It began as a national law enforcement and investigative (not police) agency and its purpose was to conduct investigations into violations of federal laws and to assist state and local enforcement and police organizations.

J. Edgar Hoover became director of the FBI in 1924. During his early tenure, the roaring 1920s into the Depression era '30s, the focus was on gangsters whose criminal activities crossed state boundaries. During those years, the FBI had very limited powers and law enforcement was generally considered to be a state or local responsibility. However, state and local law enforcement agencies were no match for criminals like John Dillinger, George "Machine Gun" Kelly, Alvin "Creepy" Karpis, and the Barker gang. The FBI was extremely successful in pursuing these criminals, but only after several agents were shot and killed was Hoover successful in getting Congress to authorize FBI agents to carry weapons and make arrests. Because of these successes, the FBI's jurisdiction was expanded by the passage of laws making it a criminal offense to cross state lines in criminal activities (stolen vehicles, prostitution, stolen property, etc.) and the FBI grew in terms of its budget and resources.

With the approach of World War II the focus of the FBI shifted significantly to espionage and counterespionage with its primary target being Nazi Germany. Again, the FBI was very successful in making many cases involving saboteurs who infiltrated into the United States as well as various espionage cases. During this period (pre-CIA), the FBI operated extensively in Central America and South America, gathering intelligence concerning German intelligence and espionage activities.

After the war, focus again shifted, this time to the Soviet Union and the Communist Party in the United States. Communists and their sympathizers had penetrated to the highest levels of government (e.g., Alger Hiss) and Hoover and many others believed communism to be a serious threat to our nation. Significant resources were allocated to domestic intelligence investigations as well as to espionage and counterespionage. The FBI was also successful in this arena, making numerous cases, including that of Julius and Ethel Rosenberg, for espionage.

During the 1980s there was another fundamental change in the FBI's priorities. Until 1982 the FBI had no jurisdiction over federal drug violations. That was the responsibility of the Drug Enforcement Administration. Because drug abuse in the United States had reached epidemic proportions, the attorney general of the United States made the decision to have the FBI share jurisdiction over federal drug offenses with the DEA. However, there were no resources initially allocated by the attorney general for this purpose. Almost overnight there was a massive reallocation of resources internally within the FBI from various programs into drug enforcement. By the time I reached FBI headquarters in 1989 and had responsibility for the budget, the reallocations were causing serious problems. The simple fact was that although the FBI had finally been allocated more resources to combat the drug problem, there was no backfilling the resources that had been moved from other programs into drug enforcement.

Other agencies were all too eager to pick up the slack but not exactly for altruistic reasons. In government, each agency is constantly seeking to expand its power and influence. By taking on additional work, the agency then has justification to ask Congress for more money and manpower—also ensuring that the agency becomes more powerful and important.

One FBI program that particularly suffered because of the priority placed on the war on drugs was the fugitive apprehension program. Since there were few resources—either manpower or money—to pursue these kinds of cases, a vacuum was created that the U.S. Marshals Service happily filled.

The U.S. Marshals Service is the country's oldest law enforcement agency—created in 1789—with the purpose of maintaining civil authority. It has a diverse portfolio of law enforcement duties including protecting witnesses, escorting prisoners, as well as executing arrest warrants and civil summonses. U.S. Marshals also serve as bailiffs to the federal courts and provide security for federal judges.

From its beginning, the Marshals Service had responsibility for executing arrest warrants that had been issued by federal authorities. However, as other federal agencies such as the FBI came into being, each agency took responsibility for executing arrest warrants issued in cases it was actively working. The reasons for this are quite simple and relate to the ability of the arresting agents to obtain a statement or possibly evidence or fruits of the crime with which the fugitive has been charged. In the case of the Marshals Service, its basic interest is the safe apprehension of the fugitive; and it has little knowledge or interest in the facts of the underlying case. Its focus is simply on ensuring that the warrant issued is valid and that the person the marshals are arresting is the person named in the warrant.

In the late 1970s and early 1980s the Marshals Service was eager to expand its operations and become a more potent force in federal law enforcement. At the same time, the FBI was experiencing serious budget deficiencies and was looking for ways to decrease its commitment to lower-priority matters. In about 1985 the FBI and the Marshals Service reached an agreement wherein the FBI basically ceded jurisdiction for certain types of fugitive cases. For example, federal warrants are issued for escaped federal prisoners and the FBI had the responsibility for their apprehension. The FBI agreed that the Marshals Service would have jurisdiction for all these cases except for individuals who had been incarcerated as a result of an FBI investigation. As a result, the Marshals Service formed teams called FISTs (Fugitive Investigative Strike Teams) that would travel around the country to major cities and conduct roundups of large numbers of fugitives. This served the public by taking potentially dangerous criminals off the streets but the publicity for the Marshals Service didn't hurt either. (Its budget somehow managed to get increased.) On certain high-profile cases there were confrontations between the Marshals Service and the agency with the underlying case (FBI, DEA, U.S. Customs, Secret Service, etc.). The agency with the substantive cases had legitimate interests in making the arrests, but the Marshals Service, eager for the publicity, would deploy the FIST team and make the arrests without the other agency.

To its chagrin, the Marshals Service was unsuccessful in taking primary responsibility for all federal fugitive cases. Federal law enforcement agencies with the substantive cases successfully convinced the attorney general that at the time of the arrest there were many instances where important evidence was recovered or statements obtained and that only the originating agency would be knowledgeable in the facts of the case.

The U.S. Marshals Service is not unique in wanting to expand into the FBI's jurisdictional areas. Another agency that got a taste of the FBI's activities in the 1980s and seems to want more is the Secret Service. The Secret Service has responsibility for protecting the president and the vice president and their families, former presidents and vice presidents and their families, and foreign heads of state while they are in the United States. It also has responsibility for the physical security of the White House and foreign embassies in the United States. As an agency of the Treasury Department, its duties include jurisdiction over U.S. currency counterfeiting as well as any fraud or counterfeiting of U.S. bonds, treasury notes, or other federal financial instruments. During the 1980s' budget crunch, the Secret Service took responsibility from the FBI for investigations concerning bankcard violations. The Secret Service has frequently expressed interest in expanding its jurisdiction into other areas currently assigned to the FBI to include any and all violations involving federally insured banks.

Another federal agency moving vigorously to expand its jurisdiction and its operations is U.S. Immigration and Customs Enforcement (ICE). While it has jurisdiction over the smuggling into the United States of illegal narcotics, it contends that since the bulk of illegal narcotics are brought in illegally that it should have jurisdiction over domestic cases as well. With the FBI shifting resources away from narcotics into terrorism, the timing may be perfect for ICE to fill the partial vacuum.

Just how large a vacuum is created by the FBI's shift in resources?

According to a Justice Department report recently issued by the department's inspector general, the FBI is investigating only about one half of the cases it did before 9/11 because of its focus on terrorism. Financial fraud, bank robberies, other reactive crimes, and drug cases have been neglected as a result. The number of investigations in criminal cases is 45 percent fewer in 2004 than it was in 2000. Drug cases are down by 70 percent. All this should be no surprise since more than twenty-two hundred special agents have been shifted from these areas into terrorism investigations.

A recent Government Accountability Office report focused on the question of whether cases were being neglected because of the FBI's shift in resources. Their answer was that they were not, because other agencies were picking up the slack. This is precisely what I have been trying to communicate. As the FBI lessens its commitment to a given area of criminal investigative activity, other agencies move in to fill the gap. The next step is for the new agency to point out to Congress that it is handling more and more cases and obtaining more prosecutions and that it needs additional resources allocated to meet these needs. In the meantime, the FBI statistics in that particular area are declining so the budgeteers happily move the resources from the FBI to the agency now doing the job. Unless there is a strong movement to backfill the FBI resources shifted away from areas of its traditional jurisdiction, this trend will accelerate and there will be a splintering of the agencies dedicated to a particular area of enforcement. The result will be a decrease in the effectiveness of the law enforcement efforts. This cycle seems to be gathering force and growing like a snowball rolling downhill.

While this splintering is taking place there are powerful people exercising their influence and pressuring the FBI to change its culture. These uninformed people believe that the FBI is not able to adapt to changing circumstances and needs to be hit over the head or substantially reorganized to conform to their mistaken idea of what the FBI should be. I, for one, pray that the FBI culture does not change. It is a culture of dedicated men and women doing their very best and risking their lives to serve the American people and protect this nation. As noted previously, the FBI has changed its focus on numerous occasions and has been phenomenally successful in combating the threat prevalent at the time. This has been true whether the challenges involved fighting gangsters in the early days of the FBI; investigating espionage or conducting counterespionage activities, as was true during World War II or the Cold War; destroying the KKK; bringing numerous massive bank fraud investigations to successful conclusions; having a significant impact on major drug trafficking cartels; bringing to prosecutors significant public corruption cases throughout the United States; or, more recently, thwarting terrorist plots against the United States. It is no accident that there has been no major terrorist attack in the United States since 9/11. While the FBI cannot and should not claim sole responsibility for this success, it is a major player working in concert with numerous other agencies to bring about that success.

Without any doubt, I believe that there will be a time when terrorism will shrink significantly as a serious threat. Who knows whether that will be in two years, five years, ten years, or more, but it will happen. I am not saying that terrorism will be completely eliminated. Not at all. It will, however, at some point in the future, cease to be a serious threat domestically. It has already been five years since 9/11 and those of us active in the security industry can see a tremendous growth of apathy and less and less concern about terrorism. Already we are seeing a slowdown of terrorist cases. According to a study by Syracuse University's Transactional Records Access Clearinghouse, terrorism cases comprise less than 1 percent of all prosecutions and they peaked in 2002. What is the attitude going to be when there has been no terrorist attack in eight or ten years? At some point Congress and the American people may well ask why such a large commitment of resources is being made to terrorism.

It is possible that we may see a repeat of what happened following the collapse of the Soviet Union. Almost immediately, Congress discovered that there was a "windfall" in terms of huge amounts of resources that had been committed to the Cold War. Legislators could not be persuaded that threats against the United States, whether they were from the Soviet Union, China, or elsewhere, were still a major concern. They therefore proceeded to decimate the CIA as well as other agencies' intelligence operations and redirect the resources elsewhere. One could argue that these thoughtless actions so crippled U.S. intelligence and counterintelligence functions that this was partially the reason for our failure to detect the 9/11 plot before the fact.

While we will not see a collapse of terrorism as dramatic as the collapse of the Soviet Union, it is possible that the shrinking of terrorism may take place over a relatively short time. It seems apparent to me that only if Muslims themselves turn on the radical Islamic terrorists will they be defeated. No matter how effective our intelligence and military operations might be, I do not believe it possible for us to defeat terrorism externally.

With the bombings in Iraq, Jordan, India, and elsewhere primarily killing Muslims, we are beginning to see some signs that moderate and even conservative Islamists are speaking out against the radical elements of Islam who are involved in terrorism. When Islam's disgust for terrorism grows and results in Muslims taking positive actions to thwart the terrorists, we will see terrorism begin to subside. The terrorists will not be able to survive if they do not have the support of the communities within which they are operating. The atrocities being perpetrated by the terrorists are beginning to backfire on them and may ultimately result in their eradication.

When the time comes to redirect the resources committed to terrorism what will happen? Will the FBI be able to redirect those resources back into white-collar crime, drug enforcement, organized crime, and so on? Probably not, because, as I have previously noted, numerous other agencies have been busy filling the gaps left when the FBI redirected resources into terrorism. Once jurisdiction has been either ceded or abandoned because of a lack of resources, it is virtually impossible to reclaim jurisdiction.

The attempts to convert the FBI from the agency that it has been since its formation—dedicated to federal law enforcement, domestic intelligence, and security—to solely an intelligence agency focused on terrorism will ultimately be extremely detrimental to our nation. The FBI's worldwide reputation as the best law enforcement agency in the world will rapidly diminish.

The effectiveness of the FBI has already been substantially adversely impacted by the reduction of resources committed to criminal investigative activities. Since there are fewer and fewer agents working criminal cases, the ability to maintain effectiveness in a given criminal investigative program shrinks. For example, other police agencies that have been accustomed to working with the FBI and to referring cases within the FBI's jurisdiction to them are forced to go elsewhere or to attempt to handle the case on their own. The sources and informants cultivated by agents working in a given program rapidly atrophy or disappear altogether. With fewer and fewer cases in a program and with the informant base drying up, a point will be reached at which the FBI will no longer be effective in some areas of its criminal jurisdiction. I cannot believe that this is what the American people want to happen. I saw firsthand how people react when they are informed that the FBI is planning to change its commitment to their community when I met with the good citizens of Savannah, Georgia, to discuss the closing of the Savannah Field Office. With what is now happening with the commitment to terrorism, the American people are probably not aware that the FBI no longer has the ability to protect them from criminal activities the same way it has in the past.

I do not mean to suggest that the other federal agencies such as the Marshals Service, the Secret Service, ICE, DEA, ATF, and others are not capable law enforcement agencies. They are very good in the areas of their primary jurisdiction, but they are not very effective in other arenas. My thesis here is that when responsibility for enforcement of a given criminal investigative program is splintered, as is happening now, the effectiveness of enforcement activities in that area is substantially diminished. Not only is the effectiveness diminished, it can become positively dangerous. It has happened in numerous drug cases that two agencies were separately working the same case and were unaware of the interest of the other agency. There have been near catastrophes when the agents of one agency conducted a raid to take down a case only to find that the people they were targeting were undercover agents from another agency.

In addition, when two or more federal agencies are competing for resources in a given investigative program each agency will strive to make the biggest and most important cases in order to garner more favorable publicity and attract the favorable attention of Congress. This situation almost guarantees that each agency will keep its information on significant cases to itself so as to steal a march on the other agency.

I specifically recall a case in Atlanta when the FBI, DEA, and U.S. Customs (now ICE) were jointly working a case involving some major drug smugglers. The DEA had placed an informant who provided information concerning aircraft coming to a small rural airport in Georgia in the middle of the night. With agents from all agencies, we set up on the identified airport on three separate nights with no success.

Since this was a smuggling case, Customs apparently felt that it should be the lead agency, not the DEA. Therefore, without informing any other agencies but using the information developed by the DEA informant, it independently inserted an undercover pilot into the case. The undercover pilot was successful in getting a load of drugs from the suspects that he flew into a different airport where the Customs agents were waiting. Major arrests were made and great headlines resulted for Customs. All the rest of us had been completely left out of this new development. Fortunately, no one was injured but what Customs did in this case was potentially extremely dangerous and could have resulted in the deaths of agents, informants, or even innocent bystanders.

For these reasons, there should be clear-cut lines of jurisdiction for federal agencies and each agency should take the lead on cases within its jurisdiction. If situations occur like that just described, the repercussions for the offending agency should be severe. By having a single agency responsible for a criminal investigative program, the enforcement activities nationwide will be coordinated and investigative activity will be focused rather than fragmented and worked with a case-by-case approach. Intelligence gathered in the program will be factored into the program and a viable informant base can be planned and developed to attack the problems.

While a single agency should have jurisdiction for a given investigative program, other agencies can and should be included in the enforcement activities in order to increase their effectiveness. I am specifically referring to the formation of task forces consisting of personnel from any agency having an interest (federal, state, or local). The FBI has employed this tactic for many years with great success.

For example, when I was in Phoenix we sponsored several task forces specializing in such topics as fugitives, health care fraud, narcotics, crimes on Indian reservations, organized crime, violent crimes, and white-collar crime. The Fugitive Task Force included personnel from the FBI, U.S. Marshals Service, Maricopa County Sheriff's Office, Phoenix Police Department, as well as the Glendale Police Department. The group was housed in the FBI offices and was under the leadership of a lieutenant from the Maricopa County Sheriff's Office. All members of the group had access to databases belonging to any of the member agencies and shared intelligence among themselves. The task force was extremely effective and apprehended large numbers of very dangerous fugitives, thereby making Phoenix a safer place to live and work. As I had previously touched upon, we were able to form the Safe Trails Task Force with participation of the Navajo Nation and the FBI to improve law enforcement on several Indian reservations. Perhaps the oldest task force is the Joint Terrorism Task Force in New York City, New York. It was created more than twenty years ago and has had responsibility for investigating major terrorism cases including the first bombing of the World Trade

Center.

The FBI is an extremely competent agency that has successfully navigated several very difficult times and emerged even better and stronger than before. It has identified and countered numerous serious threats to the United States. This is because of the highly talented and dedicated men and women who do not hesitate to sacrifice, sometimes even their lives, to make the FBI as good as it can be. In addition, the unwavering support of the American people who want and demand a strong and effective FBI is an important ingredient to its success. I (and I believe the American people do as well) sincerely hope that this success continues with regard to terrorism. At the same time, it is my belief that the FBI is facing a potentially very damaging refocusing and restructuring that could have disastrous consequences in the future. Someone once crudely but wisely said, "If it ain't broke, don't fix it." The FBI is not broken and never has been. The director and men and women of the FBI need and deserve our strong support and the allocation of resources to maintain the FBI's effectiveness in all areas of its jurisdictional responsibility.

# EPILOGUE:
## SEMIRETIREMENT IN ARIZONA AND REFLECTIONS ON LIFE AND CAREER

After I had spent more than thirty-six years in government service, including jobs in the navy and the FBI, and six years with Guardsmark, my wife, Kathy, finally convinced me to slow down a bit. We decided to move to Prescott, Arizona, so that we could not only be near our sons and their families but also escape the desert heat of Phoenix and Tucson. Mr. Lipman and I discussed my situation and agreed that I would remain affiliated with Guardsmark but that I would reduce my work schedule effective January 1, 2003.

Looking back on my forty-two years of service in intelligence, law enforcement, and private security, it gives me great pride to know that I served in three organizations that are the world's best in their respective fields: the U.S. Navy, the FBI, and Guardsmark. I always did my best to never let these organizations down, and I sincerely hope that my small contributions added to their legacies.

# INDEX

# About the Author

**Weldon L. Kennedy** retired from the FBI in 1997 as its deputy director, the organization's second-highest position and its highest nonpolitical appointment. During his thirty-three-year career, he served in Portland, Oregon; Las Vegas; Miami; San Juan, Puerto Rico; Newark, New Jersey; Boston; Jackson, Mississippi; Phoenix; Atlanta; and four tours at FBI headquarters. Now a vice chairman and group executive for the security services firm Guardsmark, Kennedy lives in Prescott, Arizona.